Crime Rate Madness

A SAPIENT Being's Guide to the Color of Crime, Antifa, BLM, SPLC & OSF Impacts on Criminal Justice

By

Corey Lee Wilson

Crime Rate Madness

Crime Rate Madness

Fratire Publishing books can be purchased in bulk with special discounts for educational purposes, association gifts, sales promotions, and special editions can be created to specifications. All inquiries for such can be made below.

FRATIRE PUBLISHING LLC
4533 Temescal Canyon Rd. # 308
Corona, CA 92883
www.FratirePublishing.com
FratirePublishing@att.net
(951) 638-5502

FratirePublishing
Relevant Books for **SAPIENT** Beings

Fratire Publishing is all about common sense and relevant books for sapient beings. If this sounds like you and you can never have enough common sense, wisdom, and relevancy, then visit us and learn more about the 50 *MADNESS* series of book titles at www.FratirePublishing.com.

Printed paperback and eBook ePUB by Ingram Spark in La Vergne, Tennessee, USA
Copyright © 2021: First Edition February 2021
ISBN 978-0-9994603-5-1 (Paperback)
ISBN 978-1-953319-31-9 (eBook)
LCCN 2021901100

Contents

Acknowledgements

I owe a debt of gratitude to the following for "heavily" borrowing at times pieces of their work and/or outright sections. I do this unashamedly to use the sapient phrase, "if it ain't broke—don't try to fix it." Most of the borrowed works and research cannot be improved upon—so why try? It's better to assemble these meaningful parts, profound messages, and eloquent arguments into a cohesive whole, told with high school and college students in mind, and that's what I've done and where my talent lies.

Below in alphabetical order are the major contributors to *The SAPIENT Being* that I borrowed verbatim, quoted, and conceptualized much of their content from a little to a lot. Wherever this happened, I did my best to acknowledge my source. If I didn't at times within the 15 chapters, I did so intentionally because doing so would have distracted from their message. Nonetheless, they are more than referenced in the Resources section.

D'Souza, Dinesh: Is a conservative author and filmmaker co-anchoring Chapter 6 with his keen analysis of the roots of Antifa's anarcho-Communist uprising and rage with his article titled "The Philosopher of Antifa" that should be a must read for every college freshman.

Latzer, Barry: Is a professor emeritus at John Jay College of Criminal Justice, CUNY and contributed content to Chapters 1, 4, 7, and 15 such as "The Facts on Race, Crime, and Policing in America Law & Liberty" and "The Need to Discuss Black-on-Black Crime" articles, the 2016 book *The Rise and Fall of Violent Crime in America*, and a final article "Do Illegal Aliens Have High Crime Rates?"

Lonergan, Brian: Is the director of communications at the Immigration Reform Law Institute (IRLI) and contributed heavily to Chapter 14 with his "Meet America's Ten Worst Sanctuary Communities," "Sanctuary California Failed to Honor Over 5,600 ICE Detainers" and "Sanctuary laws defy the will of the American people" articles.

Mac Donald, Heather: Is a law enforcement expert at the Manhattan Institute and author of the 2017 book *The War on Cops: How the New Attack on Law and Order Makes Everyone Less Safe*. Mac Donald's articles "Crime and the Illegal Alien: The Fallout from Crippled Immigration Enforcement" and "The Myth of Systemic Police Racism" were both important to Chapter 7. Her "There Is No Epidemic of Racist Police Shootings" article was included in Chapter 8, and "Crime and the Illegal Alien: The Fallout from Crippled Immigration Enforcement" was instrumental to Chapter 15.

Ngo, Andy: Is the author of the 2021 book *Unmasked: Inside Antifa's Radical Plan to Destroy Democracy* that reveals the inner workings of Antifa cells. Ngo courageously upholds journalistic standards and has gone above and beyond the call of duty covering and uncovering Antifa activities and was beaten and hospitalized for it. Nonetheless, he is resolute in exposing and confronting the anarcho-communist Antifa movement as well as exposing Rose City Antifa and infiltrating the Seattle CHAZ.

Professor X: Is an unknown UC Berkeley history professor co-anchoring Chapter 6 who penned an anonymous letter to the university's history department titled an "Open Letter Against BLM, Police Brutality and Cultural Orthodoxy" that reveals the systemic illiberalism and unsapient policies in Berkeley and their leftist academia.

Rubenstein, M.A., Edwin S.: Author of "The Color of Crime 2016: Race, Crime, and Justice in America" used extensively in Chapter 2 and throughout the rest of the book. His articles have appeared in *Harvard Business Review, New York Times, Wall Street Journal*, and *Investor's Business Daily* and he is the author of *The Right Data: The Conservative Guidebook to Busting Liberal Economic Myths.*

On a personal level, I created for my very diverse fraternity brothers in 2020 at the Delta Tau Chapter of the Phi Kappa Tau Fraternity at Cal Poly Pomona University, and our readers as well, an Adversity & Less Privileged Rankings Survey for Townhall Scoring & Discussion. This is a self-survey and points challenge to determine who has encountered the most interracial crime and suffered from that adversity and a link to it can be found in the Appendix.

The whole purpose is open dialogue with the hope of breaking down racial stereotypes related to interracial crime and adversity and there are three parts to this survey for scoring:

- Top 10 Adversity Incidents List
- Top 10 Less Privileged Scoring List
- Diversity Extra Credit Bio

All three parts can be ranked with each item scored on a scale of one to three: one being less meaningful, three being the most, and two in between or in the middle. If you cannot produce 10 items in the first two sections, that's okay, list as many as you can. Don't be intimidated with a few incidents because like basketball, three outside shots nets three points each equals nine total and five free throws at one point each only equals five total.

The third section is an extra credit or bonus section if you believe you have diversity in your life, work, or family history, etc. Please keep this diversity biography info related to this topic no more two to three paragraphs long. You can only earn 1 to 3 points for this section.

You can also do a blind survey amongst friends if you like with the identify of each contestant (so as not to influence the scoring) and let the judges in a Townhall group rate each item on a scale of 1 to 3, and see who scores the highest, and then discuss the results and conclusions. When all three sections are added together, the highest possible score is 63 (30 + 30 + 3).

And finally, how did I score you might ask? Let's just say that no one has been able to beat my score. If you think you can, I welcome any and all challengers, so please check out the Appendix link at the end of this book and follow it to the Fratire Publishing Blog where you can score me— and perhaps yourself—and let's start a discussion on the blog and see where it goes.

A SAPIENT Being's Preface

A black man in America is more likely to be struck by lightning than shot by a police officer and by the numbers, it's rare for police to kill anyone. However, when a shooting occurs, it needs to be evaluated on its own merits. The false narratives and fake news surrounding police shootings of innocent black suspects has caused law enforcement officers to be demonized, assaulted, and murdered.

Numerous scientific studies have proven that when behavioral, demographic, and other contextual factors are controlled, the racial disparity in police shootings disappears. In 2019, police shot and killed 1,003 people in the US, according to the *Washington Post's* Fatal Force database. Of those, 250 were black and 405 white. Police shot and killed 55 unarmed suspects, including 25 whites and 14 blacks and only one of the involved officers in 2019 was charged with murder.

According to the FBI's Uniform Crime Reporting (UCR), there were 686,665 sworn police officers in the United States in 2018 which equals one unarmed black male shot and killed for every 49,047 sworn police officers! Despite these facts, politicians, activists, and the media continue to misrepresent them. It's time to stop the lying and set the record straight!

In 2018, police made 10,310,960 arrests, according to the FBI, and the race was known for 5.6 million offenders. Of them, 1,548,690 (27.4%) were black and there were 229 black males shot and killed by police that year, according to the *Washington Post*, for a ratio of one out of every 6,762 black offenders. The ratio of unarmed black men shot and killed (23) in 2018 was *one* out of 67,334 black men arrested!

These hard facts, inconvenient truths, and multiple unbiased data sources used for *Crime Rate Madness*, more than prove there is no epidemic of racist police shootings in the US. Furthermore, a long list of scientific papers disproves systemic racial bias in police killings.

Nonetheless, for some of you this *MADNESS* book will be a triggering event, denial of truth, and a painful intervention. For others, it will be a revelation, an epiphany, a sapient being moment.

Crime Rate Madness offers an opportunity to be part of the solution to this problem and as the time-tested saying goes, "Everyone is entitled to their own opinions—but they're not entitled to their own facts." Facts are facts, the truth is the truth—but they can be skewed and manipulated for disingenuous methods and false narratives also covered in this textbook.

The primary focus of *Crime Rate Madness* is an analysis of racial crime rate disparities, black-on-black crime, interracial victimization rates, 'so called' police brutality, depolicing efforts, BLM and Antifa instigated riots and lawlessness, SPLC false hate group ratings, OSF anti-law enforcement funding, and fake news and false narratives from the media.

Are you interested in setting the record straight about crime and punishment and supporting our law enforcement community? If yes, please read on and if you also believe in the message of this book and willing to fight for it—please considering joining one of these two programs below sponsored by the SAPIENT Being.

Make Free Speech Again On Campus (MFSAOC) Program

Provide high school and college students the opportunity to start SAPIENT Being campus clubs, chapters, and alliances where independent, liberal, and conservative minded students can meet safely and freely as sapient beings to learn the facts and truth concerning the important issues facing us today. Learn more about the process of practicing, protecting, and promoting viewpoint diversity, freedom of speech and intellectual humility as part of the Make Free Speech Again On Campus program for on or off and/or virtual campus groups at https://www.sapientbeing.org/programs.

This is a new membership drive with independent students in mind who want to hear both sides of an issue, from any topic, without intimidation. It's also a perfect opportunity for liberal and conservative minded students to pop each other's ideological bubbles, and together, openly, and honestly, discuss and debate the hottest and most contentious issues facing America and the world today. We accomplish this by following the highest standards of civil discourse and debating each other's ideas, premises, and principles without attacking their character with malice and prejudice. This is sapience at its best!

World Of Writing Warriors (WOWW) Program

Return free speech, open dialogue and civil discourse to high school and college campuses without intimidation and threat of violence to those with differences in opinion, ideologies, and practices. Encourage open debate, dialogue, and the free expression of alternative and non-orthodox viewpoints with the goal of creating a World Of Writing Warriors (WOWW) program at https://www.sapientbeing.org/programs that upholds journalistic standards and promotes viewpoint diversity throughout all types of campus journalism and media.

The WOWW Program is a partnership between the SAPIENT Being and Fratire Publishing that provides a unique opportunity for promising and unpublished writers, student and graduate journalists, debate programs and sponsors, white paper researchers and authors of every discipline and background to contribute to any of the *MADNESS* titles and chapters and be recognized for it. Because Fratire Publishing is a small but determined independent publisher, it makes the perfect home for the WOWW Program with its 50 *MADNESS* series of titles.

Are You a Sapient Being or Want to Be One?

Sapience, also known as wisdom, is the ability to think and act using knowledge, experience, understanding, common sense and insight. Sapience is associated with attributes such as intelligence, enlightenment, unbiased judgment, compassion, experiential self-knowledge, self-actualization, and virtues such as ethics and benevolence.

Being a sapient being is not about identity politics, it's about doing what is right and borrows many of the essential qualities of Centrism that supports strength, tradition, open mindedness, and policy based on evidence not ideology.

Sapient beings are independent minded thinkers that achieve common sense solutions that appropriately address America's and the world's most pressing issues. They gauge situations based on context and reason, consideration, and probability. They are open minded and exercise conviction and willing to fight for it on the intellectual battlefield. Sapient beings don't blindly and recklessly follow their feelings or emotions.

Their unifying ideology is based on the truth, reason, logic, scientific method, and pragmatism— and not necessarily defined by compromise, moderation, or any particular faith—but is considerate of them.

Most importantly, per a letter written by Princeton professor Robert George in 2017 and endorsed by 28 professors from three Ivy League universities for incoming freshmen, "Think for yourself!"

George's letter continues:

Thinking for yourself means questioning dominant ideas even when others insist on their being treated as unquestionable. It means deciding what one believes not by conforming to fashionable opinions, but by taking the trouble to learn and honestly consider the strongest arguments to be advanced on both or all sides of questions— including arguments for positions that others revile and want to stigmatize and against positions others seek to immunize from critical scrutiny.

The love of truth and the desire to attain it should motivate you to think for yourself. The central point of a college education is to seek truth and to learn the skills and acquire the virtues necessary to be a lifelong truth-seeker. Open-mindedness, critical thinking, and debate are essential to discovering the truth. Moreover, they are our best antidotes to bigotry.

Merriam-Webster's first definition of the word "bigot" is a person "who is obstinately or intolerantly devoted to his or her own opinions and prejudices." The only people who need fear open-minded inquiry and robust debate are the actual bigots, including those on campuses or in the broader society who seek to protect the hegemony of their opinions by claiming that to question those opinions is itself bigotry.

So, don't be tyrannized by public opinion. Don't get trapped in an echo chamber. Whether you in the end reject or embrace a view, make sure you decide where you stand by critically assessing the arguments for the competing positions. Think for yourself. Good luck to you in college!

Now, that might sound easy. But you will find—as you may have discovered already in high school—that thinking for yourself can be a challenge. It always demands self-discipline, and these days can require courage.

In today's climate, it's all-too-easy to allow your views and outlook to be shaped by dominant opinion on your campus or in the broader academic culture. The danger any student—or faculty member—faces today is falling into the vice of conformism, yielding to groupthink, the orthodoxy.

At many colleges and universities what John Stuart Mill called "the tyranny of public opinion" does more than merely discourage students from dissenting from prevailing views on moral, political, and other types of questions. It leads them to suppose that dominant views are so obviously correct that only a bigot or a crank could question them.

Since no one wants to be, or be thought of as, a bigot or a crank, the easy, lazy way to proceed is simply by falling into line with campus orthodoxies. Don't do it!

To be sure, our overly-politicized culture has a hard time viewing any "verbal cacophony" as a sign of strength and vibrancy. And perhaps nowhere is this truer than on many college campuses where political correctness is rampant, groupthink is common, and social media "mobs" arise in a flash to intimidate anyone who openly strays from the prevailing orthodoxy.

At the SAPIENT Being we're not intimidated—and our primary purpose is to seek the truth by enhancing viewpoint diversity, promoting intellectual humility, protecting freedom of speech and expression while developing sapience in the process—no matter what the cost on the intellectual battlefield, campus classroom, and marketplace of ideas. This is our ethos! Is it yours?

Best regards and sapiently yours,

Corey Lee Wilson

Corey Lee Wilson

S.A.P.I.E.N.T. Being

1 – America's Embarrassing Crime Statistics & Perceptions

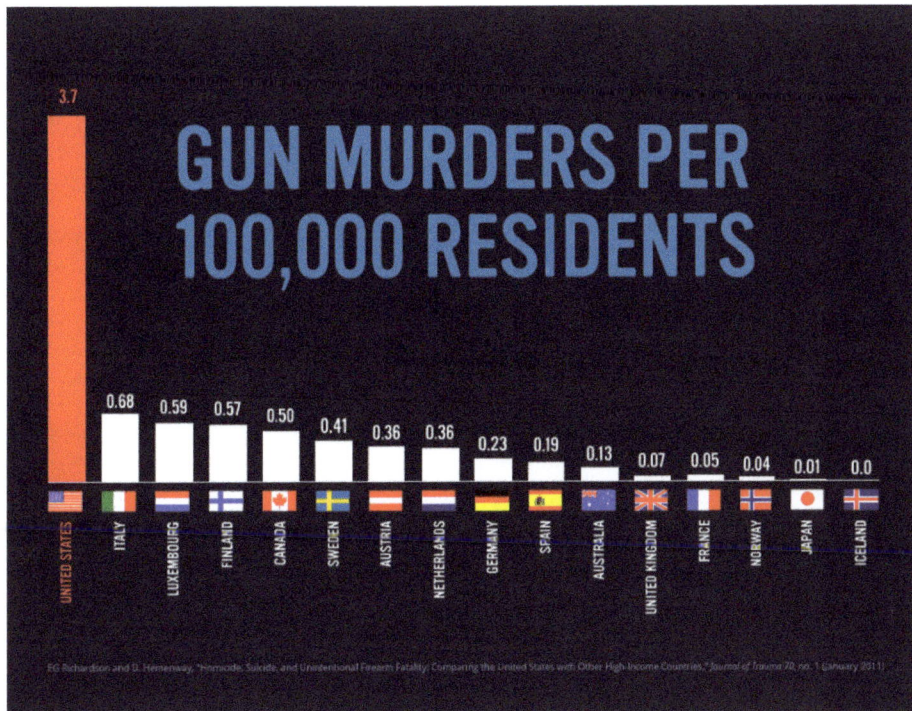

Credit: Lab Prolib in Gun Culture (2015).

Crime is a deliberate offense that a person, whether coerced or not, commits. United States crime has been monitored and reported since the 1700's. Crime rates have risen and fallen since then. Crime started increasing after 1963 and reached a peak in 1993. Since the mid-1990s during the Clinton administration, there has been a significant downward trend from 1994 to 2013, increasing slightly up through 2020.

Public perception, however, is misleading and most people believe that crime rates are up and worse than ever before. According to 17 Gallup polls, six-in-ten people say that there is more crime in the U.S. now than compared with previous years.

Other research performed by Pew Research Center shows similar findings with 57% of registered voters believe that crime has gotten worse since 2008, even though the FBI data clearly indicates rates declining in double-digits.

There are many forms of crime, and they are divided into four major classifications:

- Personal – These crimes are committed against a person, which affects them either physically or psychologically. Rape, assault, and murder are examples of personal crimes. Robbery, which is also categorized as a crime against property, is also considered a personal crime in that it causes physical and emotional distress to the victim.

- Property – Ownership of property, whether a car or savings, is one of the basic rights of a person, and preventing someone from enjoying that liberty through unlawful ways merits punishment. Fraud, forgery, theft, and robbery are categorized under crimes against property.

- Inchoate – Inchoate offenses are crimes committed to fulfill another crime. Conspiracy, attempt (i.e., to commit manslaughter, robbery, etc.) and bribery are types of inchoate offenses.

- Statutory – Statutory crimes are committed against the government as well as the laws passed by its legislative body. Insider trading, statutory rape, drug trafficking, and drunk driving are classified as statutory crimes.

There are three degrees of assault in violent crime:

- 1st Degree which is intentionally inflicted bodily harm and may result in a felony murder charge.

- 2nd Degree which differs from 1st Degree in that it may use a potentially deadly weapon, but death neither resulted nor was it intended.

- 3rd Degree which is a misdemeanor assault causing bodily injury.

Homicide, domestic violence, aggravated battery, hate crimes, rape, and physical and sexual abuse of an adult or a child all fall under the category of violent crime. Violent crimes include homicide, accidental or intentional murder, rape, or other sexual assault charges, robbery with or without a weapon, assault, inducing aggravated or simple assault and purse snatching or pickpocketing. All of these crimes include injury or threat of injury to the victim.

Property crimes are burglary with or without the intent of theft. Anyone who is not authorized to be onsite at a property and breaks in or is found there illegally is guilty of burglary. Theft is also a crime within this classification and can be as simple as theft of cash or small belongings. Motor vehicle theft is also included in this category; this includes attempted robberies that are unsuccessful.

Race, Crime, and Police Violence

In this section, Barry Latzer, professor emeritus at John Jay College of Criminal Justice, CUNY provides a number of key points from his June 2020 essay, "The Facts on Race, Crime, and Policing in America."

Big city police are deployed in high numbers to low-income African American communities. Why? Because that's where most of the crime is. That's where it has been since the 1920s, and especially since the 1960s. Such deployments were far less common prior to the 1960s, when black communities were severely under-policed. The result was impunity for many black violent criminals and, in turn, an incentive for black men to engage in more violence as a self-defense mechanism.

The late 1960s changed this pattern. As black-on-white crime rose, police departments came under mounting pressure to control crime, much of which occurred in or near minority neighborhoods where it victimized black residents. African American violent crime rates soared between the 1960s and the early 1990s. During that period, in big cities, arrests of African Americans for homicide, the most accurate measure of violent crime, accounted for 65 to 78 percent of all homicide arrests. This is an extraordinary figure when one considers that the nonwhite population of these cities ranged from only 20 percent to a bit over 35 percent.

The situation today has improved considerably. African American crime rates, and United States crime rates generally, have fallen dramatically. For all persons of all age groups, the homicide death rate fell 34 percent from 1990 to 2016. For black males in the same time frame, the decline was 40 percent.

While violent crime has fallen, it nevertheless remains disproportionally high in communities of color. The latest police data collected by the FBI indicates that blacks comprised 58 percent of all murder arrests and 40 percent of those apprehended for all violent crimes. This disproportional involvement of African Americans in violent crime turns out to be the most significant factor of all in explaining the use of force against blacks by police.

It will be no surprise that violent criminals in the United States are commonly armed and dangerous. For assaults, for instance, 71 percent of arrested persons carried firearms. Among suspected murderers, 58 percent had guns, as did 42 percent of apprehended robbery suspects. This tally doesn't include the knives or blunt instruments recovered from violent offenders, including over 48,000 cutting instruments possessed by those arrested for assault alone.

Police, of course, are well aware of this situation. Charged with a duty to apprehend offenders, they are—and must be—prepared to use force. Confrontations, often armed confrontations, in these circumstances are inevitable.

Such confrontations will frequently involve white police and black suspects. Whites are a declining proportion of police departments in the United States, but they're still close to half the force in big-city departments where white males make up 44 percent of full-time sworn officers.

Does the Criminal Justice System Treat Blacks Less Fairly Than Whites?

Barry Latzer notes: The most recent 2020 George Floyd incident has raised anew the issue of police use of force, especially against people of color. Most Americans, black and white, believe that the criminal justice system treats blacks less fairly than whites. A 2019 Pew Research poll found that 84 percent of blacks and 63 percent of whites support this view. Those numbers may rise in the wake of the George Floyd episode.

Numerous proposals to reduce police violence are now being offered, but I'm skeptical that these will change things in the short or medium term. The reason for my lack of optimism is not that American police are incurably racist. Police are probably no more racist than the average American. Rather, it is that African Americans (or blacks, both terms used interchangeable throughout this book)—low-income, young, male, urban African Americans, to be precise—engage in violent misconduct at higher rates than other groups, and violent crime begets police violence. As numerous examples, studies, and reports will show, the more a group engages in violent crime, the more the police will use violence against members of that group.

Everyone Agrees Excessive Use of Force Should Be Eliminated

On June 6, 2020, Congress introduced H.R. 7120–Justice in Policing Act of 2020 to deal with police misconduct. The bill lowers the standard to convict police officers for misconduct, limits qualified immunity against civil action, provides addition tools to investigate patterns of discrimination, creates a national misconduct registry, and creates a framework to prohibit racial profiling at all levels.

Per Barry Latzer, other constructive solutions include: Improving officer training and standards, increasing transparency and the timely release of information, enhancing shooting investigations, reevaluating carotid restraint standards, and studying the effects of both public sector unions and civilian review boards. Since each shooting must be evaluated on its own merits, the mandatory use of body cameras could provide valuable evidence.

The media and protesters claim the violent actions of a few rioters do not represent most of the peaceful group, yet they argue the actions of one bad officer represents the whole. This faulty reasoning needs to stop. People need to forgo emotional arguments for rational analysis, stop confusing correlation with causation, and understand the impact of confounding variables

For too long, the demonstrably false narrative about racially motivated police shootings has been propagated by politicians, activist groups, the media, and Hollywood. The data proves when contextual variables are considered, the racial disparity in police shootings disappears. It's time for the public to overcome their cognitive dissonance and discover the truth.

Interracial Crime

While blacks commit the majority of homicides, they are also the group with the highest percentage of homicide victims. According to the 2018 FBI UCR, there were 6,460 known-race homicide victims, of which 3,315 were white and 2,925 were black.

Whites were 51% of known race homicide victims and 76.5% of the total US population, while blacks were 45% of known race homicide victims, but only 13.4% of the US. That means the homicide rate for blacks was 3.35 times their percentage of the US population, making them over five times as likely to be homicide victims.

And who is mostly responsible for murdering these high percentages of blacks? It's not police—it's other blacks. Most crime is intraracial, where both victims and offenders share the same race, but when violent crime is interracial, blacks commit a far higher percentage than whites.

According to a Bureau of Justice Statistics 2018 study, 15.3% of crimes against whites were committed by blacks for a total of 547,948 crimes. In contrast, whites committed 10.6% of crimes against blacks for a total of 59,777 crimes. Anyone, including a fifth grader, can do the math here and arrive at the same answers.

Despite being 13.4% of the population, blacks committed nine times more interracial crimes against whites than whites committed against blacks. If racism is the cause of interracial violence, white cops are not the problem.

Scientific Studies

Furthermore, Barry Latzer found, per a 2019 research article, published by the Proceedings of the National Academy of Sciences (PNAS), detailed the findings of a study by David J. Johnson. The study analyzed fatal police shootings in 2015 and confirmed blacks, which were 12% of the population, accounted for 26% of those shot and killed by police.

But when violent crime was used as a benchmark, the anti-black disparity disappeared. The study found officers were more likely to shoot suspects of the same race, and more importantly, the number of police shootings could be predicted by race-specific violent crime rates.

The Collaborative Reform Initiative studied deadly force used by the Philadelphia Police Department from 2007 through 2013. The study determined 59% of officers involved in shootings were white and 34% were black. In these shootings, 80% of suspects were black, and the majority were young males. Unarmed suspects were 15.4% of all people shot by police, but 25% of white suspects and 15.8% of black suspects were unarmed.

The study found the shooting of unarmed suspects was most often caused by threat perception failures or physical altercations. With black suspects, white officers had a 6.8% threat perception failure and the rate for black officers was 11.6%. The study found no significant threat perception failures among different suspect racial groups.

A 2016 National Bureau of Economic Research study by Harvard Economics Professor Roland Fryer, analyzed racial differences in police use of force. It concluded that blacks and Hispanics were 50% more likely to experience non-lethal police use of force, but when controlling for contextual factors, the study found no racial disparity in the use of deadly force in police shootings. The study also debunked prior claims that implicit bias affected shooting decisions.

A 2014 study in the *Journal of Experimental Criminology*, by Dr. Lois James, used laboratory simulations to test racial and ethnic bias in police shootings. Previous research had suggested blacks were more likely to be perceived as having weapons. This study flashed images of people and objects, and test subjects were required to decide whether to shoot. Out of 827 scenarios, 588 of which required deadly force, unarmed subjects were shot 47 times.

Unarmed white suspects were shot 46 times and unarmed blacks were shot only once. Subjects also waited longer to shoot black suspects. The study found that "subconscious associations between race and threat exhibited by participants are not linked to shooting behavior."

Enough of the Lying—Just Look at the Data

As reported by Jeffrey James Higgins, a retired DEA supervisory special agent and former Hillsborough County Sheriff's Office deputy, with 25 years of law enforcement experience, with a Master of Science in Criminal Justice with a focus on research, in 2015, about 53.5 million people had at least one contact with police, and 95% of those contacts involved traffic stops, according to the Bureau of Justice Statistics (BJS).

According to a BJS special report, 91% of whites and 85% of blacks contacted by police during traffic stops said police behaved properly. Of citizens contacted during street stops, 81% said police acted properly. Only 2% of all citizens contacted by police experienced force, or the threat of force.

After the Ahmoud Arbery murder in Georgia, LeBron James tweeted: "We're literally hunted EVERYDAY/EVERYTIME we step foot outside the comfort of our homes!" That sentiment has been repeated during the recent protests, but does it reflect reality?

According to the US census, in July 2019, an estimated 328,239,523 people resided in the US. Blacks comprise 13.4%, or 43,984,096 people. That means police shot and killed one unarmed black male out of every 3,141,721 black Americans. Does that sound like an epidemic of police murders?

The numbers of unarmed blacks shot and killed by police are so low, most Americans recognize their names. Comparatively, every year police kill a larger number of unarmed whites, but almost no one knows their names.

Fig. 7: Percentage of Arrested Suspects Who Were Black, 2009–2013; Percentage of Prisoners Who Were Black, 2013

Data sources: Uniform Crime Reports (arrests); Bureau of Justice Statistics (prisoners)

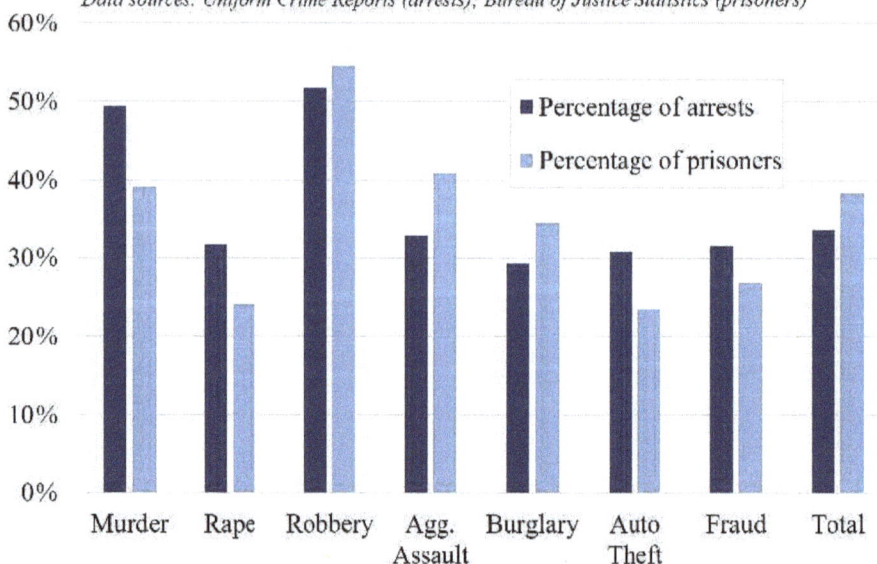

Why does the media ignore these shootings? And focus on the others? If you fall into this illiberal mind set, you'll have difficulties understanding the true cause of crime rate disparities amongst America's demographics. However, *Crime Rate Madness* can help provide a non-biased, truthful, and sapient point of view.

It's true the relative percentage of blacks killed is higher than with whites, but the press does not cover the shooting of whites to the same extent, probably because it contradicts the narrative of racist police. Shootings later determined to be justified are still trumpeted as proof of racism—as with the 2014 death of Michael Brown in Ferguson, Missouri.

Even in bad shootings, there is often scant evidence of racism, because it's difficult to determine internal motivations. It's bad science to assume racism based solely on the disparate numbers between racial populations. As an example, a study of police shootings in 2015 showed suicidal whites were more likely to be killed by police. Are police racist against whites? Of course not!

Is There Racial Bias in Law Enforcement

The past two years have seen unprecedented concern about racial bias in law enforcement. Deaths of young black men at the hands of the police led to serious rioting in Ferguson, Missouri, and in Baltimore. These and other deaths gave rise to the Black Lives Matter movement, which has carried out hundreds of demonstrations across the country and even in Canada. It is widely assumed that the police and the courts are strongly biased—certainly against blacks, and probably against Hispanics.

This problem cannot be fully understood by concentrating on a few cases, no matter how disturbing they may first appear. There were an estimated 11,300,000 arrests in the United States in 2013, the overwhelming majority of which were carried out properly. It is only in a larger context that we can draw conclusions about systemic police bias or misbehavior.

This larger context is characterized by two fundamental factors. The first is that different racial groups commit crime at strikingly different rates and have done so for many years. The second is that crime, overall, has declined dramatically over the last 20 years. Only after considering these points is it possible to draw well-founded conclusions about police bias.

In 2005 (updated in 2016), "The Color of Crime 2016: Race, Crime, and Justice in America" by Edwin S. Rubenstein, M.A., provides numerous government crime statistics that shows blacks were seven times more likely to commit murder and eight times more likely to commit robbery than people of other races, while Asians had consistently low crime rates. Hispanics appeared to be committing violent crime at roughly three times the white rate, but this conclusion was tentative because official statistics often failed to distinguish between whites and Hispanics.

The study also found that blacks were seven times more likely than whites to be in prison and Hispanics were three times more likely. It also concluded that high black arrest and imprisonment rates—often cited as evidence of a racist criminal justice system—were explained by the black share of offenders.

Denying the True Cause of Crime Rate Disparities Amongst America's Demographics?

As you will clearly see as you read through this book, the hard facts, inconvenient truths, and multiple unbiased data sources used for *Crime Rate Madness* more than prove there is NO epidemic of racist police shootings in the America. Furthermore, a long list of scientific papers disproves systemic racial bias in police killings.

Nonetheless, for some of you this textbook will be a will be a triggering event, denial of truth, and a painful intervention. For others, it will be a revelation, an epiphany, a sapient being moment. If you fall into the first category of those who refuse to accept the true cause of crime rate disparities amongst America's demographics—would you be open to hearing other and alternative points of view? If you're open to dissecting unproven and false narratives of systemic racism, white supremacy, and rampant police brutality—congratulate yourself and read on.

If it's your 'so-called' progressive point of view that the only reasonable explanation for the "unequal outcomes" of crime rate statistics is proof of racial bias and systemic racism in law enforcement—could there be other reasons you haven't considered before, heard about, or were taught?

If the answer is yes, that's a sapient decision, so let's get started with our next significant fact:

White officers are no more likely than black or Hispanic officers to shoot black civilians. It is a racial group's rate of violent crime that determines police shootings, not the race of the officer. The more frequently officers encounter violent suspects from any given racial group, the greater the chance that members of that racial group will be shot by a police officer. In fact, if there is a bias in police shootings after crime rates are taken into account, it is against white civilians.

The True Statistics of Police Killings

"The Color of Crime 2016" report exposes another aspect of race-relations that is largely ignored by the media is the fact that more whites are killed by police than blacks. On top of this, FBI data show that for every 10,000 black Americans arrested for violent crime, three are killed, yet for every 10,000 white Americans arrested for violent crime, four are killed.

Biased, newspapers make it difficult to see this fact, though clicking on categories like race or choosing "total" rather than "per million" reveals the amounts of whites killed annually can in fact be more than double or triple that of blacks. Do you know any of their names? Taking into account that blacks are far more likely to commit violent crime than whites, these figures, if anything, suggest an anti-white bias. It is possible that due to negative press in the past, police are more hesitant to shoot blacks than they are to shoot whites.

Blacks Americans are also 18 times more likely to shoot and kill a police officer than the other way around. Despite making up only 6.4% of the population of the United States, black males account for 33% of cop killers. Blacks are far more likely per 100,000 to kill police officers than any other race.

The black population in America ranged from 11.6 percent to 13 percent between 1980 to 2013. Compared to that percentage in the population, the percentage of black offenders who killed police officers per 100,000 is extremely high.

Hard Data Proves There is No Epidemic of Racist Police Shootings

There is a plethora of fake news articles and false narrative and biased studies that in one way or another, attempt to reject the overwhelming evidence of numerous scientific studies that has proven that when behavioral, demographic, and other "contextual" factors are controlled—the racial disparity in police shootings disappears. Beware of these studies!

Despite the truth, leftward bias, anti-police narratives, and fake news sources with false narratives tend to thrive in an echo chamber of unsapience that is viewpoint orthodox, statistically unsound, and to one degree or another, violate at least one of the fifteen the most important fallacies of logic as covered in Chapter 8.

Although an arguable amount of progress has been made in the general academic treatment of race, the intersection of race and crime still proves to be a problematic topic for social science as previously noted. A race and crime summary from a number of studies compiled by Criminal Justice is listed below:

As Sampson and Wilson (1995) stated, "The discussion of race and crime is mired in an unproductive mix of controversy and silence ... criminologists are loathe to speak ... for fear of being misunderstood or labeled racist." Nonetheless, the disproportionate involvement of minorities with crime, both as victims and perpetrators, demands a systematic and balanced exploration.

Many social scientists Mann (1993) and Stark (1990) complicate the matter with assertions that the perceived differential between groups with regard to crime is reducible to either systematized bias or unreliable/misapplied statistics. To counter, a number of scholars Hawkins (1986); Hindelang (1978); Katz (1988); Sampson and Wilson (1995) have provided arguments that both acknowledge the differentials while furthering the etiological debate.

Long List of Scientific Papers Disprove Racial Bias in Police Killings

Per Rubenstein (2016), there are dramatic race differences in crime rates. Asians have the lowest rates, followed by whites, and then Hispanics. Blacks have notably high crime rates. This pattern holds true for virtually all crime categories and for virtually all age groups. The high black crime rate also explains the high incarceration rate for blacks compared to whites—and are not due to unfair sentencing, police bias, or systemic racism.

Even though overall crime indices have been falling for the past 25 year, Unz (2013) noted in the case of blacks, for the last 25 years, the weighted crime correlations have steadily risen from 0.60 to around 0.80 or above, almost always falling within between 0.75 and 0.85 range.

It's important to recognize that within the world of academic sociology discovering an important correlation in the range of 0.80 or above is quite remarkable, almost extraordinary. And even these correlations between black population prevalence and urban crime rates may actually tend to significantly understate the reality.

Lott and Moody (2017), using one of the most comprehensive list of police shootings compiled, finds black suspects are not more likely to be shot by white officers than blacks after controlling for a whole host of variables and finds no support for racial based discrimination by white officers.

Per Cesario et al. (2018), we know blacks are over represented compared to their percentage of the population in police killings, but that isn't the right benchmark. Blacks also commit a significant number of crimes which makes them more likely to find themselves in scenarios involving police, and that alone means they're more likely to "act out" and lead to a justified police killing.

Using various metrics of crime (murder, violent crime, weapons violations), and looking at all fatal shootings, they found a consistent anti-white bias in police shootings. Disaggregating the data and only looking at unarmed victims shows blacks still usually not being discriminated against and, in fact, being shot less than you'd expect based on their crime indices.

James (2016) did a lab experiment with police officers and found officers took longer to shoot blacks than whites in their scenarios (1.09 to shoot a white, 1.32 seconds to shoot a black), and they were more likely to wrongly shoot non-aggressing whites than non-aggressing blacks.

Johnson et al. (2019) looked at 2015 data and found that black and white cops were equally likely to shoot blacks.

Fryer (2016, revised 2018) found no racial bias in police shootings, though he did find bias in police use of force. The data was limited to Houston, though, so it's hard to know if the data is generalizable.

Ross (2015) found a racial bias in police shootings and was widely reported in media. There are critical issues that weren't reported though: It didn't use incident level data, making it subject to the ecological fallacy. Further, it used odd metrics of crime (like assault and weapons violations), when crimes like homicide are more appropriate because those crimes typically include a body and have much less police discretion in terms of arrests etc.

Goff et al. (2016) found no bias in police shootings but did find a bias in police force (like Fryer). However, when they controlled for violent crime, whites were actually more likely to experience use of force than blacks were.

Per Barry Latzer, a professor emeritus at John Jay College of Criminal Justice, CUNY and 2016 author of *The Rise and Fall of Violent Crime in America*, there are three more studies below worth considering.

The Chicago Study

As it turns out, when it comes to the use of force, the race of the police officer may not be significant. A study of 270 police shootings in Chicago from 2006 to 2014 found that the demographics of the officers who fired their weapons matched the demographics of the police department. Whites were 51 percent of the shooters and 53 percent of the force; blacks were 23 percent of the shooters and 25 percent of the force. In other words, there is no evidence that white police were more likely to discharge their weapons or that African American officers were less likely. This is especially noteworthy given the demographics of the shooting victims: 5 percent were white, 14 percent Hispanic, and an eye-popping 80 percent were black.

Equally significant is the reason for the confrontation. In the overwhelming majority of cases (77 percent), the police were reactive, not proactive. They were responding, in the typical scenario, to a call about a violent crime. In the proactive situation (23 percent of the shootings), the officer initiated the contact, e.g., stopped a suspicious person.

One study showed that white police officers were no more likely than black officers to fatally shoot black civilians. In 80 percent of the shootings, the officer reported a gun threat, and in 60 percent a firearm was recovered. In the remaining 20 percent, the officer said (s)he was threatened with a motor vehicle (12 percent), a weapon other than a gun (10 percent), or a physical attack (8 percent).

In short, according to the Chicago data, in the overwhelming majority of police-civilian shootings, the police didn't initiate the confrontation, but rather were summoned by civilian reports, whereupon they fired in response to a direct threat of an attack, usually with a gun.

Nowadays many mistrust police accounts, suspecting a cover-up or at least a slanting of the truth. But there is empirical and unbiased support for the police version of events. It comes in a recent study of fatal police shootings and it is to this study that we cover below.

The Fatal Shootings Study

Psychologists led by David J. Johnson of the University of Maryland created a database of 917 fatal shootings of civilians by police in 2015. They correlated various factors—characteristics of the police officer, the civilian who was shot, and the county in which the incident occurred—with the race of the victim.

First, they found no evidence of bias against victims of color. "Controlling for predictors at the civilian, officer, and county levels," the analysts wrote, "a person fatally shot by police was 6.67 times less likely ... to be Black than White and 3.33 times less likely ... to be Hispanic than White. Thus, in the typical shooting, we did not find evidence of anti-Black or anti-Hispanic disparity."

This accords with national data compiled by the *Washington Post*, not exactly a pro-police publication, for a five-year period (2015-2019). The *Post* tallied 4,263 fatal shootings by police for which the race or ethnicity of the victim was known. Of these, 53 percent were white, 28 percent were black, and 20 percent were Hispanic. In other words, nearly twice as many whites as blacks were fatally shot by police.

Professor Johnson and associates examined the 2015 incidents in detail to determine the reasons for the shootings. They found that "[t]he vast majority—between 90 percent and 95 percent—of the civilians shot by officers were actively attacking police or other citizens when they were shot." This confirms the claims of police shooters in Chicago, as noted above.

It also reinforces Roland Fryer's highly publicized study on race and the use of force by police. Fryer found, after controlling for numerous factors, that blacks were 27.4 percent less likely than non-Hispanic whites to be fatally shot by police.

A second major finding of the Johnson study was the absence of any correlation between the race of the officer and that of the victim. That is, after controlling for other factors, white police officers were no more likely than black officers to fatally shoot black civilians. In fact, the more black officers on a police force, the more African Americans were fatally shot.

The most significant finding of all, though, was the correlation between violent crime and police shooting. The more violent crime by blacks in a county, the more blacks shot to death by police. In the words of the study:

Officer race, sex, or experience did not predict the race of a person fatally shot beyond relationships explained by county demographics. On the other hand, race-specific violent crime strongly predicted the race of a civilian fatally shot by police, explaining over 40% of the variance in civilian race. These results bolster claims to take into account violent crime rates when examining fatal police shootings.

It is possible, of course, that police discriminate more when nonlethal force is involved. The Fryer study drew that very conclusion, finding, for instance, that police were 18 percent more likely to shove a black person than a white in similar circumstances. But this analysis, which was limited to New York City during the aggressive "stop-and-frisk" years, did not include data on crime rates within each police precinct broken down by race or ethnicity. Unlike the Johnson study, in other words, Fryer did not correlate nonlethal force with the violent crime rate of minority groups.

Police Violence and Criminal Violence

American police must face down armed violent criminals. That's their job. Often those violent threats come from young, male, urban African Americans. As long as that is the case there will be violent confrontations between police and black civilians. Increasing the number of black police officers won't change this. Nor will study commissions, police budget reductions, chokehold prohibitions, or the elimination of qualified immunity from civil suits, to mention a few of the proposals to curb police being proposed. Some of these proposals may be wise, some not. But none will dramatically reduce the number of violent confrontations between police and African Americans.

This situation will change significantly when black violent crime rates decline significantly. That won't occur any time soon, but it will happen. It happened to Irish-Americans who committed crime at exceptionally high rates in the 19th century, and to Italian-Americans who did likewise in the early 20th century. As the United States continues to reduce obstacles to black social advancement, and as African Americans take advantage of the opportunities that this country affords them, their crime too will become a distant memory. The big questions is: When?

2 – The Color of Crime and Its Impact for All Americans

Credit: Jean Pierre Aime Harerimama/Reuters.

The definitive 2005 (updated in 2016), "The Color of Crime 2016: Race, Crime, and Justice in America" by Edwin S. Rubenstein, M.A., about race, crime, and justice in America is used extensively in this chapter and throughout *Crime Rate Madness*.

If you choose to ignore the profound crime statistics from Rubenstein's updated report (and the substantial others that follow) and believe in false ones—what is your agenda? As the timeless saying goes, "If you're not part of the solution—you're part of the problem!"

To see the stark reality of the color of crime in America, consider these glaring statistics from the chart above:

- Black on White 547,948 vs. White on Black 59,778 = 9.2:1 Ratio meaning blacks commit at least nine times more violent crimes against whites that whites commit against blacks.

- Hispanic on White 365,299 vs. White on Hispanic 207,104 = 1.8:1 Ratio meaning Hispanics commit almost twice as many violent crimes against whites as whites commit against Hispanics.

- Black on Hispanic 112,365 vs. Hispanic on Black 44,551 = 2.5:1 Ratio meaning blacks commit two and a half times more violent crimes against Hispanics as Hispanics commit against blacks.

Crime is Down in General—But Still Very High

There has been a downward long-term trend in crime taking place since 1994 clearly indicated by the broadest measure of criminality in the United States, which is the annual National Crime Victimization Survey (NCVS).

In 2013, 90,630 households and 160,040 people were interviewed for the NCVS about their experiences as crime victims—whether reported to the police or not. A 20-year compilation of the survey's findings indicates that both the number and rate of violent victimizations have declined steadily, albeit unevenly, for at least two decades per "The Color of Crime 2016" report.

Violent crime includes rape or sexual assault, robbery, simple or aggravated assault, and domestic violence—but not murder. Total violent victimizations in 2013 (the most recent year for NCVS data) were about one-third their 1994 level, which was a record high; the total number declined from 17.1 million in 1994 to 6.1 million in 2013.

This drop reflects an even steeper decline in the rate of violent crime (violent crimes per 1,000 people 12 years of age or older)—from 79.8 in 1994 to 23.2 in 2013. While violent crime is unquestionably down since the last "Color of Crime" report, the share of non-white victims.

From 2002 to 2013, the number of violent victimizations suffered by whites and blacks fell by 29.5 percent and 20.4 percent, respectively, and the white share of total violent victimizations declined from 73.2 percent to 62.6 percent. (In this report, "white," "black," and "Asian" always mean "non-Hispanic.")

Over the same period, Hispanic victimizations rose by 25.6 percent, while the "Other" category (mainly Asians) saw a 9.1 percent rise. Victimization rates for both groups declined—though not as rapidly as for whites or blacks. The rise in victimizations was the result of a rapid increase in the numbers of these groups. From 2002 to 2013, the Hispanic population age 12 and over, for example, grew 48.6 percent while the corresponding white population grew by only 1.6 percent.

The "Two or more races" category did not exist in 2002 for the NCVS, and the high victimization rates for this group probably reflect its small sample size: The rate more than doubled from 2012 to 2013.

While the black victimization rate exceeded that of whites and Hispanics in both 2002 and 2013, the gap between the black and Hispanic rates narrowed dramatically—from 6.2 victims per 1,000 people (36.1–29.9) in 2002 to just 0.3 (25.1–24.8) in 2013. If this trend continues, the Hispanic victimization rate will soon exceed the black rate.

In 2002, whites were 9 percent more likely to be victims of a crime than Hispanics. By 2013, these groups had changed places, with the white victimization rate 10.5 percent lower than the Hispanic rate. This may be due to illegal immigration of Hispanics. A disproportionate number of such immigrants are young men, who are the group most likely to commit crimes, and they may also be vulnerable as victims.

Property crimes such as burglary and motor vehicle theft also appear to be in long-term decline, falling from an estimated 35.1 million cases in 1993 to 16.8 million in 2013. As with violent crimes, property crime victims are increasingly non-white.

The overall property crime rate has declined since the last "The Color of Crime 2016" report— from 168.2 victimizations per 1,000 households in 2002 to 131.4 per 1,000 in 2013. The number of property crimes suffered by white households fell 20 percent from 2002 to 2013, and their share of such crimes dropped from 70.6 percent to 62.5 percent. Both whites and blacks suffered fewer property crimes in 2013 than in 2002.

Black and White Americans Differ Widely in Their Views of Criminal Justice

Black Americans are far more likely than whites to say the nation's criminal justice system is racially biased and that its treatment of minorities is a serious national problem.

In a recent Pew Research Center survey in May 2019, around nine-in-ten black adults (87%) said blacks are generally treated less fairly by the criminal justice system than whites, a view shared by a much smaller majority of white adults (61%). And in a survey shortly before last year's midterm elections, 79% of blacks–compared with 32% of whites–said the way racial and ethnic minorities are treated by the criminal justice system is a very big problem in the United States today.

Racial differences in views of the criminal justice system are not limited to the perceived fairness of the system as a whole. Black and white adults also differ across a range of other criminal justice-related questions asked by the Center in recent years, on subjects ranging from crime and policing to the use of computer algorithms in parole decisions.

Here's an overview of these racial differences per the Pew survey:

Crime

Black adults in the U.S. consistently express more concern than white adults about crime.

Concerns about violent crime, gun violence are higher among blacks than whites In last year's preelection survey, three-quarters of blacks–compared with fewer than half of whites (46%)– said violent crime is a very big problem in the country today. And while 82% of blacks said gun violence is a very big problem in the U.S., just 47% of whites said the same.

Blacks are also more likely than whites to see crime as a serious problem locally. In an early 2018 survey, black adults were roughly twice as likely as whites to say crime is a major problem in their local community (38% vs. 17%).

That's consistent with a survey conducted in early 2017, when blacks were about twice as likely as whites to say their local community is not too or not at all safe from crime (34% vs. 15%). Black adults were also more likely than whites to say they worry a lot about having their home broken into (28% vs. 13%) or being the victim of a violent crime (20% vs. 8%). However, similar shares in both groups (22% of blacks and 18% of whites) said they actually had been the victim of a violent crime.

Policing

Some of the most pronounced differences between blacks and whites emerge on questions related to police officers and the work they do.

A survey conducted in mid-2017 asked Americans to rate police officers and other groups of people on a "feeling thermometer" from 0 to 100, where 0 represents the coldest, most negative rating and 100 represents the warmest and most positive. Black adults gave police officers a mean rating of 47; whites gave officers a mean rating of 72.

Blacks are also more likely than whites to have specific criticisms about the way officers do their jobs, particularly when it comes to police interactions with their community.

More than eight-in-ten black adults say blacks are treated less fairly than whites by police, criminal justice system. In the Center's survey earlier this year, 84% of black adults said that, in dealing with police, blacks are generally treated less fairly than whites. A much smaller share of whites–though still a 63% majority–said the same. Blacks were also about five times as likely as whites to say they'd been unfairly stopped by police because of their race or ethnicity (44% vs. 9%), with black men especially likely to say this (59%).

Stark racial differences about key aspects of policing also emerged in a 2016 survey. Blacks were much less likely than whites to say that police in their community do an excellent or good job using the right amount of force in each situation (33% vs. 75%), treating racial and ethnic groups equally (35% vs. 75%) and holding officers accountable when misconduct occurs (31% vs. 70%). Blacks were also substantially less likely than whites to say their local police do an excellent or good job at protecting people from crime (48% vs. 78%).

Notably, black-white differences in views of policing exist among officers themselves. In a survey of nearly 8,000 sworn officers conducted in the fall of 2016, black officers were about twice as likely as white officers (57% vs. 27%) to say that high-profile deaths of black people during encounters with police were signs of a broader problem, not isolated incidents. And roughly seven-in-ten black officers (69%)–compared with around a quarter of white officers (27%)–said the protests that followed many of these incidents were motivated some or a great deal by a genuine desire to hold police accountable for their actions, rather than by long-standing bias against the police. (Several other questions in the survey also showed stark differences in the views of black and white officers.)

The Color of Crime: Major Findings

As previously noted, homicide and violent crimes committed by Black Americans in general are significantly more than those committed by white Americans. According to data from the 2017 Morbidity and Mortality Weekly Report (MMWR), between 1999 and 2015 Black Americans committed many more homicides than white Americans, approximately 10 or 11 times more.

Between 2000 and 2006 the violent crime rates of whites and Hispanics seemed to sharply diverge. According to the 2008 Bureau of Justice Statistics (BJS) report, during that half-decade, the number of whites incarcerated in state prison for violent offenses rose by just 7% while the number of Hispanics increased by a whopping 62%.

In addition to being the author of "The Color of Crime 2016: Race, Crime, and Justice in America," Edwin S. Rubenstein is the president of ESR Research and has worked as a senior economist at W.R. Grace & Co., and as research director at the Hudson Institute. His articles have appeared in *Harvard Business Review, New York Times, Wall Street Journal*, and *Investor's Business Daily*.

Throughout the rest of this chapter, various charts, figures, tables are taken directly from "The Color of Crime 2016" report and are not shown here in this chapter (but shown in the 2016 report). The foundation for Rubenstein's report comes from the Criminal Justice Information Services (CJIS), FBI: UCR–Crime in the United States, 2016, Table 21A-Arrests, by Race and Ethnicity, 2016 report and there is a link to both reports in the Appendix. Per Rubenstein:

Table 21A

Offense charged	Total arrests					
	Race					
	Total	White	Black or African American	American Indian or Alaska Native	Asian	Native Hawaiian or Other Pacific Islander
TOTAL	8,421,481	5,858,330	2,263,112	171,185	103,244	25,610
Murder and nonnegligent manslaughter	9,374	4,192	4,935	108	109	30
Rape[3]	18,606	12,571	5,412	233	309	81
Robbery	76,267	33,095	41,562	663	659	288
Aggravated assault	304,626	191,205	101,432	6,374	4,678	937
Burglary	164,641	112,651	47,991	1,613	1,925	461
Larceny-theft	833,558	575,105	231,199	14,933	10,277	2,044
Motor vehicle theft	68,170	44,970	20,955	1,018	895	332
Arson	7,767	5,593	1,813	218	120	23
Violent crime[4]	408,873	241,063	153,341	7,378	5,755	1,336

Credit: FBI: UCR, Table 21A-Arrests, by Race and Ethnicity, 2016 report (snapshot sample).

The National Crime Information Center (NCIC), has been called the lifeline of law enforcement. It's an electronic clearinghouse of crime data available to virtually every criminal justice agency nationwide. Some key points in the "The Color of Crime 2016" report are as follows:

- The evidence suggests that if there is police racial bias in arrests it is negligible. Victim and witness surveys show that police arrest violent criminals in close proportion to the rates at which criminals of different races commit violent crimes.

- There are dramatic race differences in crime rates. Asians have the lowest rates, followed by whites, and then Hispanics. Blacks have notably high crime rates. This pattern holds true for virtually all crime categories and for virtually all age groups. The high black crime rate also explains the high incarceration rate for blacks compared to whites—not due to unfair sentencing.

- In 2013, a black was six times more likely than a non-black to commit murder, and 12 times more likely to murder someone of another race than to be murdered by someone of another race.

- In 2013, of the approximately 660,000 crimes of interracial violence that involved blacks and whites, blacks were the perpetrators 85 percent of the time. This meant a black person was 27 times more likely to attack a white person than vice versa. A Hispanic was eight times more likely to attack a white person than vice versa. Whites are clearly the majority of victims.

- In 2014 in New York City, a black was 31 times more likely than a white to be arrested for murder, and a Hispanic was 12.4 times more likely. For the crime of "shooting"—defined as firing a bullet that hits someone—a black was 98.4 times more likely than a white to be arrested, and a Hispanic was 23.6 times more likely

- If New York City were all white, the murder rate would drop by 91 percent, the robbery rate by 81 percent, and the shootings rate by 97 percent. Black males are eight times more likely to commit rape than white males and this ratio hasn't moved much in 50 years.

- In an all-white Chicago, murder would decline 90 percent, rape by 81 percent, and robbery by 90 percent. There are more blacks killed by other blacks in *one* week in Chicago than all the rest of justifiable black killings by law enforcement in one year!

- In 2015, a black person was 2.45 times more likely than a white person to be shot and killed by the police. A Hispanic person was 1.21 times more likely. These figures are well within what would be expected given race differences in crime rates and likelihood to resist arrest. In other words, races/ethnicities with a higher violent crime rate (i.e. blacks and Hispanics) are more likely to be shot and killed.

- In 2015, police killings of blacks accounted for approximately 4 percent of homicides of blacks. Police killings of unarmed blacks accounted for approximately 0.6 percent of homicides of blacks. The overwhelming majority of black homicide victims (93 percent from 1980 to 2008) were killed by blacks. Police brutality is evidently not the problem—

a black man's greatest enemy is another black man, and this is clearly the problem—not so called police brutality.

- Both violent and non-violent crime has been declining in the United States since a high in 1993. 2015 saw a disturbing rise in murder in major American cities that some observers associated with "depolicing" in response to intense media and public scrutiny of police activity. We'll see the same on steroids if unsapient, depolicing measures are approved. However, the depolicing measures might be successful if major cities had low white and Asian crime rates like the New York City and Chicago examples above.

Race of Offender

It is surprisingly difficult to arrive at a definitive picture of the races of offenders as noted in "The Color of Crime 2016" report. The National Crime Victimization Survey (NCVS) categorizes crime victims by race and Hispanic ethnicity, but until recently, it did not consider Hispanics a separate offender category; it usually called them "white" or "other race."

Furthermore, beginning in 2009, the year the Obama administration took office, the NCVS stopped publishing information on race of offender, even though it continued to gather the data. In 2015, the Department of Justice (DOJ) finally released a partial set of offender-race information.

The Uniform Crime Reports (UCR) program, which is the basis of the FBI's national tabulation of arrests, includes Hispanics in the "white" category. Arrest and incarceration rates by race—to the extent they are even available—must often serve as imperfect indicators of actual offense rates by race.

As we will see in greater detail below, blacks are arrested at much higher rates than any other racial group. It is common to argue that these high rates are the result of racial bias, and that bias continues through every stage of criminal processing: indictment, plea bargain, trial, sentencing, parole, etc. In 2008, then-senator Barack Obama asserted that blacks and whites "are arrested at very different rates, are convicted at very different ... for the same crime." This view is echoed by the media but is not supported by either the scholarly literature or by government statistics.

Police, in particular, are often accused of racial bias, but is it really plausible that they arrest blacks they know are innocent but ignore white criminals? A 2008 summary of earlier research compared the races of offenders as identified by victims to the races of perpetrators arrested by the police and found that "the odds of arrest for whites were 22 percent higher for robbery, 13 percent higher for aggravated assault, and 9 percent higher for simple assault than they were for blacks, whereas there were no differences for forcible rape."

National Incident-Based Reporting System (NIBRS)

Fortunately, as noted in "The Color of Crime 2016" report there is an excellent database that shines light directly on the question of racial bias in arrests: the National Incident-Based Reporting System (NIBRS).

In 2013, 6,328 law enforcement agencies covering approximately 29 percent of the US population reported crime to the FBI using NIBRS categories, which include races of reported offenders as well as races of persons arrested. It is reasonable to assume that both the racial mix of this massive sample and the behavior of police officers are representative of the entire United States.

Unfortunately, NIBRS does not distinguish between whites and Hispanics, which means blacks are the only racial group for which we have consistent information. However, blacks are the group most frequently said to be victims of police bias, so if the police treat them fairly it is probably safe to conclude they treat other groups fairly.

Per Rubenstein, Figure 4 compares the percentages of criminals that victims say were black to the percentages of arrested suspects who were black. If police are arresting a larger proportion of blacks than the proportion of criminals victims say were black, it would be evidence of bias.

For most crimes, blacks make up a larger percentage of reported offenders than they do of those arrested. In only seven of the 22 NIBRS crime categories did blacks account for a larger share of arrests: homicides, counterfeiting/forgery, embezzlement, fraud, stolen property offenses, drug offenses, and gambling. Interestingly, these are crimes for which there may be no witnesses—such as embezzlement or stolen property—or are "victimless" crimes, such as drug offenses and gambling. The racial identification of suspects in these cases may not be reliable.

In crimes that involve direct contact with victims and in which race of offender can therefore be clearly identified, black arrest rates in Rubenstein's report are below the reported offender rates. For example, blacks were identified as 73 percent of robbery offenders but accounted for only 59 percent of robbery arrests.

When crimes from all categories are aggregated, black offenders were 14 percent less likely than non-blacks offenders to be arrested. This suggests that police do not show anti-black bias but make arrests that closely match the proportions at which people of different races commit crime.

NIBRS data come disproportionately from smaller police departments. In 2013, only 10 percent of the population covered by the system lived in cities of 250,000 and greater. What do arrest statistics show for large metropolitan areas from "The Color of Crime 2016" report?

New York City Data and Statistics

New York City, for example, does not participate in NIBRS but it records the races of arrested offenders, and consistently distinguishes between whites and Hispanics. In 2014, 374 people were arrested for murder. Their races were as follows:

- White: 2.9 percent
- Black: 61.8 percent
- Hispanic: 31.8 percent
- Asian: 2.7 percent
- Other: 0.8 percent

Police take murder very seriously and investigate all cases carefully. Press and judicial system scrutiny are high. Arrest rates for murder therefore track actual crime rates more closely than for any other crime. Murder is probably the crime for which it would be most difficult for police to make "biased" arrests even if they wanted to.

Given a population (page B1 of report) that was 32.8 percent white, 22.6 percent black, 28.9 percent Hispanic, and 13.0 percent Asian, a black was 31 times more likely than a white to be arrested for murder, a Hispanic was 12.4 times more likely than a white, and an Asian was twice as likely. These multiples and those for other crimes appear as graphs on the next page of Rubenstein's report. A "shooting" is discharge of a firearm in which a bullet strikes a person.

There is another way to express these disparities. If New York City had been all white in 2014— and the additional whites committed crimes at the same rates as the city's actual white residents—there would have been 32 murder arrests instead of 374, 1,844 robbery arrests instead of 10,163, and 16 arrests for shootings rather than 503. These figures would reflect reductions in these crimes of no less than 91, 81, and 97 percent, respectively.

There are race differences in crime rates throughout the United States, but the differences are particularly sharp in New York and other major cities. This is probably because whites who live in urban centers are often relatively wealthy whereas blacks and Hispanics who live in cities are relatively poor.

Per Rubenstein's report, in the graphs on the following page, the most serious offenses are displayed above, with the less serious offenses below (except for firearms violations, which are serious crimes). Where possible, the graphs are arranged to depict the less serious version of the same crime directly below the more serious version. Misdemeanor sex crimes, for example, do not rise to the level of rape, and include forcible touching and sexual misconduct. Grand larceny is theft of anything with a value greater than $1,000 and includes auto theft, while petty larceny is theft of anything less valuable. Felonious assault includes attack with a deadly weapon, whereas misdemeanor assault includes pushing and spitting. Misdemeanor criminal mischief includes such crimes as cemetery desecration and calling in false fire alarms.

Almost without exception, the black/white and Hispanic/white arrest multiples are lower for the less serious crimes. Whatever else this difference may mean; it is strong evidence that the police are not making biased arrests. Police have broad discretion as to whether they will arrest someone for forcible touching, shoplifting, or setting off a false fire alarm.

If racist police wanted to vent prejudices on non-whites, these are the crimes for which they could most easily do so. They can walk away if someone complains he was spat on, and if they are racist, they can walk away if the spitter is white but make an arrest if the spitter is black. Police cannot walk away if someone is lying on the sidewalk bleeding from a knife wound. They must try to make an arrest, whatever the race of the suspect. Per Rubenstein's report, the graphs that show the lowest non-white/ white arrest multiples are for crimes in which police have the greatest arrest discretion and are therefore strong evidence that New York City police are not biased in their arrest patterns.

Like New York, Chicago keeps detailed annual statistics on major crimes

Until 2010, Chicago published the race of offenders, but after the election of Mayor Rahm Emanuel, it stopped releasing that information. The 2010 report shows that, like New York City, there are stark racial differences. Arrests for murder were as follows: whites—8, blacks—190, Hispanics—48, Asians—1.

The racial mix of Chicago's population in 2010, as reported on page 25 of the police department report (whites—31.7 percent, blacks—32.4 percent, Hispanics—28.9 percent, Asians—5.4 percent) meant that a Chicago black was 24 times more likely than a Chicago white to be arrested for murder, and a Hispanic was 6.7 times more likely.

Table 3 of Rubenstein's report shows the multiples for the white arrest rates for a variety of crimes. Sharp racial differences appear not only for crimes of violence but also for property crimes, such as burglary and auto theft. The Chicago data fit the national pattern: Blacks have, by far, the highest arrest rates, followed by Hispanics. Asians have the lowest arrest rates.

Per "The Color of Crime 2016" report, If the same calculation is done as with New York City to arrive at crime rates in a theoretical all-white Chicago, murder would decline by 90.2 percent, rape by 80.8 percent, and robbery by 90.2 percent.

Chicago police also collected information on the sex of arrested criminals. Most people understand that men are more violent and dangerous than women, and this is reflected in the city's arrest statistics. In 2010, men were 12.8 times more likely than women to be arrested for murder and 19.4 times more likely to be arrested for robbery, compared to the black/white multiples for these crimes of 23.8 and 27.3, respectively. This means that although men in Chicago are more dangerous than women, by comparison, blacks are even more dangerous when compared to whites. Similar calculations for New York City are not possible because the NYPD does not release arrests by sex.

Other American Cities Release Crime Statistics But Not Always For the Same Categories

Furthermore, "The Color of Crime 2016" reports that Milwaukee records races of suspects in both homicides and "non-fatal shootings." In 2014 (the most recent year available), blacks were 12 times more likely to be murder suspects than whites, and Hispanics were four times more likely. For non-fatal shootings, blacks were 25 times more likely than whites to be suspects, and Hispanics were 7.6 times more likely.

Pittsburgh releases arrest statistics, which follow the same pattern. In 2012 (the most recent year available), blacks were 26.6 times more likely than whites to be arrested for murder. The multiples for robbery, rape, and aggravated assault were 9.8, 7.5, and 5.6, respectively. The Hispanic population was so small (2.7 percent) that comparisons were not meaningful.

St. Louis, Missouri, keeps track of homicide suspects by race (page 41 of Rubenstein's report). In 2013, 96 were black, one was white, one was Hispanic, and one was Asian. Murder victims are not a cross section of the population. In 2013, 82.5 percent had a criminal record (page 40 of the 2016 report).

A larger geographical territory, such as California, gives a broader picture of racial differences in arrest rates, and one in which racial disparities are not nearly so stark. California is one of the few states that treat whites, blacks, and Hispanics separately, so there can be no confusion about how many Hispanics are being counted as whites. The NIBRS data, together with academic studies of policing that find little racial bias in arrests, suggest that arrest figures are probably realistic indices of the different rates at which people of different races commit crime (see Table 4 of Rubenstein's report).

Consistent with national data, arrest rates of blacks, Hispanics, and "others" have all declined relative to that of whites over the past decade (see the last figures in the table: "Multiple of white rate" of Rubenstein's report). Still, in 2013, California blacks were 5.35 times more likely than whites to be arrested for violent crimes, and 4.24 times more likely to be arrested for property crimes. The corresponding figures for Hispanics were 1.42 and 1.14.

"Others," who are mostly Asians, appear to be a model group. Violent-crime arrest rates are less than half those for whites, and property crime arrest rates are 60 percent lower.

The "Total" figure indicates the multiple of the white arrest rate for the total population. Black and Hispanic arrest rates raise the multiple while arrest rates for "Others" lower it.

While black and Hispanic arrest rates have declined relative to white rates, very high black arrest rates are still the rule for most crimes (see Table 5, next page of Rubenstein's report). In 2013, the black arrest rate multiple (compared to whites) ranged from a low of 1.56 for "dangerous drugs" offenses to a high of 13.39 for robbery. Black arrest rate multiples rose for burglary, forgery, kidnaping, arson, and, especially, dangerous drugs, for which the black multiple more than doubled since 2002. Dangerous drugs are methamphetamine, phencyclidine, and barbiturates. The sharp increase, matched with a very sharp decline in arrests for "narcotics," probably reflects a shift in "War on Drugs" enforcement policy towards these drugs rather than marijuana.

California Hispanics

Per "The Color of Crime 2016" report, California Hispanics, on the other hand, were less likely than whites to be arrested for drug offenses, narcotics, and arson. At the other extreme, Hispanics were 2.50 times more likely to be arrested for homicide; for forcible rape, the figure is 2.25. Hispanics are now the single largest group in California. In 2014, there were 14.92 million whites and 14.99 million Hispanics in the state.

On average, Hispanics are younger than whites and blacks. This means there are relatively more Hispanics in the peak crime ages of 18 to 29. Some analysts have argued that when age distribution is taken into account, Hispanics are no more likely than whites to commit violent crimes.

It is not possible to test this theory with national arrest data because not all jurisdictions distinguish between Hispanics and whites. However, California distinguishes consistently between whites and Hispanics, and also includes arrest rates by age group. Table 6 on page 9 of Rubenstein's report, which is probably representative of the entire country, deserves careful study.

Hispanics of every age group are more likely than whites to be arrested for every type of violent crime. For the highest crime age group of 18 to 29, this is particularly noticeable for homicide (2.7 times the white rate), rape (2 times) and kidnapping (2 times).

Though the sample size is small, Hispanic teenagers (ages 10 to 17) were 8.2 times more likely than whites of the same age group to be arrested for homicide: In 2013, 74 Hispanic and five white teenagers were arrested for this crime. (There are more than twice as many Hispanics as whites in this age range, which brings down the multiple.) Gang violence is probably a cause.

Assaults are the most common violent crime and accounted for 80 percent of all arrests for violent crimes in California in 2013. Hispanics of every age group are arrested for assault at higher rates than whites, for an overall multiple of 1.34.

Blacks, however, are arrested at sharply higher multiples than both whites and Hispanics. Robbery is a perennial stand- out in this respect, with multiples as high as 29.8 in the 10 to 17 age group. There was only one age group, for only one crime, for which blacks were arrested at a lower rate than whites: drunk driving in the 10 to 17 age range. Again, this is a crime for which police have almost complete discretion when deciding to make an arrest, so there would be a high black/white multiple if officers were intent on targeting blacks unfairly.

Blacks are the main cause of urban crime. As Hispanics displace blacks in America's largest cities and in its largest state, crime rates should remain stable or decline because Hispanics are displacing the group with the highest crime rates.

To return to Table 5 of Rubenstein's report, it is notable that the "Other" category of offenders—which is composed largely of Asians—has the lowest arrest rates across the board. This is consistent not only with earlier versions of "The Color of Crime" but with virtually every study conducted on American crime rates. As the number of Asians in a jurisdiction rises, crime rates can be expected to fall.

Race and Drug Arrests

It is often claimed that blacks suffer unfairly from the enforcement of drug laws, and it is true that longer sentences for possession of crack cocaine rather than powder fell more heavily on blacks. As a 1997 report from the University of Chicago notes:

From 1965 through the early 1980s, blacks were approximately twice as likely as whites to be arrested for drug-related offenses. Following the federal government's initiation of the "War on Drugs," black arrest rates skyrocketed, while white arrest rates increased only slightly. By the end of the 1980s, blacks were more than five times more likely than whites to be arrested for drug-related offenses. These differences reflect the government's targeting and enforcement of specific types of drug use and trafficking.

Even setting aside the question of crack versus powder cocaine, it is often claimed that blacks suffer from police bias in drug arrests. It is common to allege that although blacks and whites use marijuana at roughly the same rate, blacks are nearly four times more likely than whites to be arrested for possession.

The assumption that whites and blacks take drugs at the same rate is based on answers to survey questions. However, there is evidence that blacks are less likely than whites to report illegal drug use. A number of studies have asked subjects about drug use and then checked their answers against the results of urine- or hair-analysis tests.

A 2005 study in the Journal of Urban Health, for example, found that blacks were ten times more likely than whites to lie about cocaine use. Hispanics were five times more likely to lie. There were similar differences in reported use of marijuana. The study concluded that "the results replicate and extend a growing body of research suggesting that African Americans underreport substance use on surveys." Studies from 2003, 2008, and as long ago as 1994 report similar findings, though one from 2001 found ambiguous results.

There is other evidence that drug use is not the same across racial groups. The US Department of Health and Human Services keeps records of how many people of different races went to emergency rooms because of an acute reaction to illegal drugs. In 2011, the most recent year for which data are available, blacks were 2.8 times more likely than whites to end up in the ER because of marijuana, and seven times more likely because of cocaine. For all drugs, the multiple was 3.5. There is no reason to think these figures reflect anything other than different rates of illegal drug use.

Ever since receiving home rule in 1975, Washington, D.C., has had a black mayor and most of its police chiefs have been black. In any given year, as many as two-thirds of its police officers are black. And yet, in 2010, a black district resident was eight times more likely than a white resident to be arrested for marijuana possession. It is hard to imagine this was because of police discrimination rather than differences in marijuana use.

Finally, it would be possible for blacks to be no more likely than whites to use drugs but still be arrested more often for using them, even by scrupulously race-neutral police. That is because blacks commit a larger number of other crimes. If someone is arrested for robbery, for example—and in California blacks were more than 13 times more likely than whites to be arrested for robbery—the police search the suspect for drugs. If they find drugs, they add a charge of possession in addition to robbery. Higher rates of illegal activity expose blacks to more intense criminal processing.

In any case, since the last "The Color of Crime 2016" report, the black/white incarceration multiple for drug offenses has declined by nearly 60 percent (see Table 8, page 12 of Rubenstein's report). This probably reflects the government's response to prison overcrowding as well as a reorientation of enforcement activity in the War on Drugs rather than a decline in police bias.

3 – Black Criminality—Not Racism or Police Brutality—Is the Problem

Credit: Chicago Tribune. Chicago police release surveillance photos, video in 2019 homicide in South Shore neighborhood.

Before we even begin this chapter with the word of "racism" in its title, we have to decide first which definition of "racist" we are using which leads to the question of, "How can you tell if someone is a racist?"

For some, racism is any kind of racial prejudice; for others it's belief in the superiority of one's own race; for others, it's being in conscious or unconscious collusion with systems of privilege based on race, etc.

The term is not universally agreed upon, nor is there a fool proof scientific method for determining a racist. Regardless, the most universally agreed upon litmus test is a person's actions and words. But when you see how actions and words (including your own) can be taken out of context, be misunderstood, or completely wrong—a sapient being can see that labeling someone as racist can be a subjective opinion—and not an objective fact.

More importantly, in this day and age it seems to be the case more often than not—that those accusing (pointing their fingers) others of being racist—have their other four fingers (of hatred, bias, prejudice and/or ignorance) pointing right back at them. Please let that sink in before you start making any accusations and pointing your finger.

As noted in Matt Margolis' June 2020 article in PJ Media, "Is There Really an 'Epidemic' of Racist Police Shootings? Several Studies Say No," in 2019 police officers fatally shot 1,004 people, most of whom were armed or otherwise dangerous. African-Americans were about a quarter of those killed by cops last year (235), a ratio that has remained stable since 2015. That share of black victims is less than what the black crime rate would predict, since police shootings are a function of how often officers encounter armed and violent suspects. In 2018, the latest year for which such data have been published, African-Americans made up 53% of known homicide offenders in the U.S. and commit about 60% of robberies, though they are 13% of the population.

The police fatally shot nine unarmed blacks and 19 unarmed whites in 2019, according to a *Washington Post* database, down from 38 and 32, respectively, in 2015. The Post defines "unarmed" broadly to include such cases as a suspect in Newark, N.J., who had a loaded handgun in his car during a police chase. In 2018 there were 7,407 black homicide victims. Assuming a comparable number of victims last year, those nine unarmed black victims of police shootings represent 0.1% of all African-Americans killed in 2019. By contrast, a police officer is 18½ times more likely to be killed by a black male than an unarmed black male is to be killed by a police officer.

The following breakdown from Law Enforcement Today also puts the issue of police brutality in perspective:

- According to 2019 data, there are 328, 240, 469 people here in the United States.

- According to stats from com, there are 670,279 full time police officers here in the United States out of a total of 900,000 sworn law enforcement officers (data from National Law Enforcement Memorial Fund).

- There are approximately 2.1 police officers per thousand people.

- Police officers are less than .21 % of population.

- Officers come into contact with 17% of the population annually.

- That means 55,800,880 contacts.

Which, at the time of the last report, led to 26,000 excessive force complaints against officers:

- That's 0.047% of contacts.

- Only 8% of those complaints were sustained.

- That's 2,080 out of 53,380,000 contacts, or .0039%.

A good friend of Matt Margolis who a chief of police put that into perspective:

- You are seven times more likely to be murdered ...

- 15 times more likely to be killed in a traffic accident ...

- 42 times more likely to be raped ...

than to have a police officer use excessive force on you.

Simply put, the narrative that police officers are overwhelmingly racist is simply not true and has likely contributed to police being assaulted or killed. During the rise of the Black Lives Matter movement, Barack Obama perpetuated the myth of systemic police racism, described by some as a "war on cops," resulting in a spike of cops killed in the line of duty from 2013-2016.

So, cooler heads must prevail when it comes to this issue. Cops who use excessive force must be dealt with appropriately but perpetuating the myth of a widespread epidemic of racist cops helps no one, and likely does more damage. We literally have people calling for the defunding of police from many powerful circles and influential people. While there may be a few bad cops out there, we rely on them to protect our communities.

Is There an 'Epidemic' of Racist Police Shootings? Several Studies Say No

A July 2016 study titled "An Empirical Analysis of Racial Differences in Police Use of Force" (revised January 2018) of over a thousand police-involved shootings found what researcher Harvard Prof. Roland G. Fryer Jr. calls "the most surprising result of my career" because there is no racial bias in police-involved shootings. Not only are blacks *not* more likely to be fired upon by police than whites in tense moments, but the study also found that, if anything, they are less likely to be shot at.

In what is one of the most comprehensive studies on the issue to date, Fryer—an African-American economist who says he began the study in response to his anger over the deaths of Michael Brown and Freddie Gray—examined 1,332 shootings that occurred between 2000 and 2015 in 10 major police departments. By the end of the exhaustive research, Fryer and his teams spent an estimated 3,000 hours poring over the data from Los Angeles, three cities in Texas (Houston, Austin, and Dallas), and four counties and two cities in Florida (Orlando and Jacksonville).

Rather than a superficial study of statistics, Fryer's team probed deeper into each case to make sure they were conducting an apples to apples investigation. In its summary of the study, the *New York Times* provides some of the key details of cases the study incorporated in its analysis, including, "How old was the suspect? How many police officers were at the scene? Were they mostly white? Was the officer at the scene for a robbery, violent activity, a traffic stop or something else? Was it nighttime? Did the officer shoot after being attacked or before a possible attack?" Some of the study's driving questions included was a black suspect more likely to be fired upon—in cases where lethal force was justified and when it was unjustified—and did the officer shoot more quickly at black suspects?

To his admitted "surprise," Fryer concluded that the racial bias narrative is demonstrably false when it comes to police-involved shootings. Here are six takeaways from Fryer's study.

1. **Police are not more likely to fire on blacks than whites.**

   In fact, blacks are 20% less likely to be fired on. When Fryer and his team dug into the details of the 1,332 officer-involved shootings, they found that officers were actually less likely to fire on black suspects without having been attacked.

   Fryer found the same to be true when he examined cases that did not result in shootings. Using data from the Houston Police Department, Fryer looked at arrests where lethal force might have been justified—where suspects were arrested for serious offenses, like resisting arrest, fleeing, or attacking an officer—and found that if a suspect was black, officers were about 20% less likely to shoot. His findings included that blacks were about 24-22% less likely to be shot at when police "might plausibly have fired."

2. **Blacks and whites involved in police shootings were equally likely to be carrying a weapon.**

As the *New York Times* highlights, Fryer also found that black and white civilians involved in police shootings "were equally likely to have been carrying a weapon." This conclusion likewise directly undermines the assumption that racial bias is a major factor in officers' use of lethal force, as some have posited that a disproportionate number of blacks were unarmed in police shootings as compared to whites.

3. **Blacks are more likely to be treated worse by officers when it comes to physical contact.**

While the study found that black men and women were not more likely to be fired upon by officers, according to a study of NYPD stop-and-frisk records from 2003-2013, they were treated worse by officers when it came to physical contact, including "use of hands" (17% more often), being pushed to the wall (18% more), use of handcuffs (16%), having weapons drawn on them (19%), being pushed to the ground (18%), and having a weapon pointed at them (24%), and being pepper sprayed (25% more, though they only assessed 9 cases).

4. **The notion that police officers' accounts are biased and unreliable is largely a myth.**

Fryer's research revealed that concerns about the reliability of police reports were also largely unfounded, his results being about the same whether or not he referred to the recounting of events provided by officers.

5. **Use of mobile video to document alleged police brutality is not impacting policing practices.**

Another conclusion of the study was that the use of cell phones and social media to document alleged police brutality does not appear to have changed policing practices, a question that many have posed in recent years following high-profile videos of police encounters.

6. **Fryer's study aligns with other research.**

Fryer's findings align with other studies that have found that the narrative of racial bias in use of lethal force by police is largely based on de-contextualized data and false assumptions.

In 2015, for example, 50% of the victims of police shootings were white, while 26% were black. Some have tried to argue that this is evidence of racial bias against blacks because they represent only 15% of the population; however, as Heather Mac Donald points out, blacks account for a disproportionate percentage of major crimes, including 62% of robberies, 57% of murders and 45% of assaults. Another example of de-contextualized data is that showing a higher percent of unarmed blacks who are shot than unarmed whites, but as both Mac Donald and Fryer found, when the details of the cases are included, such statistics turn out to be misleading.

The reality, as Fryer and others have found, is that our law enforcement is largely composed of men and women doing their best to protect the lives of citizens, handling what are often life and death situations as fairly and safely as they can.

Statistical Limitations Regarding Race and Crime in America

Per Ron Unz, author of "Race and Crime in America: The unspoken statistical reality of urban crime over the last quarter century" report published in July 2013, he aptly notes a number of limitations with his own research and it's included in this section because Unz sapiently cautions readers regarding the limitations of his own research. Unlike many researchers, he is the first to admit any inconsistencies and where updates and further research is needed.

In his own words: My central methodology is simple. I obtained the crime rates and ethnic percentages of America's larger cities from official government data sources and calculated the population-weighted cross-correlations. In order to minimize the impact of statistical outliers, I applied this same approach to hundreds of different datasets: each of the years 1985 through 2011; homicide rates, robbery rates, and violent crime overall; all large cities of 250,000 and above and also restricted only to major cities of at least 500,000.

I obtained these urban crime correlations with respect to the percentages of local whites, blacks, and Hispanics, but excluded Asians since their numbers were quite insignificant until recently (here and throughout my article, "white" shall refer to non-Hispanic whites).

It is important to recognize that within the world of academic sociology discovering an important correlation in the range of 0.80 or above is quite remarkable, almost extraordinary. And even these correlations between black population prevalence and urban crime rates may actually tend to significantly understate the reality.

All these correlations were performed on a city-wide aggregate basis. The New York City numbers include both the Upper East Side and Brownsville, Los Angeles both Bel Air and Watts, Chicago the Gold Coast and Englewood, with each city's totals averaging those of both the wealthiest and the most dangerous districts. This crude methodology tends to obscure the local pattern of crime, which usually varies tremendously between different areas, often roughly corresponding to the lines of racial segregation. It is hardly a secret that impoverished black areas do have far higher crime rates than affluent white ones.

Major Cities With Substantial Poverty But Few Blacks Tend to Have Lower Levels of Crime

As noted by Unz, consider that both blacks and Hispanics currently have similar national poverty rates in the one-third range, more than double the white figure, and each constitutes well over 20% of our urban population. However, major cities with substantial poverty but few blacks usually tend to have far lower levels of crime. For example, El Paso and Atlanta are comparable in size and have similar poverty rates, but the latter has eight times the robbery rate and over ten times the homicide rate. Within California, Oakland approximately matches Santa Ana in size and poverty but has several times the rate of crime. Thus, it seems plausible that removing the black population from our calculation might actually reduce the residual poverty/crime correlation for non-blacks to a moderate or even a low figure.

To some extent, this surprising possibility is merely a statistical syllogism. Whenever the correlation to a single factor approaches unity, no other non-equivalent item may have a large, independent impact. And failing to recognize the existence of such a single, overwhelming factor might lead us to misidentify numerous other spurious influences, whose apparent causal importance actually derives from their own correlations with the primary item. For many years, the black connection to local crime has been so strong as to almost eliminate the possible role of any other variable.

We must obviously be cautious in interpreting the meaning of these statistical findings since correlation does not necessarily imply causation. Over the last few years the crime correlation for Hispanic or Hispanic-plus-Asian numbers has been substantially more negative than the same figure for whites, but this does not necessarily prove that whites are much more likely to commit urban crime, though it would tend to rule out the contrary possibility that Hispanics or immigrants have far higher rates of criminality.

FBI Arrest Statistics Support Most Straightforward Interpretations of Racial Crime Correlations

However, as Unz notes, if we examine the official FBI arrest statistics, we find that these seem to support the most straightforward interpretation of our racial crime correlations. For example, blacks in America were over six times as likely to be arrested for homicide in 2011 as non-blacks and over eight times as likely to be arrested for robbery; the factors for previous years were usually in a similar range.

The accuracy of this racial pattern of arrests is generally confirmed by the corresponding racial pattern of victim-identification statements, also aggregated by the FBI. Indeed, several years ago the liberal Sentencing Project organization estimated that some one-third of all American black men are already convicted criminals by their 20s, and the fraction would surely be far higher for those living in urban areas.

A sense of the real world impact of these grim statistics may be found in the stratified 2011 Census-ACS data for major American cities. The three urban centers with the largest black populations are New York City, Chicago, and Philadelphia, and together they contain over one-third more adult black women than black men. The corresponding national shortfall of black males runs well into the millions, partly accounting for the notorious "marriage gap" problems faced by women of their background. Those millions of missing black men are generally dead or in prison.

Over the last few years, the official publications of the Bureau of Justice Statistics (BJS) have made it increasingly difficult to determine the racial totals of inmates in state prisons and local jails but the figures from the mid-2000s probably still provide a reasonable estimate, and I had used these in my 2010 article. Since crime is overwhelmingly committed by young males, for comparative purposes we should normalize all these incarceration totals against the base population of adult males in their prime-crime years, and the results are summarized in my previously published chart, reprinted here.

Since the mid-1990s, the issue of street crime has mostly dropped off the front pages of our national newspapers and disappeared from the public debate. Meanwhile, black Americans have gained much greater visibility in the upper reaches of our national elites, while Barack Obama has been elected and reelected as our first black president. This might seem to indicate that traditional racial cleavages in our society have become less substantial.

Furthermore, with such enormous numbers of young black men now in prison, we might naturally expect that the racial character of American urban crime rates has sharply declined over the last couple of decades. However, the quantitative evidence demonstrates the exact opposite situation, as may be seen by examining the combined twenty-five year trajectories of our various racial crime correlations, which have steadily grown more extreme. The images shown on our film screens or television sets may portray one America, but the actual data reveals a very different country.

Once we accept the reality of these stark racial facts, we must naturally wonder about the causes, and also why the historical trends seem to have been moving in exactly the wrong direction over most of the last quarter-century. Certainly, many theoretical explanations have been advanced, both from the Left and the Right, and whole library shelves have been filled with books on the subject since the urban violence of the 1960s.

Per Unz, a short article is no place for me to summarize such a vast literature on a contentious topic, especially when I can provide no original insights of my own. But good theoretical analysis requires a solid factual grounding, and my main purpose here is to establish those facts, which others may then choose to interpret howsoever they wish. Absent such information, any national dialogue becomes an exercise in empty ideological posturing.

Criminal Behavior, Not Racism, Explains 'Racial Disparities' in Crime Rates

It is widely believed that black Americans commit violent crime at substantially higher rates than whites due entirely to socioeconomic factors. This is a partly true as noted in "The Color of Crime 2016" report, however, by examining raw data provided by officially recognized institutions, it becomes clear that this is not always the case.

In 1999, the Federal Reserve Bank of New York published an economic policy review titled 'Unequal Incomes, Unequal outcomes? Economic Inequality and Measures of Well-Being.' It is shown on table 5 of page 93 of his report that people belonging to black families in the top income bracket committed up to 5 times the rate of crime whites did of the same income bracket. Moreover, from 1976 to 1995, offenders from the highest income bracket from black families committed a higher rate of violent crimes than the lowest income white families, at between 2 to 20 times the rate.

An analysis based on data provided by the U.S Bureau of Labor Statistics also proved something similar. The study 'Race, Wealth and Incarceration: Results from the National Longitudinal Survey of Youth,' released in the academic journal '*Race and Social Problems*,' reveals that "although higher levels of wealth were associated with lower rates of incarceration, the likelihood of future incarceration still was higher for blacks at every level of wealth compared to the white likelihood, as well as the Hispanic likelihood, which fell below the white likelihood for some levels of wealth." It is also notable that Native Americans have generally had higher levels of poverty over the last 30 or so years, according to a study published by The Stanford Center on Poverty and Inequality, yet still commit lower crime rates than blacks.

A *Washington Post* article titled 'Poor white kids are less likely to go to prison than rich black kids' examines the data and suggests "discrimination against people of color is more complicated and fundamental than economic inequality," implying that institutional racism is behind the phenomenon. The problem with this argument, is that the black crime rate has gotten progressively worse since segregation. Similarly, the black out-of-wedlock rate has gotten far worse since segregation.

Fig. 4: Percentage of Offenders and Arrested Suspects of Known Race Who Were Black, 2013

Data source: FBI, National Incident-Based Reporting System

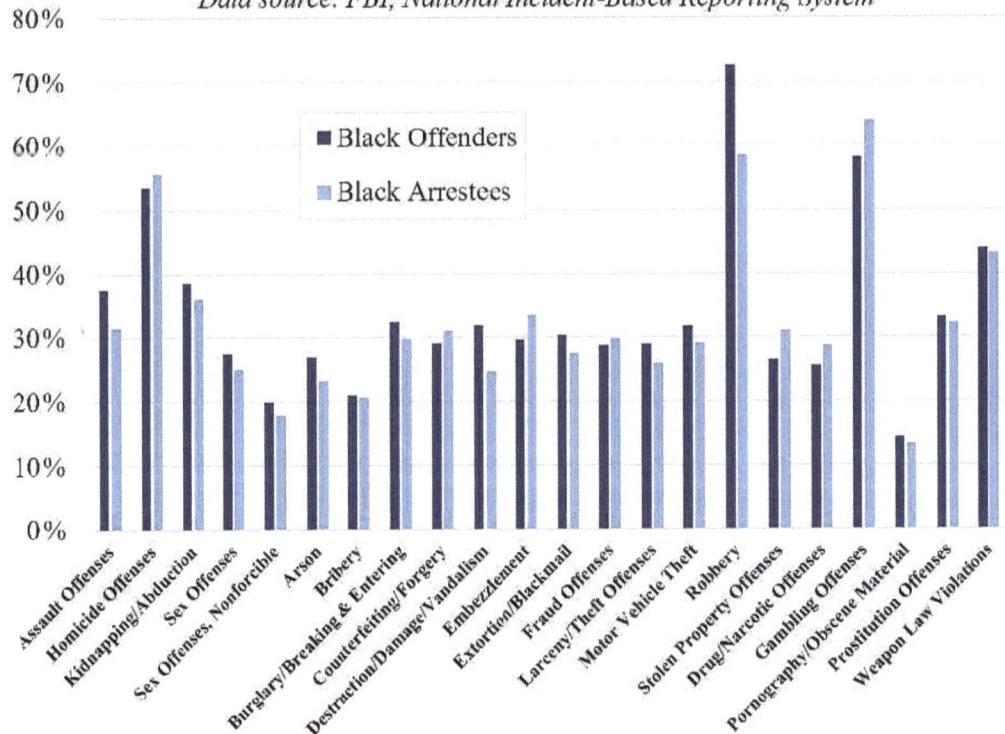

We should also consider the fact that Asians had less rights than blacks for many years, yet still commit the absolute lowest crime rate of any racial group in the United States. While blacks were granted constitutional rights of citizenship in 1865, Asians could only apply for citizenship after the Immigration and Nationality Act of 1952. Despite this, in many studies Asian people do not even have their own category in race-crime studies, often lumped in with other ethnic groups under the negligible 'others' crime rates.

Similarly, the argument for inter-generational trauma caused by slavery does not conclusively explain causation either. Both Native Americans and Jewish immigrants have experienced trauma as a result of violence and marginalization, yet crime rates for both groups are far lower than that of black Americans. The same could be said for refugees from South East Asia that arrived in the U.S during the Vietnam War.

As noted in numerous reports, data shows that the out-of-wedlock rate for black Americans has gotten increasingly worse since the era of Jim Crow and Martin Luther King Jr. In 1960, the out-of-wedlock rate for black Americans was approximately 20%. Today, the out of wedlock rate for black Americans is over 70%.

Furthermore, the violent crime rate has also gotten substantially worse for black males. According to the FBI, despite making up only 6% of the American population, black males– specifically ages 18 to 35, commit over half of all the homicides in the United States. This was *not* the case in the 1950's and 1960's.

Fatherless homes is one of the single greatest predictors of criminality, and a much greater predictors than economics. If the black household income has gotten better since the 1960's and the era of segregation, race relations have gotten better since this time as well, then why is it the case that fatherlessness and crime rates are far worse today? We'll come back to this question in the next chapter.

What New Research Says About Race and Police Shootings

A Bloomberg CityLab report by Brentin Mock in August 2019 titled "What New Research Says About Race and Police Shootings" focuses on two new studies that have revived the long-running debate over how police respond to white criminal suspects versus African Americans. In the U.S., African Americans are 2.5 times more likely to be killed by police than white people. For black women, the rate is 1.4 times more likely.

That's according to a new study conducted by Frank Edwards, of Rutgers University's School of Criminal Justice, Hedwig Lee, of Washington University in St. Louis's Department of Sociology, and Michael Esposito, of the University of Michigan's Institute for Social Research. The researchers used verified data on police killings from 2013 to 2018 compiled by the website Fatal Encounters, created by Nevada-based journalist D. Brian Burghart. Under their models, they found that roughly 1-in-1,000 black boys and men will be killed by police in their lifetime. For white boys and men, the rate is 39 out of 100,000.

In fact, people of color in general were found more likely to be killed by police than their white counterparts.

The study was published in the Proceedings of the National Academy of Sciences (PNAS), a journal that recently drew controversy for publishing another study on police killing disparities. That study, led by Michigan State University psychology professor Joseph Cesario, published in July 2019, found that violent crime rates and the racial demographics of a given location are better indicators for determining a police killing victim's race.

As Cesario explained in a press release:

Many people ask whether black or white citizens are more likely to be shot and why. If you live in a county that has a lot of white people committing crimes, white people are more likely to be shot. If you live in a county that has a lot of black people committing crimes, black people are more likely to be shot.

The two studies are just the latest salvos in a long-running debate over whether police violence towards African Americans is better explained because of racial prejudice or because black people are really violent enough to justify extra police force. The Cesario study, with its focus on crime rates, seems to fall in the latter camp. Both rely on media-generated police shootings data—Cesario's uses databases produced by The *Washington Post* and *The Guardian*.

Several academics have challenged Cesario's methodology, namely his decision to "sidestep the benchmark" of using population to calculate racial disparity. It has been questioned whether using population is an appropriate benchmark in these kinds of analyses.

Critics of this technique believe that population-benchmarking is flawed because it assumes black and white people have an equal likelihood of encountering police. (An example of population-benchmarking is, as Cesario's study explains, stating: "26% of civilians killed by police shootings in 2015 were Black even though Black civilians comprise only 12% of the U.S. population. According to this 12% benchmark, more Black civilians are fatally shot than we would expect, indicating disparity.")

Instead of using population, Cesario analyzed (contextual) variables such as the race of the police officers, crime rates, and the racial demographics of locations where police shootings happened in 2015. From that, he derived that black and Latino victims of police killings were more likely to have been shot by black and Latino cops, and that "might not be due to bias on the part of Black or Hispanic officers, but instead to simple overlap between officer and county demographics."

The problem with this, as Princeton professor Jonathan Mummolo, explained on Twitter, is that it still rests on the assumption that black and white officers encounter black civilians in equal numbers, or in even temperaments—which they don't.

What Do the Recent Mass Shootings Tell Us, If Anything, About This?

There's also something to be said for what the victims were doing when the cops shot them. Cesario points out that, "The vast majority—between 90 percent and 95 percent—of the civilians shot by officers were actively attacking police or other citizens when they were shot"—and that there were more white civilians who were committing such attacks when police killed them than were African Americans. In fact, white people were more likely to be armed when police killed them, as Cesario's study acknowledges—"if anything, [we] found anti-White disparities when controlling for race-specific crime," reads the study.

Another way to determine whether racial bias is a factor is by examining police behavior when their target is unarmed and not on the attack. This is what University of Nebraska at Omaha criminology professor Justin Nix examined in his 2017 study on police killings. Nix's research, which Cesario cites often in his own study, also focuses on police shooting-killings in 2015, when police killed nearly twice as many white people that year (495) than they did black people (258).

But 15 percent of the black people police killed that year were unarmed, compared with just six percent of white people who were unarmed when killed by police. The study also found that 24 percent of African Americans and 32 percent of other non-white racial groups were not attacking police officers when they were killed, compared to 17 percent of white people. This was interpreted as "preliminary evidence of an implicit bias effect," against African Americans and people of color.

The Limitations of the Data

Nix, however, is cautious about deriving any firm conclusions from his own findings or Cesario's because the data on police shootings in general is too limited. The FBI finally launched its database on police-involved shootings in 2019, which is why researchers rely on databases created by journalists. And even the subset of data that academics have been working with—police shooting fatalities—have their own range of limitations.

Cesario declares in his press release that "violent crime rates are the driving force behind fatal [police] shootings," but Nix says that is "pretty strong language in light of the limitations," especially if looking at when police deploy lethal force at the local level.

"I don't think the conclusions are warranted based on their analysis," said Nix. "You can't restrict the data to just fatal shootings. Another problem is that when doing these bird's-eye views, you lose nuance from city to city. Policing is a local thing and there's no reason to believe that everything is the same across the board."

For example, Nix would want numbers not only on how many times a police officer shoots their weapon, but every time they draw their gun. "You need a benchmark that says how often they were in certain circumstances where they could have shot but did not. That gets us closer to the likelihood of racial bias."

Nix recently updated his analysis on police shootings using fatal and non-fatal shootings from the 47 largest metros from 2010 to 2016, using a dataset produced by VICE. That analysis found wide variation between the cities—in St. Louis, 16.8 percent of police shootings were fatal; in Phoenix, 51.9 percent were and, in Tampa, all three of its police shootings were fatal.

What the Studies Don't Tell Us? The Race of the Police Officer Doesn't Matter

Cesario's study centers the characteristics of the police officer over the victim, concluding essentially that since black and Hispanic police are as likely or more likely to kill people of color as white officers, that the race of the police officer doesn't matter. But it's not clear whether that matters in determining whether police bias exists at all. As Philip Atiba Goff, president, and cofounder of the Center for Policing Equity, told NPR, "Racism is not a thing that white people can have and black people can't. And nobody's research would suggest that it does."

Looking at individual police characteristics doesn't tell the public anything about the links between structural racism—both within a police department and throughout society—and police violence. Boston University School of Public Health scholar Michael Siegel found that connection in his study in 2018, which analyzed data on police killings between 2013 and 2017. States that have higher rates of racial segregation, incarceration, educational attainment, economic disparity, and unemployment also tend to have higher levels of police violence against African Americans, Siegel found.

4 – The Missing Dialogue for Black-on-Black Crime Needs to Happen

Credit: Chicago Tribune. Six pictures of 18 murder victims in 24 hours: Inside the most violent day in 60 years in Chicago.

There's an assumption today that police misconduct, white supremacy, and systemic racism are responsible for thousands of innocent black lives taken wrongfully by racist white cops. We've established so far this is not the case and that black criminality is a much bigger problem than racism or police brutality. Yes, they still exist, but to what degree?

Crime is a major problem for many black communities, but how much of it can be attributed to causes such as institutional racism, systemic racism, and white privilege? According to the NAACP, from 1882-1968, there were 3,446 black people lynched at the hands of whites. Today however, being murdered by whites or a policemen is extremely rare.

For the last 35 years, there is an average of 9,252 black-on-black murders every year that translates into nearly 324,000 blacks murdered at the hands of other blacks. Only a tiny percentage of blacks are killed by police. More importantly, what's cutting black lives short is the weak black family structure, which now consists of only a third of black children living in two-parent households with illegitimacy standing at 75%.

The "legacy of slavery" is often blamed for such dire statistics. Such an explanation turns out to be sheer nonsense when one examines black history. Even during slavery, where marriage was forbidden, most black children lived in biological two-parent families. But that's rarely the case today. Before you can fix a problem—you first need to identify it as Barack Obama did in his

2008 sapient Father's Day speech in Chicago. "If we are honest with ourselves," Obama told his audience in a South Side church, Americans will admit that too many fathers are "missing—missing from too many lives and too many homes. They have abandoned their responsibilities, acting like boys instead of men."

Crime is Weakened by Family—But Thrives in a Fatherless Village

Professor Herbert G. Gutman's research in "The Black Family in Slavery and Freedom 1750-1925" found that in three-fourths of 19th-century slave families, all the children had the same mother and father. In New York City, in 1925, 85% of black households were two-parent. In fact, "Five in six children under the age of six lived with both parents." During slavery and as late as 1920, a black teenage girl raising a child without a man present was a rarity.

An 1880 study of family structure in Philadelphia shows that three-quarters of all black families were nuclear families. There were only slight differences in family structure between racial groups. The percentages of nuclear families were black (75.2%), Irish (82.2%), German (84.5%) and native white Americans (73.1%). Only one-quarter of black families were female-headed.

Female-headed families among Irish, German, and native white Americans averaged 11%. According to the 1938 *Encyclopaedia of the Social Sciences*, only 11% of black children and 3% of white children were born to unwed mothers. As Thomas Sowell reported: "Going back a hundred years, when blacks were just one generation out of slavery, we find that census data of that era showed that a slightly higher percentage of black adults had married than white adults. This fact remained true in every census from 1890 to 1940."

Walter E. Williams, a professor of economics at George Mason University, makes a compelling statement. "The absence of a father in the home predisposes children, especially boys, to academic failure, criminal behavior, and economic hardship, not to mention an inter-generational repeating of handicaps. If today's weak family structure is a legacy of slavery, then the people who make such a claim must tell us how it has managed to skip nearly five generations to have an effect."

The Pros and Cons of Black-on-Black Crime

From Barry Latzer, a professor emeritus at John Jay College of Criminal Justice, CUNY and 2016 author of *The Rise and Fall of Violent Crime in America*, enlightens us with three more studies below regarding the pros and cons in the ongoing discussion of black-on-black crime:

Thomas Abt's 2019 book *Bleeding Out: The Devastating Consequences of Urban Violence—and a Bold New Plan for Peace in the Streets* has garnered a fair amount of attention for its proposals to deal with gun violence in mainly black urban neighborhoods. The entire focus of the book is on interventions in high-crime locations to stem the violence, including hot-spots policing, working with young males at high risk of engaging in violence by offering carrots ("we're here to help you") and sticks ("we'll stop you if you don't let us help"), and locking up known violent offenders.

Lest you think this book is not about black crime, Abt states quite explicitly that "race matters when it comes to urban violence." He points out that homicide-victimization rates for black men were 3.9 times the national average and that 52 percent of all known homicide victims were black (2017 data). He might have added that the perpetrators of these crimes were overwhelmingly African Americans.

In 2018, where the homicide victim was black, the suspected killer also was 88 percent of the time. And this is not an exceptional situation. From 1976 to 2005, 94 percent of black victims were killed by other African Americans. In fact, as I will demonstrate, high rates of black-on-black killing have been the norm for well over a century. But this is not an issue Abt wants to address.

Many Push Back on "Black-on-Black" Crime and Call it Misleading

As Latzer points out, it's important to have an open and meaningful discussion on black-on-black crime: However, to the contrary, Abt abjures the phrase "black on black." He calls it "deeply misleading" and says it "perpetuates deeply harmful stereotypes about African Americans." So Abt has written an entire book addressing the problem, but he and everyone else must refrain from calling it what it is: a black-on-black phenomenon. Why?

Abt offers three reasons. First, violent crime is commonly intraracial, i.e., whites kill whites, Hispanics kill Hispanics, and so on. But, Abt says, we don't talk about white-on-white violence. Well, that's simply not true. Many analysts, Latzer included, discuss white violence, especially where it had a major impact on crime in the United States. This was the case with southern whites especially from the 18th through the 20th centuries, a situation studied extensively by crime historians and criminologists.

The reason we focus more on black-on-black violence nowadays is not racism but rather its significance to the crime problem in the United States. Presumably, this is why Abt has written an entire book on the subject. Black violent crime was a major factor in the post-1960s crime tsunami and persisted even after the wave began to ebb in the 1990s.

From 2000 to 2015, the mean African-American homicide-victimization rate, adjusted for age, was 20.1 per 100,000. That's more than three times the Hispanic rate of 6.4 (despite disadvantages comparable to those of blacks) and over seven times the average white rate, 2.7.

Moreover, as already noted, from 1976 to 2005, 94 percent of the killers of black murder victims were other African Americans. In short, this is about exceptionally high as well as overwhelmingly intraracial black violent crime. White-on-white homicide is equally intraracial, but, as Abt knows, the rates are not astronomically high.

Though Abt considers it a malign narrative, stressing that a major component of today's violent-crime problem is black-on-black underscores the tragic irony of African-American victimhood. It is, in addition, an argument for support from African-American leaders and the general black population for more-focused law-enforcement efforts in low-income neighborhoods of color—the very policies that Abt advocates.

Blacks Worry About and Disapprove of Violence in Their Communities

Barry Latzer explains further: Abt's second objection is that the expression "black on black" carries an "implicit assumption that urban violence is the result of chronic lawless behavior enabled by community tolerance for criminality." Abt says this assumption is wrong because African Americans are worried about and strongly disapprove of violence in their communities.

That is correct, but there is also a deep strain of mistrust of police in poor black neighborhoods, and this, along with fear of reprisals by black criminals, leads to a refusal to cooperate with the authorities. Such noncooperation only worsens the black-crime problem by providing impunity for the most violent.

Here are two vivid examples. Though several dozen people were present when rap star Busta Rhymes's unarmed security guard was shot to death in 2006, not one would talk to detectives. And when rapper Lil' Kim lied to police about her friends' involvement in another shooting—earning her a year in jail for perjury—she became a hero in black communities.

Actually, Abt fully recognizes the problem. The "stop snitching ethos," he says, "perpetuates itself by preventing criminals who victimize communities from being brought to justice." But if rates of black violent-crime are excessive (which they are), if these high rates have persisted over a long term (which they have), and if the stop-snitching ethos aggravates the problem (which it does), then the statement that Abt decries is at least partially correct. Urban violence is deplored by the black community, but at the same time it is enabled by a culture of noncooperation.

Now to Abt's "deeply harmful stereotypes" claim. Here he relies on Khalil Gibran Muhammad's 2011 book *The Condemnation of Blackness*, on the use of black crime statistics in the late 19th to early 20th centuries to support a racial-inferiority narrative. The Progressive era, wrote Muhammad, was "the founding moment for the emergence of an enduring statistical discourse of black dysfunctionality." Based on this narrative, adds Abt, "crime by European immigrants was explained away while crime among African Americans remained racialized as a matter of community or family values."

There Were Other Historical Crime Waves by Irish and Italian Immigrants

But immigrant crime around the turn of the 20th century, Latzer continues, was scarcely ignored, or excused and certainly was not "explained away." The prejudice against immigrants from southern Italy, for example, is notorious. In one of the most horrific incidents in American history, eleven Italian prisoners were dragged from a New Orleans jail and lynched in 1891, following the acquittal of nine of them for the murder of the city's police chief. The *New York Times* and Theodore Roosevelt expressed approval of the outrage, and one of the organizers of the mob, who later became the governor of Louisiana, wrote that Sicilian Americans were "just a little worse than the Negro, being if anything filthier in [their] habits, lawless, and treacherous."

In reality, racist ideology was common in this period and was used against Native Americans and Chinese as well as Italian immigrants, indeed against any social group with high crime rates or other antisocial behaviors. The word "race" was broadly applied to ethnic and even religious groups (such as Jews), whereas the modern concept of "culture" was in its infancy and not widely accepted. Contrary to Abt, notions of racial inferiority were widespread and certainly were not reserved solely for blacks.

In any event, the argument is a straw man. Any narrative built on a supposition of the inherent (i.e., biological) inferiority of people of color has been thoroughly discredited since the civil-rights movement of the 1960s, while the statistics on black crime during the period discussed by Muhammad remain valid. Though Abt seems unaware of it, black-on-black violent crime was excessive in the late 19th century and, despite ups and downs, has been high relative to other social groups throughout the 20th century and up to the present day.

W. E. B. Du Bois' Concern Regarding the "Vast Problem" of Negro Crime

Writing in 1899, none other than W. E. B. Du Bois, a great champion of African-American equality, was one of the first to note the "vast problem" of Negro crime, a problem that "since 1880 ... has been steadily growing." Du Bois was prescient. Rates of black violent crime continued to grow—even before the Great Migration and the "ghettos" that developed in the North in the 1920s.

Despite the lynchings and other mistreatment by whites in the late 19th century, black homicide was overwhelmingly carried out by other African Americans. In Savannah, Georgia, for example, from 1896 to 1903, researchers found 91 homicides in which the race of both the offender and the victim were known. Sixty-eight of the victims (75 percent of all those killed) were black, and 61 African Americans, or 90 percent of the alleged perpetrators, were arrested for these murders.

In the North, where the black population was small prior to the migration, the pattern of black-on-black killing was the norm. In Philadelphia, from 1839 to 1901, two-thirds of the homicide indictments of African Americans were for killing other persons of color.

In the 20th century, the number of black victims escalated while the killers remained overwhelmingly African American. In Memphis from 1920 to 1925, where African Americans were 38 percent of the population, black-on-black killings were two-thirds of all murders in the city (in which race was known).

An examination of coroner's files uncovered 500 homicide victims in Birmingham, Alabama, between 1937 and 1944. The city's population was roughly 40 percent black, but 85 percent of both the killers (418) and the killed (427) were African American.

In the 1940s, when the black migration resumed after a hiatus during the Great Depression, more northern cities began to reflect the increased black violence. In Cleveland, which was 16 percent black in the '40s, African Americans were the victims in 71 percent of the felonious homicide cases from 1947 to 1953. Whites were accused in six of the cases; blacks, in 320.

In the contemporary period, from 1976 to 2014, it is estimated that 198,288 African Americans died nationwide at the hands of black killers. That's 5,218 deaths per year on average, roughly 19 times the annual number of deaths of African Americans in confrontations with police.

This brings Latzer's discussion to Abt's third argument, which accuses "black-on-black proponents" of diverting attention from law-enforcement abuses. The forbidden phrase, he asserts, is "weaponized to absolve broader society of responsibility not just for urban violence but also for police violence."

This is Another Straw Man Argument

Per Latzer, there is no reason we can't acknowledge the black-on-black-crime problem and address police abuse. Abt himself takes a similar position without uttering the b-on-b words. Referring to urban black offenders, he says, "We can catch more killers and support the other strategies discussed in this book at the same time." These strategies include improving the fairness of law-enforcement policies in order to increase the legitimacy of police in black communities.

When he says that "broader society" is responsible for black violence, Abt means that white racism is to blame.

Racial disparities in crime and punishment are real, but they have been produced in large part by a sustained campaign of persecution by whites against disempowered minorities, particularly African Americans. Officially, that effort has ended; overt racial discrimination has been prohibited by law for decades. Nevertheless, the brutal legacy of that campaign—racism, segregation, concentrated poverty, and violence—remains.

There are problems with this white-racism theory as noted by Latzer:

First, one would expect higher levels of black crime when the racial oppression was at its maximum, and lower levels when it was less so. But that hasn't been the case. Black homicide rates were about the same as white homicide rates during slavery. They frequently were higher in the North than in the more oppressive South throughout the 20th century. And they hit new peaks in the late 1960s, a time when whites supported the most sweeping civil-rights legislation in American history.

Second, if white abuse was responsible for black violence, why weren't whites targeted more often? Why were other African Americans overwhelmingly the victims? Why was black-on-black violence elevated even after lynching and Jim Crow were no longer powerful disincentives to black-on-white crime?

Third, how do we explain levels of black violence out of all proportion to African-American disadvantage? Other groups suffer comparable adversities—Hispanics, for example—but have much lower rates of violence. Though the poverty rate for Hispanics is 92 percent of the rate for blacks, African Americans have three times the homicide rate. Indeed, many of the low-income black immigrants to the United States, such as the Haitians who flooded into southern Florida in the 1980s, had lower violent-crime rates than did the African-American residents. This despite the fact that they too were black and impoverished and had suffered a legacy of the most brutal slavery.

Southern White Penchant For Violent Responses to Perceived Insults and Affronts

Here Latzer provides some important facts for further discussion:

There are better explanations for black-on-black violence, including the cultural theories that Abt dismisses without any serious consideration. A compelling case can be made that African Americans, having spent centuries in the South, adopted the southern white penchant for violent responses to perceived insults and affronts, what Thomas Sowell once called the "black redneck" phenomenon.

On this view, black criminal violence was the product of the southern-male honor culture that, among black men of lower socioeconomic status, manifested as a violent response to petty insults, sexual rivalries, etc. Since African Americans interacted socially with other persons of color much more than with whites, the victims of such honor-culture assaults were overwhelmingly black. This violence continued when African Americans migrated to the North. Indeed, it escalated in the northern cities, where there was greater freedom and less oppression.

Racism did play a role here, but not the role usually assigned. Discrimination kept large numbers of blacks from rising to the middle class, and the middle class, black or white, eschews violence. Had blacks been permitted to advance socioeconomically, their story would have been more like the Irish and Italian immigrant narrative, with a rise from violence and poverty to affluence and law-abidingness.

Ironically notes Latzer, though he scorns cultural explanations, Abt describes just the kind of behavior depicted in the subculture-of-violence theory:

Urban violence can occur in the course of other street crimes, especially robbery, but often it is sparked by arguments, conflicts, or "beefs" of some kind. These disputes often involve long-standing rivalries between groups known as gangs, cliques, sets, crews, and so on. In 2017, 64 percent of all homicides where a motive was identified were the result of disputes of some kind, and with stronger data the percentage would probably be higher. Many of these conflicts are connected to cycles of retaliatory violence that go back years, even generations. ... For many who commit murder, it's all about payback.

This could have been describing white behavior in the 19th-century South, and it is significant that blacks came out of that very milieu. But Abt is wedded to the legacy-of-white-racism theory and indifferent to any alternative explanation.

Rejecting Progressive Thinking that Our Justice System is Irredeemably Racist

To his credit states Latzer, Abt rejects the most extreme progressive thinking, which views the entire criminal-justice system as irredeemably racist and calls for its abolition. As he acknowledges, "such extremism hurts, not helps, poor communities of color." Of course, this brings us right back to the realities of black-on-black crime and the dire need for effective law enforcement in African-American communities.

In fairness, Abt's book is not a fully developed theory of African-American crime. It is a book of policy proposals to address the problem. The proposals, described in a nutshell at the beginning of this essay, may or may not work, but they probably are worth a try. After all, as Abt says, "meaningful progress on fundamental socioeconomic conditions will take generations to achieve. People living with the reality of urban violence need relief right now."

Nor is Abt the only one looking to censor politically incorrect language. His Harvard colleague Anthony Braga and associates also warned against using the term "black-on-black violence," which, "while statistically correct, is a simplistic and emotionally charged definition of urban violence that can be problematic when used by political commentators, politicians and police executives." In fact, Abt seems to have drawn many of his arguments on the forbidden phrase from the Braga essay.

For decades now, criminologists, especially those espousing or at least harboring leftist views, have insisted that harmful social conditions are the primary cause of violent crime in general and black violent crime in particular. This hasn't gotten them very far as an explanation of the enormously high rates of black-on-black crime. Despite declines since the mid-1990s, relatively high rates have persisted even in the face of overall black socioeconomic progress.

Maybe Abt's policy proposals can succeed in reducing these rates where others have not, but his grasp of the underlying problem is flawed, and his eagerness to censor alternative views is, unfortunately, consistent with scholarly trends and cancel culture.

We're the Only Community That Caters to the Bottom Denominator of Our Society

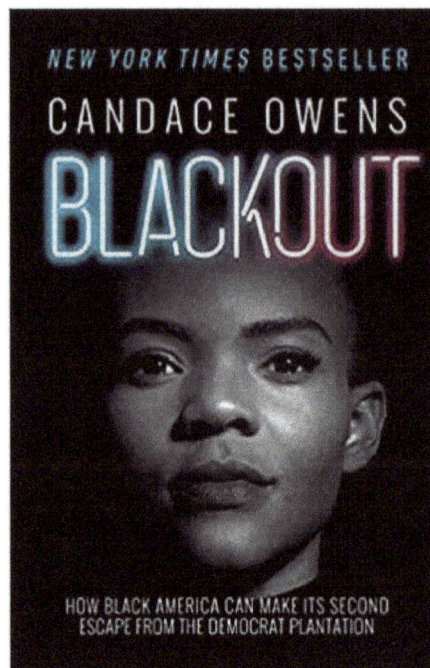

Credit: Amazon. Candace Owen's bestseller "Blackout: How Black America Can Make Its Second Escape from the Democrat Plantation."

The "Everything Candace Owens Has Said About George Floyd So Far" article in *Newsweek* by Marina Watts brings up a serious question asked by many but discussed by few in the black community. Black conservative activist and Trump supporter Candace Owens has been very vocal about George Floyd on social media and it's not the first time Owens' comments on the subject of race have made headlines.

She recently explained why she doesn't agree with the supposed narrative that is being pushed surrounding Floyd. On May 25, 2020, Floyd was killed while he was in police custody in Minneapolis. Since then, protests demanding police reform have been held in over 400 cities across the country, according to *USA Today*.

Former Minneapolis police officer Derek Chauvin, who was caught on video kneeling on Floyd's neck for nearly nine minutes, was been arrested and charged with second-degree murder and second-degree manslaughter. The three other former officers who were also on the scene have been charged with aiding and abetting second-degree murder, and with aiding and abetting second-degree manslaughter.

In a controversial 17-minute long video shared on Twitter on June 3, 2020, Owens said that she does not "support George Floyd and the media's depiction of him as a martyr for black America."

She explained that "it has been weighing very heavily" on her heart and her mind. "There was so much pressure for me to go with the popular opinion about who George Floyd was. We are being sold a lot of lies at the detriment to the black community, at the detriment to the white community and at the detriment to America as a whole."

Owens continued, "Our culture is unique from other communities because we are the only community that caters to the bottom denominator of our society. Not every black American is a criminal. Not every black American is committing crimes. But we are unique in that we are the only people that fight and scream and demand support for the people in our community that are up to no good."

The controversial commentator noted that what she was saying was not any defense for Chauvin, and that Floyd's family deserves justice of the way that he died. "Just because he was a criminal does not mean you deserve to die at the knee of a police officer. I can't say it enough, no, he did not deserve to die in that manner." She added: "But I also am not going to accept the narrative that this is the best the black community has to offer,"

"For whatever reason it has become fashionable over the last five or six years for us to turn criminals into heroes overnight. It is something I find despicable. George Floyd was not an amazing person. George Floyd is being upheld as an amazing human being." Owens alleged that Floyd was high at the time of his death and pointed to his criminal history. Floyd's criminal past included spending five years behind bars for robbery and assault.

"We shouldn't be buying t-shirts with his name on it," she said. "He was a violent criminal," she said of Floyd.

Owens added, "Everyone is pretending that this man lived a heroic lifestyle. We are embarrassing in that regard. Nobody wants to tell the truth in black America. Our biggest problem is us." She concluded the clip by saying, "Anyway, this is just a rant because I have been feeling super, super annoyed by these depictions in society. I have no apologies to make. George Floyd is not my martyr. He can be yours."

Why and How Did George Floyd, Freddie Gray & Michael Brown Die?

Shelby Steele, a conservative black author and Robert J. and Marion E. Oster Senior Fellow at the Hoover Institution, wrote and narrated a new documentary exploring race and violence in America titled, "What Killed Michael Brown?" The Federalist September 2020 article "New Documentary Examines The Death Of Michael Brown And Race In America" by Jordan Davidson covers the documentary below:

Directed by Eli Steele, it premiered on streaming platforms in October 2020. "What Killed Michael Brown?" is meant to examine race relations in the United States and the reactions to the deaths of young black men such as Michael Brown in Ferguson, Missouri, and others.

"America's original sin is not slavery. It is simply the use of race, as a means to power," the trailer states. "Was it really racism that killed Michael Brown?" At a press conference, Steele explained his decision to investigate the 2014 shooting of Brown in Ferguson and how it had implications on the way Americans view race and violence.

"What interested us in making this film was the interest of most Americans in the shooting of one young man. Media from around the globe swarmed into this little suburb of St. Louis Ferguson, Missouri and it became this huge cataclysmic cultural event," Steele said, explaining that the same attention is not drawn to regular gun violence against blacks. "Two years later in the Southside of Chicago, in one year 762 young black kids were shot and killed 3000 were wounded," he added.

The film, according to Steele, showcases the different arguments and philosophies of the movements and reactions seen in Ferguson, as well as more recent outcries in Minneapolis, and why they gained traction with the media and the American public.

"Trayvon Martin, Freddie Gray in Baltimore, Eric Garner in New York, Michael Brown, now George Floyd, and three others all seem to trigger the same sort of reflexive pattern in American life and particularly the way they're covered in the media," Steele explained. "There's this rush, this almost desperate frenzy, to see, to be an event as an example of black victimization."

Steele believes it is the culture of black victimization and the rise of "white guilt" that plays a role in the increasing amount of attention and outrage at these events. "One of the things we hope comes out of this film is that you, the viewer, sees that over and over we'll go down that road. 'We'll make race count here. We'll make it right. We'll use race to do the good thing to uplift people.' That's the worst thing you can ever hear. Then you know corruption will follow," Steele explained.

While Steele claims that growing up as a black man during segregation and the civil rights movement showed him the importance of the black advocacy craved by many of the people in Ferguson and other cities, he claims that many black leaders such as Al Sharpton and Jesse Jackson "exploit these situations" for political gain.

In the film, Steele said he avoided political and partisan and instead chose to dig into the "fictions" of race that contributed to these shootings and events. "Our main goal in this film is to simply reveal these kinds of [race] fictions. We're not partisan. We don't get into politics. It's cultural. We get into the cultures where the real contest is and that's where we try to start," Steele said.

According to Steele education and broken homes are areas that black people are ignoring in exchange for targeting racism. "We use racism and white racism as an avoid, as an escape from the real work," Steele said.

"One thing that burns me up with black relatives is that they believe in whites being the agent of black fate. They believe more in whites than they do in blacks. They believe we're weak. They believe we're inferior and that we're not gonna do anything," Steele added. "That's what black people, very often, too, believe. That's what that has to be changed."

Moving forward, Steele said he believes that black people need to embrace the freedom that they have as Americans to embrace that change. "Freedom is a frightening thing. And when the responsibility for your life is put back into your own hands, that makes us all nervous. But let's face that. Let's deal with that," he said.

In June 2020, Steele told The Federalist that today's racial tensions are caused by the explosion of a racial change during the civil rights movement and the development of "redemptive liberalism."

"The left has discovered that there's enormous power in claiming to be redemptive, claiming and putting yourself on the side of the good. And so the left always is a constant stream of political correctness and do-gooders in one kind or another and claiming the mantle of power in order to say 'We will redeem America. We will be the ones who make America achieve its dreams of equity for all,'" Steele said.

5 – Interracial Victimization, Rape, Police Deaths & Hate Crime Statistics

INTERRACIAL VIOLENT CRIME INCIDENTS 2018

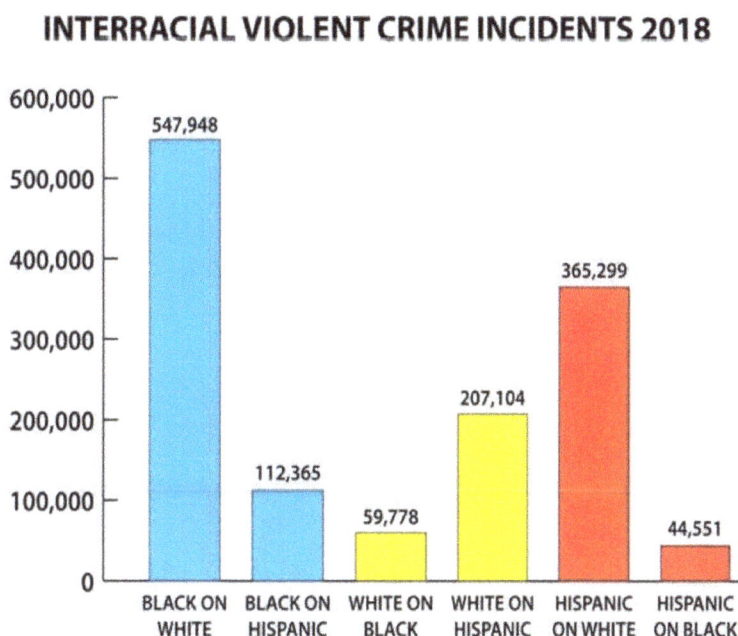

Source: Bureau of Justice Statistics, National Crime Victimization Survey, 2018 (Table 14)

While giving nonstop coverage to incidents of alleged racism committed by random white people, police officers, or businesses, the major news networks do their best to never report on racist black people who commit hate crimes against whites. They want people to believe that racism is a one-way street and that only white people can be racist, when in fact many in the black community harbor hatred for whites and frequently commit hate crimes against them.

Data shows white Americans are far more often victims of interracial crime than black Americans. In 2018, The Bureau of Justice Statistics released their survey of criminal victimization, breaking down 593,598 interracial violence between blacks and whites. Blacks committed 537,204 of those interracial felonies, or 90 percent, and whites committed 56,394 of them, or less than 10 percent.

Despite only making up 13.4% of the American population, black Americans commit more than double the number of interracial homicides on white Americans, who make up 60.4% of the American population. A great deal of violent crime—40 to 60 percent—is committed within the races. However, when violence crosses racial lines it does so in a very unequal manner.

Going farther back in time, the same lopsided scenario interracial violent crime plays out and again in the statistics. In 2012 and 2013, blacks committed an annual average of 560,600 crimes of violence against whites whereas whites committed only about 99,400 such crimes against blacks. This means blacks were the attackers in 84.9 percent of the violent crimes involving blacks and whites.

Denying Anti-White Racism and Victimization is Unsapient

In "The Color of Crime 2016: Race, Crime, and Justice in America" by Edwin S. Rubenstein, he notes that: Some observers argue that the overwhelming preponderance of black-on-white over white-on-black violence suggests that blacks deliberately target whites for violence. Others argue that since there are 4.7 times as many whites as blacks in the population, it is to be expected that black criminals are more likely to encounter white victims than vice versa.

Both positions must be evaluated in light of several considerations. First, blacks who commit assault, robbery, and rape are likely to be members of the underclass, who live in largely black neighborhoods. If they chose victims without regard to race, they should be more likely to encounter other blacks rather than whites.

Second, black/Hispanic interracial crime fits the same lopsided pattern: Of the 256,074 violent crimes involving those two groups, blacks were perpetrators 82.5 percent of the time. Unlike the nearly five-fold difference in numbers between blacks and whites, there are only about 30 percent more Hispanics than blacks. The high black-aggressor figure suggests that blacks may also deliberately target Hispanics—perhaps even more than they target whites.

Interracial Crime and Violence

Rubenstein notes the imbalance can be expressed differently: When whites commit violence, they target other whites 82.4 percent of the time, blacks 3.6 percent of the time, and Hispanics 7.8 percent of the time. In other words, white violence is directed overwhelmingly at other whites. When blacks commit violence only a minority—40.9 percent—of their victims are black. Whites are 38.6 percent and Hispanics are 14.5 percent. Hispanic assailants also attack their own group less often than they attack others. Their victims are Hispanics—40.1 percent, whites—50.7 percent, and blacks—4.7 percent.

Finally, interracial crime can be expressed in terms of the greater or lesser likelihood of a person of one race to commit violence against a member of the other. In 2012/2013, the actual likelihood of attack was extremely low in all cases, but statistically, any given black person was 27 times more likely to attack a white and six times more likely to attack a Hispanic than vice versa. A Hispanic was eight times more likely to attack a white than the reverse.

The Department of Justice keeps national records on murder. In 2013, it reported 5,621 single-offender, single-victim cases in which the race of the murderer was known. Like most federal statistics, there is no clear distinction between whites and Hispanics, so the only meaningful racial categories are black and non-black. Blacks killed 2,698 people—48 percent of the total—and non-blacks killed 2,923 or 52 percent. Since blacks were just 13.3 percent of the population, it meant a black was six times more likely than a non-black to commit murder. Although most murders are within the same race, blacks were 13.6 times more likely to kill non-blacks than non-blacks were to kill blacks.

The Mainstream Media Suppresses or Ignores Black-on-White Crime

If you're not aware of the color of crime statistics and victimization rates that have been fairly consistent for five decades, it's most likely not your fault because the fake news media focuses on one statistic and that is the white on black one (in the middle of the chart at the beginning of this chapter) while ignoring the rest. Here are but a few examples that stand out:

- When a Nation of !slam member gunned down three white people in Fresno, California because he hated whites, the story barely made a blip on the mainstream media's radar.

- New York City law enforcement confirms that a 62-year-old man has died from injuries suffered at the hands of a suspect who declared he was "going to punch the first white man that I see."

- At San Francisco State University, a black student was caught on video assaulting a white student simply because he had dreadlocks. The black person was upset that a white person had a 'black hairstyle' and claimed it was "cultural appropriation."

Mainstream media ignored these stories, and thousands of others, but if a white student attacked a black student because they didn't like their hair, it would have been the story of the week all across the country. Have you heard of the following incidents?

- In New York City, a black man was arrested for trying to shove a random white person onto the tracks of the subway train because he "hated white people."

- A group of black thugs were caught on video beating up a white man at an intersection in Chicago yelling, "You voted Trump," and then stole his car.

- A 13-year-old is doused in gasoline and set on fire by perpetrators in Kansas City telling him, "You get what you deserve, white boy."

Most Americans are completely unaware of the incident, but painfully remember the months of coverage after the Confederate flag-loving Dylann Roof opened fire inside an African American church, which sparked the beginning of the Confederate flag being banned and even Dukes of Hazzard reruns being pulled from TV because the Duke boys' car, the General Lee, has the flag painted on it.

In late 2013 a disturbing trend surfaced when random and unsuspecting white people were being sucker-punched in the face by black kids hoping to knock them out. It was dubbed the "knockout game" or "polar bear hunting" (polar bear being a slang term for white people), and the victims were of all ages, including senior citizens, chosen at random, when they were just walking down sidewalks of city streets, simply because they were white.

Some of the incidents were captured on video by nearby security cameras, and some of the perpetrators' friends videotaped the attacks themselves and posted the footage on social media or World Star Hip Hop, a website that caters to black fight videos.

Most of these attacks were only reported on the local news where they occurred, and they usually left the racial elements out of their stories. It wasn't until word of these incidents began spreading through social media that the 'knockout game' phenomenon, and its anti-white racist patterns became clear."

Have You Heard About These Stories? Probably Not

The previously mentioned incidences are not rare, isolated incidents of interracial violence and crime, but are part of a disturbing pattern of racist hate crimes against white people that number in the thousands each year. Most Americans are unaware of these incidents as well:

- After a black man shot up a white church in Tennessee during their Sunday service to get 'revenge' for white supremacist Dylann Roofs massacre at a black church two years earlier in South Carolina, it was barely mentioned in the media.

- A black serial killer in Kansas City murdered five random white men, four of them on biking and hiking trails over the course of a few months between 2016 and 2017, by walking up to them and shooting them in the back of the head. There was no motive for the attacks other than he wanted to "kill all white people," as he had admitted to police while in custody during a previous incident involving harassment charges.

- After four black thugs were arrested in Chicago for torturing a mentally handicapped white man while broadcasting it on Facebook Live, the disturbing video went viral on social media and then mainstream media reluctantly covered the incident briefly, once, and then never made any mention of it again.

If it had been white perpetrators torturing a black man while broadcasting it on Facebook, it would have stayed in the news cycle for weeks, perhaps months. The networks would have devoted prime time specials to their "exclusive" interview with the victim, and he would have become the left's poster boy and rallying cry against racism and hatred perpetrated from white people. We would have heard his name as often as Trayvon Martin or Michael Brown or George Floyd, but instead this incident, and the victim, was immediately forgotten.

White Victims, Black Criminals, and White Guilt

The media have relentlessly fanned the flames of racial hatred, while engaging in a systematic pattern of misinformation and blatant suppression of facts surrounding the perpetrators and victims of crime. The James Simpson article in February 2015 in Accuracy in Media titled "Black Criminals, White Victims, and White Guilt" explains why:

The figures come quickly but are never subjected to the necessary scrutiny. Last fall, for example, the George Soros-funded ProPublica published a claim that black youths are killed by the police at a rate 21 times higher than white youths. Mass media parroted that claim, but the data are incomplete and biased. They represent just 1.2 percent of police departments nationwide, and most reports come from urban areas, where the population is disproportionately black.

More reliable data from the Centers for Disease Control (CDC) suggest that in 2012, 123 blacks were killed by police using firearms while 326 whites, including 227 non-Hispanic whites, were killed. These data, however, are also not entirely reliable, but represent a larger data set than the FBI's Uniform Crime Reporting (UCR).

CNN's Marc Lamont Hill, a racial agitator fired by Fox News for defending cop-killers, spread misleading statistic about police shootings, claiming that "Every 28 hours, an unarmed black person is killed by police." This too was trumpeted in the media. It became a twitter hashtag, "#every28hours," and another mantra like "hands up, don't shoot." But it is demonstrably false.

There were 313 blacks killed by police, security guards and other "vigilantes" in 2012. Dividing 313 into the number of hours in a year (8,760) yields 28. However, 177 of these "unarmed black persons" were actually armed with firearms. That leaves 136. Others may have been technically "unarmed" but were threatening the officer's life, for example with their car—or as in Michael Brown's case, attempting to take the officer's gun. Many more were not the result of shootings, but accidents, e.g., during vehicular chases. Finally, some of the shooters were not police.

When the hyperbole is removed, the facts present a much more reasonable explanation. Barring a small number of tragic mishaps, police shootings are usually justified.

Black-on-White Crime in America

These acts of unspeakable violence perpetrated by black offenders on white victims rarely get much media attention, for fear of "subjecting an entire group of people to suspicion," as Jason Lewis' September 2013 *Star Tribune* article "Black-on-white crime in America" reports:

While most violent crime is indeed intraracial, 26.7 percent of homicides where the victim is a stranger are interracial. And in 2008, the offending rate for blacks (24.7 offenders per 100,000) was seven times higher than the rate for whites (3.4 offenders per 100,000), according to the latest figures from the Bureau of Justice Statistics (BJS).

Accounting for population differences, whites are simply far more likely to be victims of interracial crime than blacks. This is no statistical anomaly and the data, once again, suggest something quite different. Regardless, that didn't stop Jesse Jackson from telling the *Los Angeles Times* at the height of the George Zimmerman frenzy that "targeting, arresting, convicting blacks and ultimately killing us is big business."

A Censored Race War?

From his May 2012 "A Censored Race War" article in the *National Review* by Thomas Sowell, a black senior fellow at the Hoover Institution, he explains the almost total exclusion of black-on-while victimization incidences in mainstream and social media, as well as local news stations:

When two white newspaper reporters for the *Virginian-Pilot* were driving through Norfolk and were set upon and beaten by a mob of young blacks—beaten so badly that they had to take a week off from work—that might sound like news that should have been reported, at least by their own newspaper. But it wasn't.

The O'Reilly Factor on Fox News Channel was the first major television program to report this incident. Yet this story is not just a Norfolk story, either in what happened or in how the media and the authorities have tried to sweep it under the rug.

Similar episodes of unprovoked violence by young black gangs against white people chosen at random on beaches, in shopping malls, or in other public places have occurred in Philadelphia, New York, Denver, Chicago, Cleveland, Washington. D.C., Los Angeles, and other places across the country. Both the authorities and the media tend to try to sweep these episodes under the rug

In Milwaukee, for example, an attack on whites at a public park a few years ago left many of the victims battered to the ground and bloody. But when the police arrived on the scene, it became clear that the authorities wanted to keep this quiet.

One 22-year-old woman, who had been robbed of her cell phone and debit card, and had blood streaming down her face, said, "About 20 of us stayed to give statements and make sure everyone was accounted for. The police wouldn't listen to us, they wouldn't take our names or statements. They told us to leave. It was completely infuriating." The police chief seemed determined to head off any suggestion that this was a racially motivated attack by saying that crime is color-blind. Officials elsewhere have said similar things.

A wave of such attacks in Chicago were reported, but not the race of the attackers or victims. Media outlets that do not report the race of people committing crimes nevertheless report racial disparities in imprisonment and write heated editorials blaming the criminal-justice system.

What the Authorities and Media Seem Determined to Suppress

What the authorities and the media seem determined to suppress is that the hoodlum elements in many ghettoes launch coordinated attacks on whites in public places. If there is anything worse than a one-sided race war, it is a two-sided race war, especially when one of the races outnumbers the other several times over.

It may be understandable that some people want to head off such a catastrophe, either by not reporting the attacks in this race war, or by not identifying the race of those attacking, or by insisting that the attacks were not racially motivated—even when the attackers themselves voice anti-white invective as they laugh at their bleeding victims.

Trying to keep the lid on is understandable. But a lot of pressure can build up under that lid. If and when that pressure leads to an explosion of white backlash, things could be a lot worse than if the truth had come out earlier, and steps taken by both black and white leaders to deal with the hoodlums and with those who inflame them. These latter would include not only race hustlers like Al Sharpton and Jesse Jackson but also lesser-known people in the media, in educational institutions, and elsewhere who hype grievances and make all the problems of blacks the fault of whites.

Some of these people may think that they are doing blacks a favor. But it is no favor to anyone who lags behind to turn their energies from the task of improving and advancing themselves to the task of lashing out at others.

These others extend beyond whites. Asian-American schoolchildren in New York and Philadelphia have for years been beaten up by their black classmates. But people in the mainstream media who go ballistic if some kid says something unkind on the Internet about a homosexual classmate nevertheless hear no evil, see no evil, and speak no evil when Asian-American youngsters are victims of violence.

Those who automatically say that the social pathology of the ghetto is due to poverty, discrimination, and the like cannot explain why such pathology was far less prevalent in the 1950s, when poverty and discrimination were worse. But there were not nearly as many grievance mongers and race hustlers then as there are now.

The Brutal Reality of Black on White Rape Statistics

This media blackout trend also carries over to interracial rape statistics as posted in the May 2007 Front Page Magazine article by Lawrence Auster "The Truth Of Interracial Rape In The United States:"

In 2008, the Bureau of Justice released its crime victimization survey for race of victim and race of offender, specifically recording rape and verbal threats of rape. It concluded that white-on-black instances were statistically zero, and it continues to stay at or around this mark every year in every analysis since 2008.

The Bureau of Justice extrapolated an estimate of 117,640 white women who say they were sexually assaulted or threatened with sexual assault. Of those victims, 16.4% reported their assailant as black. The final numbers were 19,293 white women sexually assaulted or threatened by black men in a 24 month period. Again, the reverse was near zero for a black woman being raped by a white man.

There are similar findings in the 2005 report in (frequently used) Table 42, entitled "Personal crimes of violence, 2005, percent distribution of single-offender victimizations, based on race of victims, by type of crime and perceived race of offender."

From that report we learn that there were 111,590 white victims and 36,620 black victims of rape or sexual assault in 2005. (The number of rapes is not distinguished from those of sexual assaults; it is maddening that sexual assault, an ill-defined category that covers various types of criminal acts ranging from penetration to inappropriate touching, is conflated with the more specific crime of rape.)

In the 111,590 cases in which the victim of rape or sexual assault was white, 44.5 percent of the offenders were white, and 33.6 percent of the offenders were black. In the 36,620 cases in which the victim of rape or sexual assault was black, 100 percent of the offenders were black, and 0.0 percent of the offenders were white. The table explains that 0.0 percent means that there were under 10 incidents nationally.

The table does not gives statistics for Hispanic victims and offenders. But the bottom line on interracial white/black and black/white rape is clear and the fact checkers have skipped this fact along with many others.

In the United States in 2005, 37,460 white females were sexually assaulted or raped by a black man, while between zero and ten black females were sexually assaulted or raped by a white man. What this means is that every day in the United States, over one hundred white women are raped or sexually assaulted by a black man. And no more than once a month a black woman is raped by a white man.

The Department of Justice statistics refer, of course, to verified reports. According to the Wikipedia article on rape, as many as half of all rape charges nationally are determined by police and prosecutors to be false: If we cut the two stats in half above, we still approach close to zero, and the black/white disparity is just as glaring.

But even when news media's reports of black on white rape make the race of the perpetrator evident (which the media only does in a minority of instances), no explicit reference is ever made to the racial aspect of the case. Each story of black on white rape is reported in isolation, not presented as part of a larger pattern.

There is never the slightest mention of the fact that white women in this country are being targeted by black rapists. In the inverted world of illiberalism, the phenomenon does not exist.

Police Officers Killed Surged 28% in 2020

On July 7, 2016, a gunman in Dallas opened fire on police officers working at a protest of back-to-back killings of black men by police in Minnesota and Louisiana. The attacker, Micah Johnson, killed five officers and wounded nine others and two civilians before police killed him with a robot-delivered bomb when negotiations failed. Authorities say Johnson, who was black, told negotiators he wanted to kill as many white police officers as he could. It was the deadliest day for American law enforcement since Sept. 11, 2001.

In the wake of George Floyd's death at the hands of Minneapolis police in late May, tremendous scrutiny was placed on policing with peaceful protests broadly calling for reform. But accompanying that was a rise in an anti-police sentiment that, experts say, manifested itself in attacks on officers, patrol vehicles and precinct stationhouses, leaving cops around the country feeling under siege.

An ABC News review in July 2020 by Bill Hutchinson found that in recent years, periods of civil unrest coincided with an increase in police killings. While the sample size is small and a multitude of factors come into play in each situation, some experts say that an anti-police sentiment helps embolden offenders.

Police Killings Rise in Times of Civil Unrest

Per Hutchinson, police killings are a complicated matter—involving a multitude of factors, this year primarily being linked to traffic stops and responses to domestic violence calls.

While FBI data doesn't directly link the slayings to the civil unrest or anti-police rhetoric, police advocacy groups and many law enforcement officials say the protests–particularly when they become unruly–can contribute to an anti-police atmosphere that puts officers in danger from those looking to exploit the situation.

Two years earlier in 2014, 51 police officers were slain in the line of duty up from 27 in 2013, an 89% jump. Seven of the officers were ambushed. However, the number of police officer killings in 2013 was the lowest in decades, according to the data, and the number of officer deaths due to felonious acts in 2014 was representative of what was seen in an average year.

The 2014 police officer slayings happened amidst the backdrop of protests that erupted across the country over the police shooting of Michael Brown, a black teenager, in Ferguson, Missouri, and the police-involved chokehold death of Eric Garner, a 43-year-old black man, in New York City. The officer who shot Brown and those involved in Garner's death were not criminally charged.

And in 2011, the year where Occupy Wall Street protesters clashed with police, law enforcement officers killed increased 28% to 72, including 15 who were ambushed.

'People Feel Vindicated Attacking Law Enforcement'

Following the surge in shootings of police officers in 2011, Maria "Maki" Haberfeld, a professor of police science at John Jay College of Criminal Justice in New York, said while she cannot definitively say that the increase in police officer slayings are related to the mass protests or the increase in anti-police rhetoric by demonstrators and politicians alike, police have become "scapegoats" for broader anger.

Haberfeld participated in a study sponsored by the FBI to examine reasons for the deadly streak. What she found was a myriad of reasons, but hatred for police was not among the top motives.

"I think it was different back then. It was more related to issues of people who were trying to avoid going back to prison, or people with mental issues," Haberfeld told ABC News of the findings. "It was less related to what I am seeing right now. Right now it's just violence against the police."

Haberfeld also said some suspects recently accused of perpetrating violence against law enforcement officers also vary from those seen in the past. She noted that in late June 2020, two attorneys from Brooklyn, New York, were among three people arrested and charged with tossing Molotov cocktails inside occupied New York Police Department vehicles.

The Often Distorted Reality of Hate Crime in America

Racism remains a blight, but one-sided reporting and misrepresented facts don't help as reported by Gerard Baker in the May 2020 *Wall Street Journal* article "The Often Distorted Reality of Hate Crime in America."

You will have heard by now of Ahmaud Arbery, the 25-year-old black man shot dead on a street outside Brunswick, Georgia, in February. Prosecutors initially declined to press charges in the case, saying that the alleged perpetrators, a white father and son, Gregory, and Travis

McMichael, had used legitimate force. Then video surfaced of the incident in which the unarmed black man is seen running down the street, seems to be confronted by the McMichaels, and is shot at point-blank range by the men, both of whom have now been charged with murder.

You probably haven't heard of Paul and Lidia Marino. The couple, 86 and 85 years old, were shot dead a week ago while visiting a veterans' cemetery in Bear, Delaware, where their son, who died in 2017, is buried. The authorities have so far been unable to establish a motive for the killing, but they identified a suspect, Sheldon Francis, a 29-year-old black man, later found dead after an exchange of fire with the police.

As far as I can tell, from news databases and online searches, other than local newspapers and TV, and a brief story by the *New York Post*, the death of the Marinos, who were white, has gone as unremarked as their lives. Arbery's death, by contrast, has become one of those crimes that some who control our public discourse have decided is a "teachable moment."

Some who control our public discourse have decided that Ahmaud Arbery's death is a 'teachable moment.'

Millions of words have been devoted to exploring and explaining the moral of the killing. It has been widely described as a "lynching." We have been reminded once again of the prevalence of unequal and violent treatment of minorities. We've been told once again that the killing reflects the daily reality of life in America for young blacks. This teaching moment has turned into a continuous, ubiquitous lecture series on the unalterably racist nature of America.

We don't yet know the full facts behind either of these killings. Arbery's certainly looked ugly, and whatever his killers and some neighbors allege he may have been doing on that street on a sunny afternoon, he clearly did not deserve to be gunned down. We will learn no doubt soon whether his killers did indeed have racist motives.

Perhaps, meanwhile, the murder of the Marinos was a random act of violence, a deranged killer, a robbery that savagely escalated. But whatever the motive, per Baker, "I'd be willing to wager a small fortune that we won't hear much more about it."

Is Arbery's Killing More Representative Than the Marinos'?

Some will say that's as it should be. Arbery's killing is simply more representative of the nature of race relations in America. By the numbers it clearly is not!

But from the simple perspective of hate crimes, this isn't right. According to the latest official data from the Justice Department, there were indeed more than twice as many antiblack hate crimes as there were antiwhite hate crimes in 2018. But if you adjust the figures for the relative size of each group in the total U.S. population, they show that blacks are 50% overrepresented among perpetrators of hate crimes, while whites are about 25% underrepresented.

In a larger sense, some will say, the much greater attention given to white attacks on blacks is justified because of the nature of socioeconomic relations between the races. Certainly, given the nation's history and continuing social inequalities, a heightened sensitivity should be accorded evidence of racist violence by white people.

But we have gone way beyond heightened sensitivity, to the point of complete distortion of reality. Almost every instance of white violence against minorities is held up now as a bleak model of the state of the nation, while almost every instance of black violence against whites is ignored.

This selective, exclusive narrative isn't just confined to the typical media channels. It's embedded in the very way in which most of us acquire knowledge of the world today and here's an experiment to show why. If you Google "blacks shot by whites" you get a predictable list of results heavily populated with articles about police violence. Google "whites shot by blacks" and, curiously, you get essentially the same set of results. The Google algorithm doesn't even seem to acknowledge the possibility of black-on-white violence.

No fair person disputes the proposition that racism remains a continuing reality and blight on American life. But the systematic misrepresentation of the facts, the highly selective choice of stories, the one-sided nature of the reporting and the routine exclusion of countervailing evidence only risk making it worse.

The True Statistics of Hate Crime and Hate Groups

In a list compiled of all of the attacks on Asians in the US where the offender was known and reported, most of the perpetrators of the crimes were black Americans. The most vicious attack of them all, a mass stabbing of an Asian family at a Sam's Club supermarket, was carried out by a Hispanic man.

The media also fails to mention that black Americans are vastly overrepresented among perpetrators of hate crimes—by 50 percent—according to recent Justice Department data from 2017; whites are underrepresented by 24 percent.

This is particularly true for the anti-Jewish hate crimes occurring mainly in New York City. Additionally, black Americans commit hate crimes at a rate that is three times higher than whites per 100,000 according to FBI crime data from 2016 and 2017. All of this data available, and yet the numerous congressional hearings on "White Nationalism" may have made you believe otherwise.

Black Americans are also more than twice as likely to be in a hate group than white Americans, according to the Southern Poverty Law Center's (SPLC) own data. They state on the website that "The black nationalist movement is a reaction to centuries of institutionalized white supremacy in America," which supposedly justifies their actions.

The Execution Style Murder of the Interracial Pietrzak Newlyweds

It was a real life NCIS investigation and murder crime story that unfortunately eclipsed any fictionalized TV crime show and it rocked the nation and at first baffled detectives and real-life NCIS agents. When the case broke open, it was reported that four African American Marines entered the Pietrzak home, sexually assaulted Jenkins-Pietrzak and tortured the interracial couple before killing them.

Two of the four accused Marines worked under Pietrzak's command and it seemed implausible that Sgt. Jan Pietrzak, a young, decorated Marine and his wife, Quiana Jenkins-Pietrzak, an aspiring doctor, married just 67 days, had their young lives ended in such a horrific manner in their suburban Riverside County home.

But on October 15, 2008, the newlyweds failed to report to their jobs and when Riverside sheriff's deputies arrived at their home to conduct a welfare check, they found the couple's lifeless bodies–they had been shot execution-style and their home ransacked.

Sergeant Pietrzak was known as a tough disciplinarian. It was also known around the base that he had gotten a $30,000 bonus months earlier and had told some people he had kept the money at their home, which was near Camp Pendleton. "This case involved torture. It involved greed," says NCIS Special Agent Matthew Timmons. "It involved anger. It involved double lives." Why would anyone kill the Pietrzaks, a beloved couple was open to speculation.

District Attorney Rod Pacheco emphasized the robbery motive, commenting, "To burglarize their home and then to treat them in the way they did before they died and to murder them— it's hard for our minds to comprehend this kind of savagery."

After hearing and reviewing evidence and confessions from the four Marine suspects, a June 2013 a jury rendered a verdict of death for two of the four assailants and life in prison without parole for a third. The fourth assailant was later also sentenced to death.

As we end this chapter, aware of the Marine motto semper fi "always faithful," you have to ask yourself this question: What could motivate four fellow marines to execute one of their own? You can decide for yourself by watching the 45-minute NCIS exclusive news story in the Appendix.

Credit: CBS News. Jan Pawel Pietrzak and Quiana Jenkins Pietrzak

6 – The Leftist Roots of Anti-Law Enforcement Bias and Rage

Credit: AP. Mario Savio, a New York philosophy student and a leader of the Free Speech Movement.

The outbreak of mass rioting and looting across America in 2020 is alarming in its own right, but equally chilling is the public's support for the violence. As first reported by the *Washington Examiner's* Paul Bedard, a new poll finds that college students in particular overwhelmingly believe that rioting and looting is justified.

The poll was conducted by Mclaughlin & Associate in conjunction with Yale University's conservative William F. Buckley Program. It surveyed a nationally representative sample of 800 college students on a wide array of issues, from the coronavirus to race in America. One key finding from the poll was that 64 percent of college students agreed that "the recent rioting and looting is justified to some degree." Only 28 percent disagreed with this assessment.

GQ Pan's August 2020 *Epoch Times* article titled "Law Professor at Senate Hearing: Antifa Is Winning on College Campuses" quotes Jonathan Turley, a George Washington University law professor who warned the Senate regarding the free speech suppression movement taking place on college campuses.

Turley testified in August 2020 before a Senate subcommittee during a hearing that aimed to examine the protection of free speech and prevention of violent demonstrations against it. According to Turley, far-left anarcho-communist group Antifa, unlike other extremist groups that also commit violence during protests, is particularly dangerous because it's part of a nationwide anti-free speech movement that uses intimidation tactics to prevent ideological opponents from expressing their views.

"If you go through the Antifa handbook and look at their literature, it's quite express, as stated in the handbook, they reject the premise of what they call a classical liberal view of free speech," Turley said. "Specifically they object to statements like, 'I may disagree with what you have to say, but I would give my life to defend it.' They reject that. They believe that free speech itself is a tool of oppression."

Antifa is Winning on College Campuses

"Many of us on campuses have been dealing with Antifa for years, and Antifa is winning," Turley said, adding that he had never seen the same level of fear and intimidation on campuses today throughout his 30 years of higher education career.

"Faculty are afraid to speak out about issues," he continued. "We can't have a dialogue about the important issues occurring today because there's a fear that you might be accused of being reactionary or racist. We've had law professors who have been physically attacked, have required police protection. That's the environment that we're developing."

Turley moved on to warn those who see these self-proclaimed anti-fascists as allies that they don't know Antifa. "Those of us who have been teaching on campuses can tell you about these groups," he said. "And the alarm that I have is because I'm watching my profession, the teaching profession, die, with free speech."

When asked by Sen. Ted Cruz (R-Texas) if he thought it was harmful for Minnesota Attorney General Keith Ellison to post a picture of himself holding an "Anti-Fascist Handbook" on Twitter, Turley said he noted that some Democratic politicians have not only failed to denounce Antifa but endorsed it.

"Ellison said that they would put the fear in the heart of Donald Trump, but what he doesn't see is that Antifa is putting the fear in the hearts of many people, other than Donald Trump," Turley said. "If you go to campuses today, you will find more advocates for limiting speech than protecting it. They're winning."

"And when you see pictures like Ellison's picture with Antifa, it's very disturbing because Antifa's not coming after him," he continued. "They're not even coming after Democrats. They're coming after Republicans, conservatives, and those of us in the free speech community.

"They're coming after us. But don't think we'll be the last ones. That's not how this works."

UC Berkeley History Professor's Open Letter Against BLM, Police Brutality & Cultural Orthodoxy

Tracy Beanz's UncoverDC.com article in June 2020 titled "UC Berkeley History Professor's Open Letter Against BLM, Police Brutality and Cultural Orthodoxy" that published the anonymous UC Berkeley history professor's open letter written in June 2020 against BLM, police brutality and cultural orthodoxy covers half of this chapter (with subsections added by me and a few paragraphs omitted for brevity). In the professor's own words:

Dear profs X, Y, Z:

I am one of your colleagues at the University of California, Berkeley. I have met you both personally but do not know you closely, and am contacting you anonymously, with apologies. I am worried that writing this email publicly might lead to me losing my job, and likely all future jobs in my field.

In your recent departmental emails you mentioned our pledge to diversity, but I am increasingly alarmed by the absence of diversity of opinion on the topic of the recent protests and our community response to them. In the extended links and resources you provided, I could not find a single instance of substantial counter-argument or alternative narrative to explain the under-representation of black individuals in academia or their over-representation in the criminal justice system.

The explanation provided in your documentation, to the near exclusion of all others, is univariate: the problems of the black community are caused by whites, or, when whites are not physically present, by the infiltration of white supremacy and white systemic racism into American brains, souls, and institutions.

Many cogent objections to this thesis have been raised by sober voices, including from within the black community itself, such as Thomas Sowell and Wilfred Reilly. These people are not racists or 'Uncle Toms.' They are intelligent scholars who reject a narrative that strips black people of agency and systematically externalizes the problems of the black community onto outsiders. Their view is entirely absent from the departmental and UCB-wide communiques.

The claim that the difficulties that the black community faces are entirely causally explained by exogenous factors in the form of white systemic racism, white supremacy, and other forms of white discrimination remains a problematic hypothesis that should be vigorously challenged by historians. Instead, it is being treated as an axiomatic and actionable truth without serious consideration of its profound flaws, or its worrying implication of total black impotence. This hypothesis is transforming our institution and our culture, without any space for dissent outside of a tightly policed, narrow discourse.

If we claim that the criminal justice system is white-supremacist, why is it that Asian Americans, Indian Americans, and Nigerian Americans are incarcerated at vastly lower rates than white Americans? This is a funny sort of white supremacy. Even Jewish Americans are incarcerated less than gentile whites. I think it's fair to say that your average white supremacist disapproves of Jews. And yet, these alleged white supremacists incarcerate gentiles at vastly higher rates than Jews.

None of this is addressed in your literature. None of this is explained, beyond hand-waving and ad hominems. "Those are racist dog whistles." "The model minority myth is white supremacist." "Only fascists talk about black-on-black crime," ad nauseam. These types of statements do not amount to counterarguments: they are simply arbitrary offensive classifications, intended to silence and oppress discourse.

Any serious historian will recognize these for the silencing orthodoxy tactics they are, common to suppressive regimes, doctrines, and religions throughout time and space. They are intended to crush real diversity and permanently exile the culture of robust criticism from our department.

Antifa and BLM Are the Natural Product of Our Educational System

Alarmingly, she adds: Increasingly, we are being called upon to comply and subscribe to BLM's problematic view of history, and the department is being presented as unified on the matter. In particular, ethnic minorities are being aggressively marshaled into a single position. Any apparent unity is surely a function of the fact that dissent could almost certainly lead to expulsion or cancellation for those of us in a precarious position, which is no small number.

I personally don't dare speak out against the BLM narrative, and with this barrage of alleged unity being mass-produced by the administration, tenured professoriate, the UC administration, corporate America, and the media, the punishment for dissent is a clear danger at a time of widespread economic vulnerability. I am certain that if my name were attached to this email, I would lose my job and all future jobs, even though I believe in and can justify every word I type.

The vast majority of violence visited on the black community is committed by black people. There are virtually no marches for these invisible victims, no public silences, no heartfelt letters from the UC regents, deans, and departmental heads. The message is clear: Black lives only matter when whites take them. Black violence is expected and insoluble, while white violence requires explanation and demands solution.

Please look into your hearts and see how monstrously bigoted this formulation truly is. No discussion is permitted for non-black victims of black violence, who proportionally outnumber black victims of non-black violence. This is especially bitter in the Bay Area, where Asian victimization by black assailants has reached epidemic proportions, to the point that the SF police chief has advised Asians to stop hanging good-luck charms on their doors, as this attracts the attention of (overwhelmingly black) home invaders.

The claim that black interracial violence is the product of redlining, slavery, and other injustices is a largely historical claim. It is for historians, therefore, to explain why Japanese internment or the massacre of European Jewry hasn't led to equivalent rates of dysfunction and low SES performance among Japanese and Jewish Americans, respectively. Arab Americans have been viciously demonized since 9/11, as have Chinese Americans more recently.

However, both groups outperform white Americans on nearly all socio-economic status (SES) indices–as do Nigerian Americans, who incidentally have black skin. It is for historians to point out and discuss these anomalies. However, no real discussion is possible in the current climate at our department. The explanation is provided to us, disagreement with it is racist, and the job of historians is to further explore additional ways in which the explanation is additionally correct. This is a mockery of the historical profession.

Captured by the Interests of the Democratic Party

She goes on to say: Most troublingly, our department appears to have been entirely captured by the interests of the Democratic National Convention (DNC), and the Democratic Party more broadly. To explain what I mean, consider what happens if you choose to donate to Black Lives Matter, an organization UCB History has explicitly promoted in its recent mailers.

All donations to the official BLM website are immediately redirected to ActBlue Charities, an organization primarily concerned with bankrolling election campaigns for Democrat candidates. Donating to BLM today is to indirectly donate to Joe Biden's 2020 campaign. This is grotesque given the fact that the American cities with the worst rates of black-on-black violence and police-on-black violence are overwhelmingly Democrat-run. Minneapolis itself has been entirely in the hands of Democrats for over five decades; the 'systemic racism' there was built by successive Democrat administrations.

The patronizing and condescending attitudes of Democrat leaders towards the black community, exemplified by nearly every Biden statement on the black race, all but guarantee a perpetual state of misery, resentment, poverty, and the attendant grievance politics which are simultaneously annihilating American political discourse and black lives. And yet, donating to BLM is bankrolling the election campaigns of men like Mayor Jacob Frey, who saw their cities devolve into violence. This is a grotesque capture of a good-faith movement for necessary police reform, and of our department, by a political party. Even worse, there are virtually no avenues for dissent in academic circles. I refuse to serve the Party, and so should you.

There also exists a large constituency of what can only be called 'race hustlers': hucksters of all colors who benefit from stoking the fires of racial conflict to secure administrative jobs, charity management positions, academic jobs and advancement, or personal political entrepreneurship. Given the direction our history department appears to be taking far from any commitment to truth, we can regard ourselves as a formative training institution for this brand of snake-oil salespeople. Their activities are corrosive, demolishing any hope at harmonious racial coexistence in our nation and colonizing our political and institutional life. Many of their voices are unironically segregationist.

MLK would likely be called an Uncle Tom if he spoke on our campus today. We are training leaders who intend, explicitly, to destroy one of the only truly successful ethnically diverse societies in modern history. As the People's Republic of China (PRC), an ethnonationalist and aggressively racially chauvinist national polity with null immigration and no concept of jus solis increasingly presents itself as the global political alternative to the US, I ask you: Is this wise? Are we really doing the right thing?

Floyd Was a Multiple Felon Who Once Held a Pregnant Black Woman at Gunpoint

As a final point, she adds: Our university and department has made multiple statements celebrating and eulogizing George Floyd. Floyd was a multiple felon who once held a pregnant black woman at gunpoint. He broke into her home with a gang of men and pointed a gun at her pregnant stomach. He terrorized the women in his community.

He sired and abandoned multiple children, playing no part in their support or upbringing, failing one of the most basic tests of decency for a human being. He was a drug-addict and sometime drug-dealer, a swindler who preyed upon his honest and hard-working neighbors. And yet, the regents of UC and the historians of the UCB History department are celebrating this violent criminal, elevating his name to virtual sainthood.

A man who hurt women. A man who hurt black women. With the full collaboration of the UCB history department, corporate America, most mainstream media outlets, and some of the wealthiest and most privileged opinion-shaping elites of the USA, he has become a culture hero, buried in a golden casket, his (recognized) family showered with gifts and praise.

Americans are being socially pressured into kneeling for this violent, abusive misogynist. A generation of black men are being coerced into identifying with George Floyd, the absolute worst specimen of our race and species. I'm ashamed of my department. I would say that I'm ashamed of both of you, but perhaps you agree with me, and are simply afraid, as I am, of the backlash of speaking the truth. It's hard to know what kneeling means when you have to kneel to keep your job.

But For the Record, I Write as a Person of Color

She continues: It shouldn't affect the strength of my argument above, but for the record, I write as a person of color. My family have been personally victimized by men like Floyd. We are aware of the condescending depredations of the Democrat party against our race. The humiliating assumption that we are too stupid to do STEM, that we need special help and lower requirements to get ahead in life, is richly familiar to us. I sometimes wonder if it wouldn't be easier to deal with open fascists, who at least would be straightforward in calling me a subhuman, and who are unlikely to share my race.

The ever-present soft bigotry of low expectations and the permanent claim that the solutions to the plight of my people rest exclusively on the goodwill of whites rather than on our own hard work is psychologically devastating. No other group in America is systematically demoralized in this way by its alleged allies. A whole generation of black children are being taught that only by begging and weeping and screaming will they get handouts from guilt-ridden whites.

No message will more surely devastate their futures, especially if whites run out of guilt, or indeed if America runs out of whites. If this had been done to Japanese Americans, or Jewish Americans, or Chinese Americans, then Chinatown and Japantown would surely be no different to the roughest parts of Baltimore and East St. Louis today. The History department of UCB is now an integral institutional promulgator of a destructive and denigrating fallacy about the black race.

I hope you appreciate the frustration behind this message. I do not support BLM. I do not support the Democrat grievance agenda and the Party's uncontested capture of our department. I do not support the Party co-opting my race, as Biden recently did in his disturbing interview, claiming that voting Democrat and being black are isomorphic.

I condemn the manner of George Floyd's death and join you in calling for greater police accountability and police reform. However, I will not pretend that George Floyd was anything other than a violent misogynist, a brutal man who met a predictably brutal end. I also want to protect the practice of history. Cleo is no groveling handmaiden to politicians and corporations. Like us, she is free.

The Philosopher of Antifa and BLM

Dinesh D'Souza's June 2020 *Epoch Times* commentary titled "The Philosopher of Antifa" provides a unique clarity regarding today's socialists who want an America that integrates the groups seen as previously excluded while excluding the group that was previously included.

Using D'Souza's quote of blogger Rod Dreher, "If you are white, male, heterosexual, and religiously and/or socially conservative…there's no place for you" on the progressive left. On the contrary, it should now be expected that in society "people like you are going to have to lose their jobs and influence."

In other words, per D'Souza: for identity socialists and for the left more generally, blacks and Latinos are in; whites are out. Women are in; men are out. Gays, bisexuals, transsexuals, together with other, more exotic types are in; heterosexuals are out. Illegals are in; native-born citizens are out. One may think this is all part of the politics of inclusion, but to think that is to get only half the picture. The point, for the left, is not merely to include but also to exclude, to estrange their opponents from their native land.

How did we get here? To understand identity socialism, we must meet the man who figured out how to bring its various strands together, Herbert Marcuse.

Credit: Getty Images. Herbert Marcuse speaks at UC San Diego.

Marcuse's Revolution

A German philosopher partly of Jewish descent, Marcuse studied under the philosopher Martin Heidegger before escaping Germany prior to the Nazi ascent. After stints at Columbia, Harvard, and Brandeis, Marcuse moved to California, where he joined the University of California–San Diego and became the guru of the New Left in the 60s.

Marcuse influenced a whole generation of young radicals, from Weather Underground co-founder Bill Ayers to Yippie activist Abbie Hoffman to Tom Hayden, president of the activist group Students for a Democratic Society (SDS). Angela Davis, who later joined the Black Panthers and also ran for vice president on the Communist Party ticket, was a student of Marcuse and also one of his proteges. It was Marcuse, Davis said, who "taught me that it was possible to be an academic, an activist, a scholar, and a revolutionary."

Per D'Souza, Marcuse egged on the activists of the 1960s to seize buildings and overthrow the hierarchy of the university, as a kind of first step to fomenting socialist revolution in America. Interestingly, it was Ronald Reagan—then-governor of California—who got Marcuse fired. Still, Marcuse retained his celebrity and influence over the radicals of the time. He did not, of course, create the forces of identity socialism, but he saw, perhaps earlier than anyone else, how they could form the basis for a new and viable socialism in America.

That's the socialism we are dealing with now.

To understand the problem Marcuse confronted, we have to go back to Karl Marx. Marx saw himself as the prophet, not the instigator, of the advent of socialism. We think of Marx as some sort of activist, seeking to organize a workers' revolution, but Marx emphasized from the outset that the socialist revolution would come inevitably; nothing had to be done to cause it. The Marxist view is nicely summed up by one of Marx's German followers, Karl Kautsky, who wrote, "Our task is not to organize the revolution but to organize ourselves for the revolution; it is not to make the revolution, but to take advantage of it."

But what happens when the working class is too secure and contented to revolt? Marx didn't anticipate this; in fact, the absence of a single worker revolt of the kind Marx predicted, anywhere in the world, is a full and decisive refutation of "scientific" Marxism. In the early 20th century, Marxists across the world were fully aware of this problem. Lenin solved it by assembling a professional cadre of revolutionaries. If the revolution would not be done by the working class, he insisted, it would have to be done for them.

Marcuse defined the problem in the same way Lenin did: If the working class isn't up for socialism, where can one find a new proletariat to bring it about? Marcuse knew that modern industrialized countries such as the United States couldn't assemble the types of landless peasants and professional soldiers—the flotsam and jetsam of a backward feudal society—that Lenin relied on. So who could serve in the substitute proletariat that would be needed to agitate for socialism in America?

'Raising Consciousness'

D'Souza notes that: Marcuse looked around to identify which groups had a natural antipathy to capitalism. Marcuse knew he could count on the bohemian artists and intellectuals who had long hated industrial civilization, in part because they considered themselves superior to businessmen and shopkeepers. These self-styled "outcasts" were natural recruits for what Marcuse termed the Great Refusal—the visceral repudiation of free-market society.

The problem, however, was that these bohemians were confined to small sectors of Western society: the Schwabing section of Munich, the Left Bank of Paris, Greenwich Village in New York, and a handful of university campuses. By themselves, they were scarcely enough to hold a demonstration, let alone make a revolution.

So Marcuse had to search further. He had to think of a way to take bohemian culture mainstream, to normalize the outcasts and to turn normal people into outcasts. He started with an unlikely group of proles: the young people of the 1960s. Here, finally, was a group that could make up a mass movement.

Yet what a group! Fortunately, Marx wasn't around to see it; he would have burst out laughing. Abbie Hoffman? Jerry Rubin? Mario Savio? How could people of this sorry stripe, these slack, spoiled products of postwar prosperity, these parodies of humanity, these horny slothful loafers completely divorced from real-world problems, and neurotically focused on themselves, their drugs and sex lives and mind-numbing music, serve as the shock troops of revolution?

To do this, Marcuse answered: By "raising their consciousness." The students were already somewhat alienated from the larger society. They lived in these socialist communes called universities.

Here, Marcuse recognized, was the very raw material out of which socialism is made in a rich, successful society. Perhaps there was a way to instruct them in oppression, to convert their spiritual anomie into political discontent. Marcuse was confident that an activist group of professors could raise the consciousness of a whole generation of students so they could feel subjectively oppressed even if there were no objective forces oppressing them. Then they would become activists to fight not someone else's oppression, but their own.

To Marcuse's good fortune, the 60s was the decade of the Vietnam War. Students were facing the prospect of being drafted. Thus they had selfish reasons to oppose the war. Yet this selfishness could be harnessed by teaching the students that they weren't draft-dodgers; rather, they were noble resisters who were part of a global struggle for social justice. In this way, bad karma could itself be recruited on behalf of left-wing activism.

Marcuse portrayed Ho Chi Minh and the Vietcong as a kind of Third World proletariat, fighting to free itself from American hegemony. This represented a transposition of Marxist categories. The new working class were the Vietnamese "freedom fighters." The evil capitalists were American soldiers serving on behalf of the U.S. government. Marcuse's genius was to tell leftist students in the 1960s that the Vietnamese "freedom fighters" could not succeed without them.

"Only the internal weakening of the superpower," Marcuse wrote in "An Essay on Liberation," can finally stop the financing and equipping of suppression in the backward countries." And indeed America turned sour on the Vietnam War from within—not from losing at the beginning of the war.

In his vision, the students were the "freedom fighters" within the belly of the capitalist beast. Together, the revolutionaries at home and abroad would collaborate in the Great Refusal. They would jointly end the war and redeem both Vietnam and America. And what would this redemption look like? In Marcuse's words, "Collective ownership, collective control and planning of the means of production and distribution." In other words, classical socialism.

Transposing Class

OK, so now we got the young people D'Souza explains. Who else? Herbert Marcuse looked around America for more prospective proles, and he found, in addition to the students, three groups ripe for the taking. The first was the Black Power movement, which was adjunct to the civil rights movement. The beauty of this group, from Marcuse's point of view, is that it would not have to be instructed in the art of grievance; blacks had legitimate grievances that dated back centuries.

Consequently, here was a group that could be mobilized against the status quo, and if the status quo could be identified with capitalism, here was a group that should be open to socialism. Through a kind of Marxist transposition, "blacks" would become the working class, "whites" the capitalist class. Race, in this analysis, takes the place of class. This is how we get Afro-socialism, and from there it's a short step to Latino socialism and every other type of ethnic socialism.

Another emerging source of disgruntlement was the feminists. Marcuse recognized that with effective consciousness raising, they too could be taught to see themselves as an oppressed proletariat. This of course would require another Marxist transposition: "Women" would now be viewed as the working class and "men" the capitalist class; the class category would now be shifted to gender.

"The movement becomes radical," Marcuse wrote, "to the degree to which it aims, not only at equality within the job and value structure of the established society ... but rather at a change in the structure itself." Marcuse's target wasn't just the patriarchy; it was the monogamous family. In Gramscian (Antonio Gramsci) terms, Marcuse viewed the heterosexual family itself as an expression of bourgeois culture, so in his view, the abolition of the family would help hasten the advent of socialism.

Marcuse didn't write specifically about homosexuals or transgender people, but he was more than aware of exotic and outlandish forms of sexual behavior, and the logic of identity socialism can easily be extended to all these groups. Once again, we need some creative Marxist transposition. Gays and transgender people become the newest proletariat, and heterosexuals—even black and female heterosexuals—become their oppressors.

Roots of Intersectionality

Per Dinesh D'Souza's keen observations, we see here the roots of "intersectionality." As the left now holds, one form of oppression is good, but two is better, and three or more is best. The true exemplar of identity socialism is a black or brown male transitioning to be a woman with a Third World background who is trying illegally to get into this country because his/her—own country has allegedly been devastated by climate change.

These latest developments go beyond Marcuse. He didn't know about intersectionality, but he did recognize the emerging environmental movement as an opportunity to restrict and regulate capitalism. The goal, he emphasized, was "to drive ecology to the point where it is no longer containable within the capitalist framework," although he recognized that this "means first extending the drive within the capitalist framework."

Marcuse also inverted Sigmund Freud to advocate the liberation of eros. Freud had argued that primitive man is single-mindedly devoted to "the pleasure principle," but as civilization advances, the pleasure principle must be subordinated to what Freud termed "the reality principle." In other words, civilization is the product of the subordination of instinct to reason. Repression, Freud argued, is the necessary price we must pay for civilization.

Marcuse argued that at some point, however, civilization reaches a point where humans can go the other way. They can release the very natural instincts that have been suppressed for so long and subordinate the reality principle to the pleasure principle. This would involve a release of what Marcuse termed "polymorphous sexuality" and the "reactivation of all erotogenic zones." We are a short distance here from the whole range of sexual orientations, from bisexuality to transsexuality, and beyond.

Marcuse recognized that mobilizing all these groups—the students, the environmentalists, the blacks, the feminists, the gays—would take time and require a great deal of consciousness raising or reeducation. He saw the university as the ideal venue for carrying out this project, which is why he devoted his own life to teaching and training a generation of socialist and left-wing activists.

Over time, Marcuse believed, the university could produce a new type of culture, and that culture would then metastasize into the larger society to infect the media, the movies, even the lifestyle of the titans of the capitalist class itself.

Marcuse's project—the takeover of the American university, to make it a tool of socialist indoctrination—did not succeed in his lifetime. In fact, as mentioned above, he got the boot when Reagan pressured the regents of the university system not to renew Marcuse's contract. In time, however, Marcuse succeeded as the activist generation of the 1960s gradually took over the elite universities. Today, socialist indoctrination is the norm on the American campus, and Marcuse's dream has been realized.

'Repressive Tolerance'

Marcuse is also the philosopher of Antifa. He argued, in a famous essay called "Repressive Tolerance," that tolerance is not a norm or right that should be extended to all people. Yes, tolerance is good, but not when it comes to people who are intolerant. It is perfectly fine to be intolerant against them (i.e., Republicans, conservatives, Trumps supporters, etc.) to the point of disrupting them, shutting down their events, preventing them from speaking, even destroying their careers and property.

D'Souza admits that Marcuse didn't use the term "hater," but he invented the argument that it's legitimate to be hateful against haters. For Marcuse, there were no limits to what could be done to discredit and ruin such people; he wanted the left to defeat them "by any means necessary." Marcuse even approved of certain forms of domestic terrorism, such as the Weather Underground bombing the Pentagon, on the grounds that the perpetrators were attempting to stop the greater violence that U.S. forces inflict on people in Vietnam and other countries.

Our world is quite different now from what it was in the 1960s, and yet there is so much that seems eerily familiar. When it comes to identity socialism, we are still living with Marcuse's legacy. The natural outgrowth and unsapient conclusion to this philosophy is "critical race theory."

Critical Race Theory

Then President Trump issued an executive order in September 20202 prohibiting federal agencies from using "critical race theory" as part of their personnel-training programs. The president acted in response to Christopher F. Rufo's *City Journal* article "Against Wokeness: Conservatives must understand the threat posed by critical race theory," exposing the use of "diversity, equity, and inclusion" training courses in federal agencies.

These programs, based on a neo-Marxist ideology that originated in law schools a generation ago, purport to expose and correct "unconscious racial bias" and "white privilege" among their employees. Critical race theory treats "whiteness" as a moral blight and maligns all members of that racial group as complicit in oppression.

Critical race theory now forms the basis of personnel-training programs around the country, from corporate America and universities to churches and nonprofits. The racial narrative that underlies these initiatives poses a grave threat to the ideal of colorblind justice under the law enshrined in the American constitutional system.

Many have been slow to oppose the radical demands of groups such as BLM, either out of fear of being labelled racists or because of ignorance about the ideological agenda of these groups. Instead, conservatives have continued to "fight the last war" against the familiar enemies of cultural relativism or tax-and-spend liberalism, not recognizing that a new, virulent form of radicalism now animates the American Left.

Under the dogma of critical race theory, the neo-Marxist Left now treats members of "oppressor" groups (whites, males, Christians, Jews, conservatives) as inherently guilty by virtue of their group membership; conversely, members of victim groups are considered morally innocent. By this logic, claims of victimization by members of victim groups necessarily must be believed, while members of oppressor groups are already guilty by virtue of their group membership. This formula eliminates any need for due process since the mere perception of victimization constitutes proof of same.

One can trace a direct line from the critical race theory trainings in government, education, and universities to the recent violence and destruction in the streets of so many American cities. Many committed to the cultural Marxist narrative are now entrenched in vital American institutions. The recent riots have exposed the extent to which leaders in the Democratic Party have embraced the ideology of the woke Left.

With such widespread penetration of that ideology, the crisis is unlikely to fade away.

7 – No Systemic Racism or Police Brutality—Only Systemic Rioting & Lawlessness

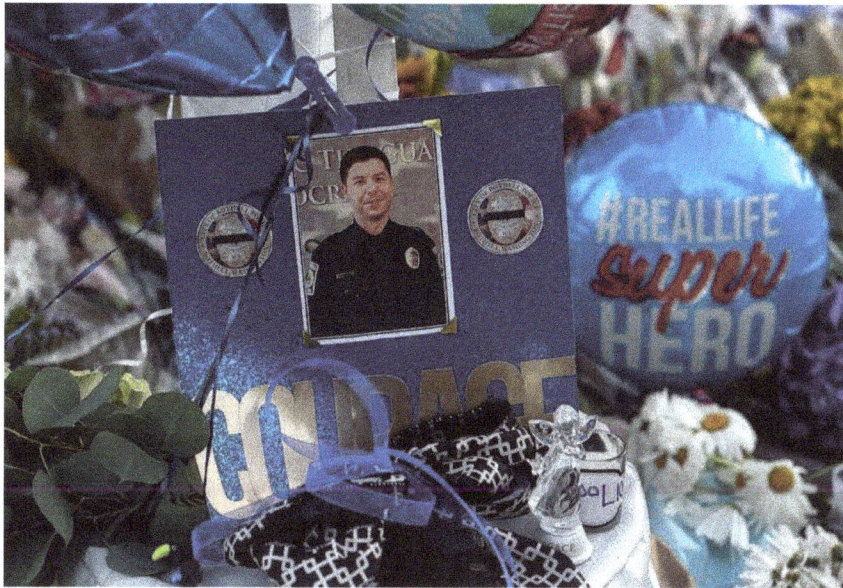

Credit: David Ryder/Getty Images. Police Officer Jonathan Shoop is displayed at a memorial outside the Bothell Police Department in July 2020.

The persistent belief that we are living through an epidemic of racially biased police shootings is a creation of selective reporting. The "policing is racist" discourse is poisonous. It exacerbates anti-cop tensions in minority communities and makes cops unwilling to engage in the proactive policing that can save lives and fulfil their mission and visions statements to protect and serve.

The anti-cop narrative deflects attention away from solving the real criminal-justice problem, which is high rates of black-on-black victimization. Blacks die of homicide at eight times the rate of non-Hispanic whites, overwhelmingly killed not by cops, not by whites, but by other blacks. Police shootings are not the reason that blacks die of homicide at eight times the rate of whites and Hispanics combined; criminal violence is.

Heather Mac Donald, a law enforcement expert at the Manhattan Institute, released her latest article "The Myth of Systemic Police Racism: featured in *The Wall Street Journal* in June 2020.

Per Mac Donald: The latest in a series of studies undercutting the claim of systemic police bias was published in August 2019 in the Proceedings of the National Academy of Sciences (PNAS). The researchers found that the more frequently officers encounter violent suspects from any given racial group, the greater the chance that a member of that group will be fatally shot by a police officer. There is "no significant evidence of antiblack disparity in the likelihood of being fatally shot by police," they concluded.

It is a racial group's rate of violent crime that determines police shootings, not the race of the officer. The more frequently officers encounter violent suspects from any given racial group, the greater the chance that members of that racial group will be shot by a police officer. In fact, if there is a bias in police shootings after crime rates are taken into account, it is against white civilians, the study found.

A 2015 Justice Department analysis of the Philadelphia Police Department found that white police officers were less likely than black or Hispanic officers to shoot unarmed black suspects. Research by Harvard economist Roland G. Fryer Jr. also found no evidence of racial discrimination in shootings. Any evidence to the contrary fails to take into account crime rates and civilian behavior before and during interactions with police.

The Duties of Police Carry a Great Deal of Risk

Law enforcement officers are commissioned to keep citizens safe 24 hours a day and seven days a week. The duties of police carry a great deal of risk, but many people pursue a career as a police officer because they feel a moral calling to protect and serve others.

As noted in the June 2018 "Obligations & Job Duties of Police" article in Officers Chron by Rose Johnson: A typical day varies depending on the jurisdiction and agency type. For example, a police officer in the inner city typically spends more time responding to 911 calls and investigating crimes than a small town sheriff in a remote area.

Ethics, integrity, accountability, and honesty are important values for a police officer to possess. At all times, police officers must follow the law and departmental regulations. For example, use of force must be reasonable and necessary. They are expected to carry out their duties and responsibilities equitably and justly. Police must not show favoritism or act in a discriminatory manner recognizing that all citizens deserve respectful treatment regardless of race, ethnicity, sexual orientation, socioeconomic status, national origin, or religion, for instance.

The police code of ethics prohibits dishonesty and corruption. Police officers who engage in serious misconduct on duty or in their personal life can face disciplinary action and legal prosecution. When assisting crime victims, police have a duty to be caring, compassionate and responsive by taking the report seriously, pursuing the offender and explaining victim services available in the community.

There is No Epidemic of Racist Police Shootings

Heather Mac Donald's earlier July 2019 report from Manhattan Institute titled "There Is No Epidemic of Racist Police Shootings" debunks another common myth.

Mac Donald notes that the authors, faculty at Michigan State University and the University of Maryland at College Park, created a database of 917 officer-involved fatal shootings in 2015 from more than 650 police departments. Fifty-five percent of the victims were white, 27 percent were black, and 19 percent were Hispanic.

Between 90 and 95 percent of the civilians shot by officers in 2015 were attacking police or other citizens; 90 percent were armed with a weapon. So-called threat-misperception shootings, in which an officer shoots an unarmed civilian after mistaking a cellphone, say, for a gun, were rare.

Earlier studies have also disproven the idea that white officers are biased in shooting black citizens. The Black Lives Matter narrative has been impervious to the truth, however. Their efforts to increase minority representation will not reduce racial disparities in shootings, concludes the PNAS study, since white officers are not responsible for those disparities; black crime rates are.

Moreover, lowered hiring standards risk bad police work and corruption. A 2015 Justice Department study of the Philadelphia Police Department found that black officers were 67 percent more likely than white officers to mistakenly shoot an unarmed black suspect; Hispanic officers were 145 percent more likely than white officers to mistakenly shoot an unarmed black suspect. Whether lowered hiring standards are responsible for those disparities was not addressed.

The False Narrative of Systemic Police in America

The false narrative of systemic police bias resulted in targeted killings of officers and may be repeating itself from one racially charged police shooting to another. Heather Mac Donald's 2016 bestseller *The War on Cops: How the New Attack on Law and Order Makes Everyone Less Safe* explains why:

Officers are being assaulted and shot at while they try to arrest gun suspects or respond to the growing riots. Police precincts and courthouses have been destroyed with impunity, which will encourage more civilization-destroying violence. If the Ferguson effect of officers backing off law enforcement in minority neighborhoods is reborn as the Minneapolis effect, the thousands of law-abiding African-Americans who depend on the police for basic safety will once again be the most likely victims and the ones who suffer the most.

The Minneapolis officers who arrested George Floyd must be held accountable for their excessive use of force and callous indifference to his distress. Police training needs to double down on de-escalation tactics. But Floyd's death should not undermine the legitimacy of American law enforcement, without which we will continue on a path toward chaos.

In 2019 police officers fatally shot 1,004 people, most of whom were armed or otherwise dangerous. African-Americans were about a quarter of those killed by cops in 2018 (235), a ratio that has remained stable since 2015.

That share of black victims is less than what the black crime rate would predict, since police shootings are a function of how often officers encounter armed and violent suspects. In 2018, the latest year for which such data have been published, African-Americans made up 53% of known homicide offenders in the U.S. and commit about 60% of robberies, though they are 13% of the population.

The police fatally shot nine unarmed blacks and 19 unarmed whites in 2019, according to a *Washington Post* database, down from 38 and 32, respectively, in 2015. The *Post* defines "unarmed" broadly to include such cases as a suspect in Newark, N.J., who had a loaded handgun in his car during a police chase.

In 2018 there were 7,407 black homicide victims. Assuming a comparable number of victims last year, those nine unarmed black victims of police shootings represent 0.1% of all African-Americans killed in 2019.

In fact, a police officer is 18.5 times more likely to be killed by a black male than an unarmed black male is to be killed by a police officer. And the fact that "2016's increase in gunfire deaths so far came after decades of decline" is precisely what makes the increase so striking. That it reverses decades of decline is not a point in Black Lives Matter's favor.

Economist and black conservative author Thomas Sowell told "Life Liberty & Levin" in a July 2020 interview that the left's claim that America is beset by "systemic racism" has no definitive meaning and cannot be "tested" in any empirical manner.

"You hear this phrase, 'systemic racism' [or] 'systemic oppression'," host Mark Levin told Sowell. "You hear it on our college campuses. You hear it from very wealthy and fabulously famous sports stars. What does that mean? And whatever it means, is it true?"

"It really has no meaning that can be specified and tested in the way that one tests hypotheses," answered Sowell, who added that the currency of the phrase reminds him of the "propaganda tactics" of Nazi Germany, where Sowell claimed that if a lie was "repeated long enough and loud enough" it would be widely believed.

The Myth of Systemic Police Racism and Killings

There has always been considerable concern about police killings of blacks, more recently especially after Officer Darren Wilson shot Michael Brown on Aug. 9, 2014, in Ferguson, Missouri. Officer Wilson is white, and Brown was black and unarmed. Although an extensive investigation by the Department of Justice found that Officer Wilson acted appropriately in response to Brown's physical attacks and subsequent threats, the shooting provoked riots and gave impetus to the Black Lives Matter movement, which claims that racist police officers routinely kill unarmed blacks.

This claim has been difficult to verify since there are no national statistics on police shootings. Moreover, as noted above, broad arrest statistics and academic studies do not support the view that arrests are biased, so there is little reason to think shootings would be biased. The Black Lives Matter movement has not been driven by data but by the deaths of specific people such as Michael Brown, Eric Garner, Tamir Rice, Sandra Bland, and Freddie Gray.

Freddie Gray's death, due to injuries after his arrest in Baltimore, also provoked riots and was taken up with great energy by Black Lives Matter. Three of the six officers charged in Gray's death were black—and they were charged with the most serious crimes—but the incident is still cited as an example of police racism.

Police Killings of Blacks

In the absence of government data, the *Washington Post* investigated every reported case of a fatal shooting by the police during 2015. It found 990 cases, with the following racial distribution of victims:

- White: 50.0 percent (495 victims)
- Black: 26.1 percent (258)
- Hispanic: 17.4 percent (172)
- Asian: 1.4 percent (14)
- Other/Unknown: 5.2 percent (51)

Given their proportions in the population, a black person was 2.45 times more likely than a white person to be shot and killed by police, a Hispanic was 1.24 times more likely, and an Asian was only one third as likely. It is reasonable to expect people of different races to find themselves in potentially lethal confrontations with the police in proportion to their likelihood to commit violent crime, with blacks most likely and Asians least likely.

In California—a large state that keeps consistent statistics on race and ethnicity—blacks are arrested for violent crimes at 5.35 times the white rate, and Hispanics at 1.42 times the white rate. The low likelihood of Asians being killed by police is in keeping with low Asian arrest rates for violent crime. The black and Hispanic multiples for police shooting deaths are well within the arrest multiples—the black multiple is less than half—and certainly do not suggest undisciplined police violence.

Moreover, FBI data show that from 2005 to 2014, blacks accounted for 40 percent of police killings. Since blacks were approximately 13 percent of the population, it meant they were 4.46 times more likely than people of other races to kill a police officer.

In its study, the Post found that men were 22.9 times more likely than women to be shot and killed by officers. No one suggests that law enforcement bias accounts for this huge multiple, which is undoubtedly caused by differences in behavior between men and women. In the case of racial multiples, police bias cannot be ruled out, but it is reasonable to assume that the multiples are explained by race differences in behavior.

The *Washington Post* noted further that all but 93 of the 990 people fatally shot by police were armed, usually with a firearm or knife. The unarmed victims had the following racial distribution:

- White: 34.4 percent (32 victims)
- Black: 40.8 percent (38)
- Hispanic: 19.4 percent (18)
- Asian: 0 percent (0)
- Unknown: 5.4 percent (5)

An unarmed black was therefore 5.6 times more likely than an unarmed white to be shot by police, and a Hispanic was 2.6 times more likely. The black multiple is certainly high, though not that much higher than the California violent-arrest multiple of 5.35 noted above.

Washington Post Investigates Every Reported Case of Fatal Shooting by Police

There is no obvious explanation for why unarmed blacks were shot and killed at a white multiple that was twice that for armed blacks. If police bias is the cause, there is no clear reason why it should be worse in the case of unarmed suspects. The sample size of 93 is small, so random events produce a large effect.

It may be that race differences in how suspects behave when they are arrested explain at least part of the difference. There are no national data, but a five-year study of non-felony arrests in San Francisco found that blacks were 9.6 times more likely than whites (including Hispanics) to be charged with resisting arrest, and whites were 8.6 times more likely than Asians to be so charged.

In Chicago, from September 2014 to September 2015, blacks accounted for 77 percent of arrests for obstruction of justice and resisting arrest (page 4 of report), meaning they were 6.8 times more likely than non-blacks to be arrested on these charges. If these findings are typical, they help explain why the arrest of a black non-felony suspect—who would more than likely be unarmed—could escalate into potentially lethal violence.

The *Post's* analysis was intended to throw light on police bias but failed to indicate the races of the officers involved in fatal shootings. This would be useful information. A 2015 Department of Justice study of police shootings in Philadelphia found racial differences in "threat perception failure," that is, cases in which an officer shot an unarmed suspect because the officer thought the suspect was armed.

Black officers were nearly twice as likely as white officers to shoot an unarmed black (11.4 percent of all shootings by black officers vs. 6.8 percent of all shootings by white officers). The percentage of such errors by Hispanic officers—16.7 percent—was even higher.

Black officers may be somewhat more prone to error in general. About 12 percent of police officers in the United States are black. Between 2005 and 2015, 16.6 percent of the 54 officers criminally charged for fatally shooting someone while on duty were black.

Homicide is a serious problem for black men. Since at least 2002 and up to 2013 (the latest data available), murder was the leading cause of death for black men, ages 15 to 34. Their murderers are almost always other black men. According to a Department of Justice report, (page 13), from 1980 to 2008, 93 percent of black homicide victims were killed by blacks.

The point of this statistic is there is no "open season" of whites killing blacks as mainstream media, BLM, and the Democratic Party would have you believe.

By contrast, the 256 police judicial killings of blacks in 2015 would be only 4.2 percent of the 6,095 blacks who were murdered in 2014 (the most recent year for which national data are available). The 38 unarmed blacks killed by police accounted for just 0.6 percent. Police shootings of unarmed blacks is a very small problem compared to murder in the black community.

Attorney General Believes There's No Systemic Racism in US Policing

As reported by Sam Dorman of Fox News in July 2020, former Attorney General William Barr told Congress in July 2020 that he doesn't believe police departments are systemically racist, pushing back against Democrats' overarching justification for implementing sweeping police reforms after high-profile, police-involved deaths of Black Americans.

His comments came during a House Judiciary Committee hearing where Rep. Sheila Jackson Lee, D-Texas, pressed Barr on the administration's efforts to counter systemic racism. "I don't agree there's systemic racism in the police department, generally, in this country," Barr said, and his comments came as House Democrats passed policing reform legislation that has been painted as a way to address systemic racism.

The Justice in Policing Act of 2020 includes cooperation from Barr's department, including in the creation of a task force overseeing law enforcement in the U.S. In his opening statement, Barr said it was "understandable" that African Americans harbored distrust towards the police and acknowledged perceptions of bias during police encounters. "At the same time, I think it would be an oversimplification to treat the problem as rooted in some deep-seated racism generally infecting our police departments," he added.

"It seems far more likely that the problem stems from a complex mix of factors, which can be addressed with focused attention over time. We in law enforcement must be conscious of the concerns and ensure that we do not have two different systems of justice."

Conservatives have generally pushed back on the term, arguing that law enforcement statistics indicate racism isn't systemic. Based on the overwhelming evidence as presented in *Crime Rate Madness*, their position seems to be the most sapient.

The Long, Hot, and Dangerous Summer of 2020

Despite overwhelming and abundant evidence that leftist, anarchist, and some right-wing groups are heavily involved in these protests and riots, very few journalists have been willing to expose the truth.

One notable exception is Antifa expert Andy Ngo. On May 30, 2020, Ngo wrote on Twitter:

"We are witnessing glimpses of the full insurrection the far-left has been working on for decades. Within hours, militant Antifa cells across the country mobilized to aid BLM [Black Lives Matter] rioters. The first broken window is the blood in the water for looters to move in. The fires come next."

Ngo later added:

"Media, politicians, public—all of us—have underestimated the training, purpose & capability of left-wing extremists. Every part of the rioting has a purpose. Fires destroy economy. Riots can overwhelm police & even military. All of it leads to a destabilized state if maintained."

The Democratic Socialists of America (DSA) now has 66,000 members nationwide and locals in almost every state. Other communist groups such as Communist Party USA, Liberation Road,

Socialist Alternative, Workers World Party, Party for Socialism and Liberation, Socialist Unity Party, and Revolutionary Communist Party and their allies in Black Lives Matter and Antifa can mobilize tens of thousands of militants and organizing cadre on short notice.

During the Ferguson riots of 2014, the pro-China Freedom Road Socialist Organization (now Liberation Road) and its allies claim to have brought nearly 10,000 activists into St. Louis, Missouri, to swell the ranks of the rioters.

Attorney General Conducts Comprehensive Investigations Into Antifa

"We have some investigations underway and very focused investigations on certain individuals that relate to Antifa," Barr said during an interview with Fox News in June 2020. "But in the … initial phase of identifying people and arresting them, they were arrested for crimes that don't require us to identify a particular group or don't necessitate that."

An *Epoch Times* June 2020 article by Bowen Xiao, Ivan Pentchoukov, and Jack Phillips quoted Barr who added, "this is why the group Antifa hasn't been mentioned in criminal complaints related to the rioting amid protests following the death of George Floyd." Barr also said in a press conference earlier that month that Antifa and other similar groups and "actors of a variety of different political persuasions" have been behind the recent violent activities in order to carry out their own separate agendas.

He said these actors had "hijacked" the protests to "engage in lawlessness, violent rioting, arson, looting of businesses, and public property assaults on law enforcement officers and innocent people, and even the murder of a federal agent." The government has made 51 arrests so far for federal crimes in connection with the rioting, the attorney general said.

Barr's comments were echoed by FBI Director Christopher Wray, who said these individuals have "set out to sow discord and upheaval rather than join in the righteous pursuit of equality and justice." Barr said their investigation will look into the sources of funding behind the extremist groups and will also focus on the coordinated tactics used by these groups during the protests.

"Some of it relates to an Antifa. Some of it relates to groups that act very much like an Antifa. As I said, there's a witch's brew of extremist groups that are trying to exploit this situation on all sides," Barr said.

Antifa and Other Far-Left Groups Exploit Protests for 'Revolution'

An *Epoch Times* article titled "Antifa, Other Far-Left Groups Exploit Protests for 'Revolution'" by Bowen Xiao and Ivan Pentchoukov in June 2020 noted that communist groups—including the extremist organization Antifa—are hijacking what started out as peaceful protests over the death of an unarmed black man to usher in a revolution, according to officials, experts, videos, and anarchists' own words.

That charge comes amid an unprecedented and coordinated effort behind the riots, the likes of which have never been seen before and which span across multiple states and involve often violent street-level tactics.

Officials from both sides say that outside groups have exploited the recent momentum to further their own agenda. Minnesota Gov. Tim Walz, a Democrat, noted that "bad actors continue to infiltrate the rightful protests" and that 80 percent of the rioters have come from outside the state. Federal officials including President Donald Trump have pointed to Antifa.

Bernard B. Kerik, former police commissioner of the New York City Police Department, said Antifa "100 percent exploited these protests," noting that their various websites control and dictate where protests start. "It's in 40 different states and 60 cities; it would be impossible for somebody outside of Antifa to fund this," he told The Epoch Times. "It's a radical, leftist, socialist attempt at revolution."

"What Antifa is doing is they're basically hijacking the black community as their army," Kerik said. "They instigate, they antagonize, they get these young black men and women to go out there and do stupid things, and then they disappear off into the sunset." Photos later pulled offline appeared to show protesters with military-grade communications radios and earpieces, Kerik said, noting: "They have to be talking to somebody at a central command center with a repeater. Where do those radios go to?"

Andy Ngo, a journalist who has covered Antifa extensively, said the group is organized in "multiple units" with scouts that monitor the perimeter of an area, providing live audio or text updates. Others carry out violent missions with weapons and firebombs. The extremist group is "horizontally" organized; it doesn't have a public leader, since it's part of their ideology that there should be no authority, Ngo said.

Author Andy Ngo's new book *Unmasked: Inside Antifa's Radical Plan to Destroy Democracy* released in February 2021, reveals the inner workings of Antifa cells, and he is known for aggressively covering and video-recording demonstrators. Ngo describes himself as the editor at large at The Post Millennial, a Canada-based conservative web publication and has drawn

According to John Miller, the NYPD's deputy commissioner of Intelligence and Counterterrorism, these outside radical groups have organized scouts, medics, and even supply routes of rocks, bottles, and accelerants "for breakaway groups to commit vandalism and violence." These groups have planned for violence in advance, using encrypted communications, he said.

Mike Griffin, a longtime political activist from Minneapolis, told The *New York Times* there were people he never witnessed before demonstrating, including "well-dressed young white men in expensive boots carrying hammers and talking about torching buildings. I know protests, I've been doing it for 20 years," he said. "People not affiliated with the protests are creating havoc on the streets."

Communism expert Trevor Loudon, meanwhile, told *The Epoch Times* that Antifa is only one part of the picture, noting that "every significant communist or socialist party in the United States has been involved in these protests and riots from the beginning." According to Loudon, "Communist Party USA, Liberation Road, Freedom Road Socialist Organization, Democratic Socialists of America, Revolutionary Communist Party, Workers World Party, and the Party for Socialism and Liberation" have been involved, among others.

Gabriel Nadales, a former Antifa member, told Jan Jekielek, host of *The Epoch Times*' "American Thought Leaders" series, that to really be a part of Antifa is to do two things: "One is to share their violent ideology and be willing to fight for them at any turn, and the second is to actually do it. It's not just about having anti-conservative beliefs," he said.

Majority of Americans Support Use of National Guard to Suppress Riots

Credit: Click2Houston.com. Protestors demonstrate outside of a burning fast food restaurant, May 2020 in Minneapolis.

A majority of American voters told Morning Consult pollsters that they support the use of the National Guard and the U.S. military to assist law enforcement in addressing protests over George Floyd's death in police custody, some of which have morphed from peaceful demonstrations into rioting, looting, and violence.

The poll shows that 71 percent of voters are in favor of the deployment of the National Guard to shore up local law enforcement in coping with the riots, many of which started out as peaceful expressions of grief and opposition to police brutality but then devolved into chaos. A smaller majority, 58 percent, of registered voters said they support calling in the U.S. military to supplement city police forces to address rioting

The new poll was conducted between May 31 and June 1, 2020, on a nationwide sample of 1624 registered voters and reported on in Tom Ozimek's June 2020 *Epoch Times* article titled "Majority of Americans Support Use of National Guard, Military to Help Address Riots."

The growing chaos that year prompted Donald Trump and members of his administration, most notably Attorney General William Barr, to call for a more forceful response. "It is time to stop watching the violence and to confront and stop it. Preventing reconciliation and driving us apart is the goal of radical groups. We cannot let them succeed," Barr said in a statement.

While the strategy of getting tough on violent protesters has been met with some criticism, chiefly from Trump's political opponents, the new Morning Consult poll suggests most everyday Americans look favorably on more forceful methods to deal with protests that get out of hand.

The poll also shows that support for a tougher response is bipartisan. While 86 percent of respondents who said they voted Republican in the 2018 House vote said they either "strongly support" or "somewhat support" calling the National Guard to supplement city police forces, 65 percent of those who voted Democrat two years ago also expressed their support for such reinforcements.

George Floyd Riots Caused Record-Setting $2 Billion in Damage

Even beyond face-value insurance costs, riots leave a lasting shadow on a city that haunts its economy for decades. Brad Polumbo's September 2020 report "Here's Why the True Cost Is Even Higher" from the Foundation for Economic Education (FEE) explains why:

Dozens of people were killed or injured in the violent unrest, and thousands of businesses and properties, many minority-owned, were looted, torched, or otherwise vandalized. Only now are we beginning to realize the full cost of the destruction. New reporting from Axios reveals that the total insured property losses incurred during the George Floyd riots will come in at $1 billion to $2 billion.

The US has experienced rioting over racial tensions before, but this report shows that the damage from the latest unrest will far exceed any historical precedent. However, there are many reasons that this figure vastly underestimates the true damage wrought by the looting and violence that has broken out in recent months. For one, the Axios report only measures insured losses. The obvious problem here is that not all the damages were insured.

Moreover, a 2005 study examining similar riots in the 1960s found 'negative, persistent, and economically significant effects of riots on the value of black-owned housing' to the degree of 'a 10 percent decline in the total value of black-owned property in cities.' And seeing as the new reporting shows that the George Floyd riots were more destructive than the riots in either of the above periods, we can reasonably expect that the long-term economic consequences will be more severe as well.

Seattle's Anarchist 'Capitol Hill Autonomous Zone' (CHAZ)

Various "Occupy"-type protests have occurred across the US since the original occupation near Wall Street in 2011. But the CHAZ is nothing like the mostly peaceful tent city in privately owned Zuccotti Park that was corralled and closely monitored by the NYPD.

CHAZ occupants, ranging from several hundred to 10,000, depending on the day, with many openly armed, controlled all of the Capitol Hill neighborhood near downtown during the peak of the George Floyd protests and subsequent riots. The neighborhood is the heart of Seattle's gay and counter-culture district and is densely filled with businesses and apartment buildings. The CHAZ now claims all of it.

Again at ground zero documenting Antifa violence, Andy Ngo's June 2020 *New York Post* article titled "My terrifying five-day stay inside Seattle's cop-free CHAZ" is a chilling firsthand account inside the zone. In Ngo's own words:

Before the takeover, violent clashes between rioters and police defending the East Precinct resulted in dozens of officers injured by rocks and other projectiles. Protesters and rioters complained of police brutality, leading Seattle Mayor Jenny Durkan to ban cops from using tear gas, pepper spray and flash-bangs for 30 days.

The CHAZ is having reverberating effects elsewhere as Antifa and other left-wing protesters established an "autonomous zone" in downtown Portland. Protesters in Nashville and other cities have attempted to recreate their own "autonomous zones" modeled after the CHAZ but have so far been stopped by law enforcement.

Mainstream media reports have focused on the "block party" atmosphere of the occupation, repeating a talking point from the Mayor Durkan. She, along with Gov. Jay Inslee, a fellow Democrat, have gone to great lengths to emphasize the "peaceful" nature of the occupation. For media crews that arrive during the day, that is certainly what they will see. People have barbecues in the street. Many bring their children to make street art. People walk their dogs.

But at Night, a Whole Different Side of the CHAZ Emerges

Those unfortunate enough to have homes or businesses within the CHAZ, Ngo notes—an estimated 30,000 residents—have no say over their new overlords. Residents have discreetly voiced their concerns to local media. Gunshots and "screams of terror" at night have been reported. A resident of an apartment building came out twice to ask protesters to leave the alley where the entrance is. They brushed him off.

Every business and property inside the CHAZ has been vandalized with graffiti. Most messages say some variation of "Black Lives Matter" or "George Floyd," but other messages call for the murder of police. Most businesses are boarded up. "ACAB"—"All cops are bastards," an Antifa slogan—is written over them.

Despite the pleas from those who live and work inside Capitol Hill for law and order to be restored, Seattle's city council has determined that the CHAZ should continue. On Tuesday, the city even provided upgrades to the CHAZ, including street blockades that double as graffiti canvases, along with cleaning services and porta-potties.

It is difficult to decipher what CHAZ occupants want. Each faction, whether liberal, Marxist or anarchist, has its own agenda. But one online manifesto posted on Medium demands no less than the abolishment of the criminal justice system.

8 – Fake News Narratives About the Police, Crime Statistics & American Racism

Credit: The Epoch Times. George Floyd mural.

If you're not aware of this statistics and victimization rate ratios that have been fairly consistent for five decades, it could be because the fake news media focuses on the only statistic that matters (i.e., the white on black crime rates) and ignores the rest. "The Color of Crime 2016" report along with so many others clearly demonstrate with unbiased/factual reporting, research, and analysis—that there is a profound bias in this regard with mainstream media (MSM).

If you choose to ignore these atrocious black crime rate statistics and believe in false ones perpetrated by fake news media and BLM—what is your agenda? It's certainly not the truth and it can't be addressing one of the three major issues adversely affecting black Americans: Exponentially high crimes rates, the fatherless black family, and low education attainment rates.

Focusing on these self-evident issues shows you understand the three major problems facing black America, and the key to their overall success (if you truly and honesty want to fix these problems and help black Americans in the process), is truthfully and honestly identifying the source of the problems, working to fix them, and stop blaming institutional racism, white supremacy and privilege, and racist cops as the cause. No more excuses!

Could these same excuses be valid if we rewind our racial justice history clock back fifty years or so? Hell yes! They were valid then and much less so today—so please remind yourself—are you living in the present—or living in the past? There's a huge difference in time and tide!

Since the mid-1990s, the high tide of street crime has mostly dropped off the front pages of our national newspapers and disappeared from the public debate. The economic and political tide of black America's success has gained much greater visibility and indicate that traditional racial cleavages in our society have become less substantial.

Furthermore, with such enormous numbers of young black men now in prison, we might naturally expect that the racial character of American urban crime rates has sharply declined over the last couple of decades. In terms of the actual number of crimes in general—it has. But in terms of racial crime rate disparities—it hasn't.

The Color of Crime Reality vs. the Mainstream Media Fantasy

The "hasn't" part can be seen from the quantitative evidence by examining the combined twenty-five year trajectories of our various racial crime correlations, which have steadily grown more extreme.

The images shown on our film screens, television sets, and computer monitors most always portray a false image of racial America (with uncontrolled racist white cops, bigoted law enforcement agencies, neo-Nazi Aryan conspiracy groups, Caucasian villains of all stripes down to casting most high-school bullies as white supremacists) but the actual data reveals a very different country and reality.

George Floyd's death in Minneapolis has revived the Obama-era narrative that law enforcement is endemically racist. After the incident, Barack Obama tweeted that for millions of black Americans, being treated differently by the criminal justice system on account of race is "tragically, painfully, maddeningly 'normal.'" Obama called on the police and the public to create a "new normal," in which bigotry no longer "infects our institutions and our hearts."

Joe Biden released a video the same day in which he asserted that all African-Americans fear for their safety from "bad police" and black children must be instructed to tolerate police abuse just so they can "make it home." That echoed a claim Obama made after the ambush murder of five Dallas officers in July 2016 by a BLM activist and sympathizer.

This charge of systemic police bias was wrong during the Obama years and remained so during the Trump years. However sickening the video of Floyd's arrest, it is *not* representative of the 375 million annual contacts that police officers have with civilians. A solid body of evidence finds no structural bias in the criminal-justice system with regard to arrests, prosecution or sentencing.

Crime and suspect behavior, not race, determine most police actions.—and we cannot fix that problem until we identify it first. And because MSM refuses to identify and report it—the truth about the rare instance of police brutality—or the overt violence of Antifa and Marxist nature of BLM—and the three underlying issue facing black America—we cannot let that happen if we love, respect, and cherish all Americans regardless of the color of their skin, ethnic background, political ideology, sexual orientation, and so on.

In order to get at the truth we must first expose and/or correct the sins of fake news and errors of false narratives from MSM and the preconditioning it may have had on our readers. And to that end goal, with essential information from non-fake, un-biased, and reliable news sources, I listed ten relevant fake news and false narratives about law enforcement, crime statistics and American racism, and more, that need to be told before proceeding to the next chapters.

Top 10 Fake News and False Narratives About Law Enforcement, Crime Statistics & Racism

In this section are various examples of unsapient positions, unsubstantiated claims, and false narratives; summarily noted as "fake news" that in one way or another violate the principles of the scientific method and/or guilty of committing any of these 15 common fallacies of logic, reason, and argument, outlined below.

- **Fallacy of argument from analogy** is an inductive argument in which a known similarity that two things share is used as evidence for concluding that the two things are similar in other respects.

- **Fallacy of ad hominem** is an argument that attacks the person who makes an assertion rather than the person's argument.

- **Fallacy of biased sample** is an argument that contains a sample that is not representative of the population being studied.

- **Fallacy of concealed evidence** is an argument that presents only facts that are favorable to its conclusion while suppressing relevant but non-supportive facts.

- **Fallacy of false analogy** is an argument that makes an erroneous comparison.

- **Fallacy of false authority** is an argument that violates any of the criteria for a justifiable appeal to authority.

- **Fallacy of false dilemma** is an argument that erroneously reduces the number of possible positions for alternatives on an issue.

- **Fallacy of hasty conclusion** is an argument that draws a conclusion based on insufficient evidence.

- **Fallacy of invincible ignorance** is an argument that insists on the legitimacy of an idea or principle despite contradictory fact.

- **Fallacy of questionable causation** is an argument that asserts that a particular circumstance produces that it causes a particular phenomenon when there is in fact little or no evidence to support set contention.

- **Fallacy of questionable classification** is an argument that classifies somebody or something on the basis of insufficient evidence.

- **Fallacy of unknown fact** is an argument that contains premises that are unknowable either in principle or in this particular case.

- **Guilt by association fallacy** is an argument in which people are judged guilty solely on the basis of the company they keep or the places they frequent.

- **Scientific method** is a way of investigating a phenomenon that's based on the collective analysis and into interpretation of evidence to determine the most probable explanation. The five basic steps in scientific method: 1) statement of the problem, 2) collection of facts, 3) formulating a hypothesis, 4) making further inferences, and 5) verifying the inferences.

- **Universal generalization** is a statement that asserts that something is true of all members of a class.

Based on what you've learned and read so far, try to the best of your abilities to determine which of the transgressions listed above are being committed below. For item 7, the fallacies are noted to help fathom this lesson. For a complete list of fallacies, please reference in the Appendix the Journalism Code of Ethics, Practical Logic & Sapience Guidelines.

1. Hiding the 3 Fundamental Issues as the Cause of High Black Crime Rates

Daniel Patrick Moynihan's 1965 report titled "The Negro Family: The Case For National Action, Office of Policy Planning and Research" on the terrible deterioration in the condition of the black American family—aroused such a firestorm of denunciation and outrage in liberal circles that the topic was rendered totally radioactive for the better part of a generation.

Eventually the continuing deterioration reached such massive proportions that the subject was taken up again by prominent liberals in the 1980s, who then declared Moynihan a prophetic voice, unjustly condemned.

The fundamental problem, in which this is most clearly the case, is that of family structure. The evidence—not final, but powerfully persuasive—is that the Negro family in the urban ghettos is crumbling. A middle-class group has managed to save itself, but for vast numbers of the unskilled, poorly educated city working class the fabric of conventional social relationships has all but disintegrated. There are indications that the situation may have been arrested in the past few years, but the general post-war trend is unmistakable. So long as this situation persists, the cycle of poverty and disadvantage will continue to repeat itself.

Without a stable family structure, regardless of race, there are three, and only three fundamental issues "today" in America created by this situation and these fundamental issues are in partial to full denial by SPLC, OSF, BLM, Antifa, MSM and others that explain the black centric issues covered so far in Chapters 1 through 7.

In 2008, Barack Obama was able to connect such lawlessness to family breakdown. "Children who grow up without a father are five times more likely to live in poverty and commit crime; nine times more likely to drop out of schools and twenty times more likely to end up in prison," he pointed out in his Chicago speech.

Furthermore, these three fundamental issues for the most part are being ignored by SPLC, OSF, BLM, Antifa, MSM and other programs as you will see in Chapters 9 through 15 when it comes to priorities, resource allocation, and public policies needed to fix the problems.

If these organizations, groups, and constituents continue to ignore and downplay the problems and/or refuse to be part of the solutions—the ongoing problems and issues for a large segment of black America, particularly high crime rates, will continue to persist, as they have been for more than 50 years since the beginning of the Great Society measures of the 1960s.

Without a stable family structure, regardless of race, these are the three fundamental issues at the root cause of high black crime rates that no sapient being can deny.

- Low black education attainment rates.
- Low black fatherhood rates.
- High poverty rates.

Exploring in detail these three issues is reserved for future *MADNESS* books and above and beyond the early call to action pointed out in *Crime Rate Madness*.

2. Did You Know That BLM is a Self-Prescribe Marxist Organization and Anti-American?

Leo Terrell is an author, commentator and civil rights attorney based in Los Angeles. He has served as an attorney for the NAACP, as former chairman of the Black-Korean Alliance, as an advisory board member for the Equal Employment Opportunity Commission and as a former member of California's Statewide Commission Against Hate Crimes.

He's spent over 20 years as a civil rights attorney in California and is well known for not taking a back seat to anyone on police misconduct cases. And yet, his commitment to justice and substantial track record of putting racially driven criminals behind bars should deserve special merit—considering Terrell is calling out the farce that is Black Lives Matter—and doing so loudly and proudly.

Why? In Terrell's own words: Because, this organization does not speak for me, as an African-American, and if you truly believe that Black lives DO matter, you should reconsider taking your cues from this group's self-serving agenda. Terrell continues:

In reality, Black Lives Matter is comprised of modern day-charlatans who learned the profitable way to protest from the Al Sharptons of the world. Style over substance. Chaos over real change. Some revealing questions about them are as follows:

- Is BLM setting up urban outreach and mentoring? No.

- Is BLM demanding better schools and safe community activities? No.

- Is BLM paying for the funerals of these Black babies killed by violence? No.

- Has BLM set up a GoFundMe or made donations to any of the destroyed—minority-owned—businesses in Minneapolis? Of course not.

To make it even worse, the Democratic Party is literally taking a pandering knee to them. What has Nancy Pelosi done for African-Americans? What has Joe Biden done? Nothing. In fact, the president they love to hate, Donald Trump, has done more in three years for Black Americans and police reform than Joe Biden has done in decades. With one recent executive order,

President Trump accomplished more for police reform than the Obama/Biden administration did over all of its eight years in office.

3. Antifa: A 'Fascist' Organization Claiming to be Fighting Against Fascism!

Antifa's mission statement is an oxymoron perpetuated by the left-leaning media narrative that the great threat to civil liberties comes from the right, a rationale used for censoring conservatives—and doing it in a fascist manner.

If a lone sociopath with right-wing leanings turns violent, commentators rush to blame it on the "climate" created by then President Trump and Fox News, which makes no more sense than blaming Elizabeth Warren for the killing spree in Dayton by a supporter of hers or blaming MSNBC for the Rachel Maddow fan who opened fire on Republican members of Congress in Alexandria, Virginia.

Violent young men certainly exist on the right, but no conservative academic or journalist tries to rationalize their attacks as "self-defense." They can post online threats and domination fantasies, but they don't have the numbers or the institutional power to silence their opponents.

As noted by John Tierney from the *City Journal*, most journalists obsess over right-wing dangers while ignoring or downplaying the actual violence on the left.

There are exceptions, like Peter Beinart of *The Atlantic*, who has warned about Antifa and criticized The Nation and Slate for celebrating one of its assaults (the punching of white nationalist Richard Spencer). But few others have paid much heed to Antifa. Some, like Carlos Maza and the New Republic's Matt Ford, have praised its milk-shaking tactic (as used on Andy Ngo).

While working at Vox, Maza tweeted, "Milkshake them all. Humiliate them at every turn. Make them dread public organizing." He has also tweeted, "Deplatform the bigots," and put that idea into practice with the outspoken support of Vox's executives. His pressure on YouTube triggered the "Vox Adpocalypse," in which YouTube cut off advertising revenue to Steven Crowder and other conservative commentators.

Outside of conservative and libertarian outlets, Antifa hasn't attracted much scrutiny, even as its followers have assaulted journalists. (They also stood outside Carlson's home, chanting, "Tucker Carlson, we will fight! We know where you sleep at night!").

4. The Fake News by MSM and Others Report That Illegal Immigrants Commit Less Crime

Advocates of open borders are fond of claiming that illegal aliens commit fewer crimes than native-born U.S. citizens. That makes perfect sense, they assert, because illegal aliens do not wish to be brought to the attention of law enforcement and risk deportation from the United States. In reality, however, this is a weak argument and a false narrative, based on bad data from multiple sources.

Why are the majority of studies of illegal alien criminality so flawed? First, as Peter Kirsanow, of *National Review* notes, "Illegal-immigrant crime calculations conveniently and invariably steal a base by leaving out the millions of crimes committed by illegal immigrants related to procuring fraudulent social security numbers, obtaining false drivers' licenses, using fraudulent green cards, and improperly accessing public benefits." That error is then compounded when researchers intentionally elect to leave out broad classes of crimes for example, drug offenses—as the Cato Institute frequently does.

Secondly, most federal, state, and local government agencies do not collect data on the rates at which illegal aliens are convicted of crimes. Most likely, this is due to political correctness, and a desire to keep the truth about the number of crimes committed by illegal aliens from coming to light. Kirsanow is one of the few who has commented openly on this tendency. He states, "Unfortunately, almost every public official not named Jeff Sessions guards against disclosure of illegal-immigrant crime data more tenaciously than disclosure of nuclear launch codes." Regardless of why this information is not collected, the end result is that there are a limited number of sources for obtaining data on crimes committed by known illegal aliens.

Finally, most researchers tend to ignore the few established sources that provide data on criminal acts by known illegal aliens. They point to all types of alleged, and typically baseless, "flaws" in this data, ranging from "limited sample size" to an inability to determine whether illegal aliens are being counted more than once. In actuality, however, the only real flaw, from the perspective of mainstream research organizations, is that examinations of data on criminal activity by known illegal aliens tend to establish that those who enter the U.S. in violation of our immigration laws also commit other crimes at a higher rate.

This should not be surprising to anyone. The simple fact that illegal aliens violated American immigration laws–and must continuously violate other federal, state, and local laws in order to mask their ongoing illegal presence in this country–demonstrates a blatant lack of respect for the rule of law.

5. The False Premise There Should Be 'Equal Outcomes'

America's foremost black economist Thomas Sowell notes, "Just who made this promise (of equal outcomes) is unclear, and why equity should mean equal outcomes despite differences in behavior is even more unclear. If black males get punished more often than Asian-American females, does that mean that it is somebody else's fault?

Nobody in their right mind believes that, but that is unspoken premise of 'so-called' progressive thinking. The biggest hoax of the past two generations is still going strong—namely, that statistical differences in outcomes for different groups are due to the way other people treat them (i.e., due to systemic racism).

Per the *War on Cops* by Heather Mac Donald, the race industry and its elite enablers take it as self-evident that high black incarceration rates result from discrimination. If a listener didn't know anything about crime, such charges of disparate treatment might seem plausible. After all, in 2006, blacks were 37.5 percent of all state and federal prisoners, though they're under 13 percent of the national population . About one in 33 black men was in prison in 2006, compared with one in 205 white men and one in 79 Hispanic men. Eleven percent of all black males between the ages of 20 and 34 are in prison or jail. The dramatic rise in the prison and jail population over the previous three decades- to 2.3 million people at the end of 2007-amplified the racial accusations against the criminal-justice system.

The favorite culprits for high black prison rates include a biased legal system, draconian drug enforcement, and even prison itself. None of these explanations stands up to scrutiny. The black incarceration rate is overwhelmingly a function of black crime. Insisting otherwise can only worsen black alienation and further defer a real solution to the black crime problem.

6.   Opportunists Fan the Flames of Racial Unrest

Violence following the recent fatal shooting of an unarmed robbery suspect in Ferguson, Missouri, has tragically followed a predictable script seen all too often by Victor Davis Hanson.

On average, more than 6,000 African-Americans are killed by gun violence each year. That startling figure is nearly equal to all of the U.S. combat fatalities incurred in both Afghanistan and Iraq over some 13 years. African-Americans are the victims in about half of the homicides in America each year despite the fact that blacks represent only about 13 percent of the U.S. population.

One would think that these alarming statistics would provoke the sort of protests that we've seen in Ferguson and most major Democratic controlled cities in 2020, but that is not the case. Nor does racial unrest automatically follow cases in which white police officers fatally shoot black criminal suspects. Only a small handful of such instances trigger outrage in the black community.

Instead, the sort of civil unrest we're seeing ignited by the infrequent and disparate cases in which someone white, whether a police officer or not, fatally shoots an unarmed African-American.

Controversy, for example, arose over George Zimmerman's fatal shooting of unarmed teenager Trayvon Martin in Florida. Then, small-town Ferguson is in an uproar over a police officer's fatal shooting of unarmed 18-year-old Michael Brown. More recently, Floyd George is made a martyr while mainstream media and racial justice activists ignore his long and disturbing police records.

There is a second theme in such cases. The media almost invariably distorts the facts, sometimes deliberately seeking to incite tensions. In the Trayvon Martin case, journalists published photos of Martin as a diminutive adolescent, not more recent pictures of Martin as a 17-year old who was much taller than Zimmerman.

Zimmerman was referred to by the *New York Times* as a "white Hispanic" (a term not usually accorded those of mixed ancestry). ABC News was accused of airing footage of Zimmerman shortly after his encounter with Martin that concealed the severity of Zimmerman's head injuries. NBC edited a recording of Zimmerman's 911 call to police in a way that suggested Zimmerman was a racist. CNN falsely speculated that Zimmerman may have used the racial slur "coon" during his 911 call.

In the Brown case, the media has rushed to portray the victim as a "gentle giant" who was almost certainly gunned down by a racist, trigger-happy cop. Only days later it was reported that just minutes before his death, the 6-foot-4, 292-pound Brown had allegedly committed a strong-armed robbery, bullying and assaulting a store owner half his size—and had been almost immediately been stopped not far away for walking down the middle of the road.

A third theme is the entrance of Al Sharpton, Jesse Jackson, and the New Black Panther Party. Almost immediately, they incite tensions by issuing wild, unfounded charges. Jackson said of the Martin shooting that "targeting, arresting, convicting blacks and ultimately killing us is big business." Jackson just called the Brown shooting a "state execution." Sharpton called the legal acquittal of Zimmerman an "atrocity. After the George Floyd death, nightly riots rock 470 American cities and Hawk Newsome, chairman of Black Lives Matter of Greater New York, during an interview with Fox News states, "If this country doesn't give us what we want, then we will burn down this system and replace it."

7. SPLC Tries to Defame "The Color of Crime 2016" Report Using Unethical Journalism Tactics

The SPLC tries to discredit and defame "The Color of Crime 2016" report by distinguished author Edwin S. Rubenstein, that was published by the New Century Foundation (NCF).

The Southern Poverty Law Center's (SPLC) June 2018 report by Cassie Miller titled "The Biggest Lie in the White Supremacist Propaganda Playbook: Unraveling the Truth About 'Black-on-White Crime,'" is this textbook's most glaring example of bias and unethical journalism and it used here as an object lesson.

Miller took great efforts in an attempt to defame and discredit "The Color of Crime 2016" report (through guilt-by-association) that was published by the New Century Foundation (NCF), a non-profit organization founded by Yale educated writer and white nationalist Jared Taylor, creator of the American Renaissance magazine.

Miller violated no less than 12 fallacies starting with the most obvious: guilt by association fallacy as noted, followed by the fallacy of argument from analogy, fallacy of ad hominem, fallacy of biased sample, fallacy of concealed evidence, fallacy of false analogy, fallacy of hasty conclusion, fallacy of invincible ignorance, fallacy of questionable classification, fallacy of unknown fact, didn't utilize the scientific method, and universal generalization.

Buried (most likely intentionally and I italicized the key revelations because they are easy to miss and/or misunderstand) in the "Spinning crime statistics" section of the SPLC report, is this paragraph from Miller stating, verbatim:

"The findings of the report drew on an *authoritative source*: the "1994 Crime Victimization Survey" released by the U.S. Department of Justice's Bureau of Justice Statistics. While Taylor's *reporting of the statistics was accurate*—there were, in fact, higher rates of violent crime committed by black people, and crimes committed by blacks against whites than the reverse—his interpretation of the data was flawed."

The "Color of Crime" report is not being discredited by Miller and the SPLC per their own admission ... "reporting of the statistics was accurate ... ." The SPLC objects to Taylor's "...interpretation of the data (that) was flawed." Please note that nowhere in *Crime Rate Madness* is Jared Taylor's interpretation of the data being used or sourced. *Only* the rock-solid data from Rubenstein's report is being used throughout this textbook and the readers of that data are left to come to their own conclusions.

To view the flawed and deceptive SPLC report by Miller, visit the Appendix for the link and test yourself on the number of fallacies violated within their report.

8. Failure to Discuss George Soros is Actively Working to 'Undermine the American System'

Former Speaker of the House Newt Gingrich said in September 2020 that billionaire left-wing disrupter George Soros is actively working to undermine the American political system.

In the same month, radio host Eric Kripke of Revolution and Metaxas asked Gingrich to explain the bizarre incident that occurred on Fox News when they cut Gingrich off after he brought up the role of Soros in funding the election of left-wing district attorneys in local races over the past several years.

Gingrich was arguing that the rise in crime in many Democrat-governed cities was partly the result of the presence of anti-police, pro-criminal district attorneys who had been elected thanks to substantial funding from Soros.

On a September 2020 edition of Outnumbered, co-host Melissa Francis and contributor Marie Harf attempted to silence Gingrich, telling him he did not need to bring Soros into the conversation. "I know that it looked very strange on television," Gingrich told Metaxas. "I think part of it was because we were all remote, so we weren't on the couch, which is the normal pattern for Outnumbered."

"Look, one of the members—Marie Harf—was actually John Kerry's press person so her visceral reaction made perfect sense," Gingrich added. "If you are a left-wing Democrat, you know that if the country learns how much George Soros is doing to undermine and destroy America that is a huge and indefensible position. We checked back channel and there is no Fox pressure against mentioning George Soros," the former Speaker clarified.

"I think people need to realize that this is a billionaire who actively works every day to undermine the American system and who has spent millions of dollars electing district attorneys who are anti-police and pro-criminal," he said. "And it's a major part of why, for example in New York, they had a 107 percent increase in shootings in August (2020) over last year, because the system is just breaking down."

9. Black Criminality is a Much Bigger Problem Than Racism or Police Brutality

With the number of racialized stories coming from the media, as pointed out by RYCIreland, one could easily assume Ben Crump (an American attorney who specializes in civil rights cases such as Trayvon Martin's, Michael Brown's, and George Floyd's) was telling the truth when he claimed that it was "open season on black people."

The media convincingly and continuously subjects many Americans to this idea. Professional basketball player for the Los Angeles Lakers, Lebron James once tweeted that blacks are being quite literally "hunted" by whites. This tweet received tens of thousands of retweets.

Similarly, former President Barack Obama's statement on the death of George Floyd, which sparked nationwide riots, received hundreds of thousands of retweets. This narrative of blacks being the victims of white violence, and that this victimization explains away any wrongdoing on the part of black criminals is nothing new. This idea has been perpetuated for many decades.

However, with little effort, one can study widely available crime statistics to reveal the truth which this textbook has provided in great detail. Racism against black Americans by white Americans has very little or nothing to do with black criminality, black criminality is a much bigger problem than racism or police brutality.

In the mid-1990s, the Center for Equal Opportunity analyzed 55,512 felony cases filed in state courts for the 75 largest counties, representing 37 percent of the U.S. population. The weighted data, taken from the BJS, revealed that juries actually acquit blacks at a higher rate than whites for 12 of the 14 types of crime studied—including murder, rape, robbery, and assault. The only category that had a higher conviction rate for African-Americans was felony traffic offenses.

10. Trump's First Step Act for Black Americans: Do You Know About It?

Then President Trump was "eager" to sign the bipartisan First Step Act into law on Dec. 21, 2018 that affects only federal prisoners, who make up less than 10 percent of the country's prison population. During his 2019 State of the Union address, Kaitlyn Schallhorn from Fox News noted how eager Trump was to tout the new law's success.

"This legislation reformed sentencing laws that have wrongly and disproportionately harmed the African-American community," Trump explained. "The First Step Act gives nonviolent offenders the chance to reenter society as productive, law-abiding citizens. Now, states across the country are following our lead. America is a nation that believes in redemption."

The First Step Act—or the formerly Incarcerated Reenter Society Transformed Safely Transitioning Every Person Act—is, at its core, a directive for the Justice Department to establish a system to assess the risk of a person to re-offend as well as to create housing or other incentives for offenders to participate in recidivism reduction programs.

The bill, which passed the Senate 87-12, culminates years of negotiations, and gave the Trump administration a signature policy victory. It's been heralded by conservatives and liberals, celebrities, and Jared Kushner, the president's son-in-law, who worked the halls of Congress for months to forge a compromise.

Non-Fake News and Unbiased Videos' Talking Points About Racism

Because most every story, topic, and agenda that MSM touches "these days" are tainted and stained with liberal and leftist bias, Prager U has hundreds of unbiased and non-fake news videos covering America's and the world's most controversial topics, starting with racism.

In this topic alone, "Is America Racist?—What is Systemic Racism?" there are dozens of 5-minute videos prepared by Prager U's team of experts (most narrators in this video series are people of color) in a variety of fields to choose from. These poignant videos cover the facts, truth, and sapient talking points regarding racism in America in an easy to comprehend format where the viewer is left to make their own decisions.

Although Prager U is indeed a conservative, faith based, and right leaning organization—their facts and figures don't lie or deceive and are spot on with no bias, no journalism code of ethics violations, and most importantly, no fake news and/or false agendas. Check out the Prager U videos listed below per the link provided in the Appendix and decide for yourself.

- Racism Is Not in America's DNA

- Is Harvard Racist?

- Is America Racist?

- Values Matter. Race Doesn't.

- Does Systemic Racism Exist?

- Who Are the Racists?

- Calling Good People "Racist" Isn't New: The Case of Ty Cobb

- Are the Police Racist?

9 – The Southern Poverty Law Center (SPLC) is an Anti-Conservative Defamation Machine

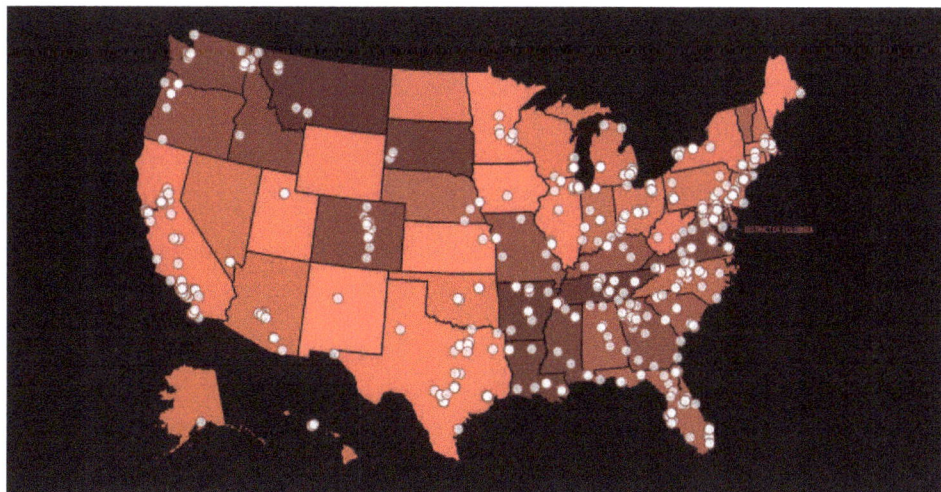

Credit: Southern Poverty Law Center (SPLC) Hate Map.

The Southern Poverty Law Center (SPLC) started as a group to oppose racist terrorism, and its first legal action valiantly targeted the Ku Klux Klan. However, in recent decades, the organization has begun marking mainstream organizations as "hate groups" on par with the KKK. In 2020, 47 nonprofit leaders denounced the SPLC's "hate list" in an open letter to the media. The SPLC has admitted that its "hate group" list is based on "opinion."

The 2010 Spring edition of *The Social Contract* reported that, by vastly exaggerating the number of KKK/neo-Nazi groups and the alleged number of "hate crime" incidents, and by falsely tying these violent groups and incidents to legitimate, law-abiding organizations, the SPLC is attempting to demonize and criminalize, in the eyes and minds of law-enforcement personnel, those with whom the SPLC disagrees.

Laird Wilcox, a recognized expert on extremist groups, is one of many critics spanning the political spectrum who see the SPLC as a danger to civil liberties. He is the founder of the Wilcox Collection on Contemporary Political Movements at the University of Kansas's Kenneth Spencer Research Library and an award-winning journalist, scholar, and author. The meticulous research provided by his *Guide to the American Left* and *Guide to the American Right* has made these works standard reference tools for serious journalists, political scientists, and law-enforcement intelligence personnel

In 2005 Wilcox noted that shoddy—even fraudulent—"research" methodology is standard operating procedure at the SPLC. He told *The New American* that "with minimal effort I went through a list of 800-plus 'hate groups' published by the SPLC and determined that over half of them were either non-existent, existed in name only, or were inactive."

Wilcox, black Professor Carol Swain, and other researchers have pointed out that the SPLC's practice of exaggerating the "extremist" and "hate group" threat actually helps draw recruits to the groups they claim to be fighting. And the SPLC, notes Wilcox, has "everything to gain: fundraising goes up, they get more media exposure, their credibility increases, and their political usefulness to the far left surges."

Over the past four decades, founder Morris Dees of the SPLC have parlayed their political and media connections into close ties with law-enforcement agencies. These ties are more troubling—and potentially far more dangerous—than their often-criticized fundraising scandals.

The Southern Poverty Law Center (SPLC) Misdirection of Law Enforcement

The Humanist, a left-liberal journal, has also scorched Morris Dees and his associates for their anti-American attacks on constitutionally protected rights, noting:

The Southern Poverty Law Center campaigns for laws that will effectively deny free speech and freedom of association to certain groups of Americans on the basis of their beliefs. Six times a year, the SPLC's letter boasts, the center reports its findings to over 6,000 law-enforcement agencies; then, with no discernible irony, it goes on to justify its Big Brother methods in the name of tolerance.

The SPLC, says Wilcox, specializes in "a highly developed and ritualized form of defamation, however—a way of harming and isolating people by denying their humanity and trying to convert them into something that deserves to be hated and eliminated. They accuse others of this but utilize their enormous resources to practice it on a mass scale themselves."

In his 1999 book, *The Watchdogs: A Close Look at Anti-Racist "Watchdog" Groups*, Laird Wilcox takes particular aim at the SPLC, writing:

Watchdog groups can have a profound influence on law enforcement tactics in a number of ways. Both the Anti-Defamation League and Southern Poverty Law Center publish newsletters and other material directed at law enforcement, often giving these agencies names from their files accompanied by suggestions of dangerousness.

Like all witch hunting operations, they occasionally find a real witch—which enhances their credibility, especially in high-profile media cases. But mixed with those few witches are thousands upon thousands of people whose politics may be extreme, but with no illegal intent whatsoever.

The SPLC's penetration of certain law-enforcement circles is especially alarming. In 2009, Homeland Security Secretary Janet Napolitano was forced to apologize to military veterans for a DHS report to law enforcement entitled "Rightwing Extremism" that warned of the danger of terrorism posed by "returning military veterans from the wars in Iraq and Afghanistan."

The same report similarly smeared pro-life, pro-gun, and pro-Constitution activists with the terrorist label. When DHS was forced, under the Freedom of Information Act, to release the sources for its report, it was revealed that most of its information had come from the SPLC's discredited "research."

At roughly the same time, in March 2009, the Missouri State Highway Patrol issued a report entitled "The Modern Militia Movement," which was the product of a federal-state law-enforcement "Fusion Center."

The authors of the report clearly were attempting to create in the minds of law-enforcement personnel an association between violent "right-wing extremists" and the millions of law-abiding Americans who oppose gun control, the United Nations, the Federal Reserve System, the income tax, illegal immigration, and abortion.

Sensationalizing Racial Conflict Issues

Wilcox adds: In looking over their fundraising stuff, I could see that they were sensationalizing racial conflict issues, and when their reports on "extremist" groups began appearing it was obviously a bogus fundraising scheme that was into demonizing and blacklisting. It reminded me so much of similar operations that were aimed at leftists during the fifties and sixties, that I concluded it was basically modeled after them.

Moralizing crusades that demonize and stereotype the opposition can be very damaging, even when they claim to be working on behalf of what objectively seems to be a "good" cause—and the more venerated the cause the more excessive and extreme tactics are seen to be justified. Movements to right wrongs are very dangerous when they let the end justify the means.

The SPLC has listings I had never heard of and I know this area pretty well. Even my own contacts in various movements had never heard of some on SPLC's list. After 1995, I had calls from police agencies trying to locate some of the SPLCs 'hate groups.' They couldn't find them either. I concluded that a lot of them were vanishingly small or didn't exist or could even be an invention of the SPLC.

If the SPLC was actually going after racial violence they would go after the racial and ethnic gangs. Many of the gangs are racially biased and the killings often reflect that fact. In southern California, Hispanic gangs have been driving blacks out of some neighborhoods for years. Imagine if whites tried to do that. The SPLC is very choosy in what it complains about. This kind of selective attention and biased reporting simply illustrates their unscrupulousness.

Wilcox adds, "The SPLC needs a watchdog itself."

Another person who takes this general kind of approach is Carol Swain, a law professor at Vanderbilt University. Swain, who happens to be black, authored *The New White Nationalism in America* (Cambridge University Press, 2002). Swain believes that there should be much more dialogue between white nationalists and blacks in the hope of clarifying issues, easing tensions, and finding common ground. It sounds like a good idea to me, but the SPLC hates it—along with Swain whom they've publicly attacked and tried to stigmatize and marginalize. She says that the SPLC has become a hate group itself.

In conclusion, Wilcox states:

When you get right down to it, all the SPLC does is call people names. It's specialized a highly developed and ritualized form of defamation, however—a way of harming and isolating people by denying their humanity and trying to convert them into something that deserves to be hated and eliminated. They accuse others of this but utilize their enormous resources to practice it on a mass scale themselves with groups whom they disagree with ideologically.

Anyone attacked by the SPLC is basically up against a contest of resources, from the ability to engage legal counsel, to the access to fairness in media treatment, to the ability to survive the financial destruction of a reputation or a career. What they do is a kind of bullying and stalking. They pick people who are vulnerable in terms of public opinion and simply destroy them. Their victims are usually ordinary people expressing their values, opinions, and beliefs—and they're up against a very talented and articulate defamation machine.

I believe Americans really need to ask themselves if they are willing to tolerate this kind of operation in a free society. Even if you agree with the SPLC's stated goals, remember that sooner or later they might start looking at you or someone you love. Don't imagine they can be contained by good will alone. What the Southern Poverty Law Center can get away with, eventually others can too.

Many Conservative Organizations Considering Lawsuits Against the SPLC

No fewer than 60 organizations branded "hate groups" or otherwise attacked by the Southern Poverty Law Center (SPLC) are considering legal action against the left-wing smear factory, a Christian legal nonprofit leader confirmed by Tyler O'Neil in his June 2018 PJ Media article titled "'About 60 Organizations' Are Considering a Lawsuit Against the SPLC Following $3M Nawaz Settlement." He suggested that the $3.375 million settlement and apology the SPLC gave to Maajid Nawaz and his Quilliam Foundation in June 2018 would encourage further legal action.

"We haven't filed anything against the SPLC, but I think a number of organizations have been considering filing lawsuits against the SPLC, because they have been doing to a lot of organizations exactly what they did to Maajid Nawaz," Mat Staver, founder and chairman of Liberty Counsel, told PJ Media in 2018.

Liberty Counsel filed a lawsuit against the charity navigation organization GuideStar for defamation after GuideStar adopted the SPLC's "hate group" list. That lawsuit is ongoing.

In 2016, the SPLC published its "Field Guide to Anti-Muslim Extremists," listing Muslim reformer Maajid Nawaz, a practicing Muslim, as one such extremist. The left-wing group listed various reasons for including him, changing the reasons every so often, and even at one point mentioning that he had gone to a strip club for his bachelor party.

SPLC President Richard Cohen extended his group's "sincerest apologies to Nawaz, Quilliam, and our readers for the error, and we wish Nawaz and Quilliam all the best." In settling the suit, the SPLC paid Nawaz's organization $3.375 million. "This is a significant settlement," Staver told PJ Media. $3.375 million dollars, and it did not even go to litigation; it was a result of a demand letter."

Importantly, "the allegations that were at issue here were very similar to the allegations against the other groups," the Liberty Counsel chairman explained. "The SPLC promotes false propaganda, demonizes and labels groups they disagree with, and that labeling has economic as well as physical consequences."

Staver insisted that the settlement with Nawaz "will encourage further legal action." He suggested that the settlement "helps our lawsuit against GuideStar" and may encourage organizations that were considering suing the SPLC to actually file the paperwork. "There are probably about 60 organizations that we're talking to—there's at least 60," Staver told PJ Media. He mentioned the group of 47 nonprofit leaders who denounced the SPLC last year and said, "that group has grown since then."

Disagreeing With the Left-Wing SPLC Organization's Political Views

Furthermore, many of the "hate groups" attacked by the SPLC do not encourage hate or violence, but merely disagree with the left-wing organization's political views. Tyler O'Neil also stated that other organizations attacked by the SPLC also told PJ Media they are "considering their options" regarding a lawsuit.

Many—like the Family Research Council (FRC), the Ruth Institute, and Alliance Defending Freedom (ADF)—merely stand for marriage as between one man and one woman. The SPLC has twisted 30-year-old arguments to smear these groups, and in one egregious case the group actually quoted as hateful the Catechism of the Catholic Church. "We are reviewing all our legal options," J.P. Duffy, a spokesman for the Family Research Council, told PJ Media.

"Truthfully, I have not been following the activities of the SPLC too closely," Jennifer Roback Morse, founder and president of the Ruth Institute, an organization that lost its credit card processor, Vanco Payments, over the SPLC's "hate group" labeling last year, told PJ Media. "Pursuing our mission is more important than attempting to take on the behemoth of the SPLC. I must say, though, this apology to Nawaz has caused us to consider our options," Morse added, cryptically.

A spokesman for Prager University, another organization attacked by the SPLC, said that "at this point" the group had "no intention to sue," but they "reserve the right to change their mind as the situation evolves." Jeremy Tedesco, senior counsel at Alliance Defending Freedom (ADF), echoed this trend, saying his organization is "evaluating all our options," including a potential lawsuit.

"It's appalling and offensive for the Southern Poverty Law Center to compare peaceful organizations which condemn violence and racism with violent and racist groups just because it disagrees with their views," Tedesco told PJ Media. "That's what SPLC did in the case of Quilliam and its founder Nawaz, and that's what it has done with ADF and numerous other organizations and individuals."

"This situation confirms once again what commentators across the political spectrum have been saying for decades: SPLC has become a far-left organization that brands its political opponents as 'haters' and 'extremists' and has lost all credibility as a civil rights watchdog," the ADF senior counsel added.

Tedesco defended the good name of Alliance Defending Freedom, which SPLC falsely maligns as a "hate group." "With eight wins in the last seven years at the U.S. Supreme Court and hundreds of victories for free speech at America's public universities, ADF is one of the nation's most respected and successful legal advocates, working to preserve our fundamental freedoms of speech, religion, and conscience for people from all walks of life," he said.

SPLC's 'Hate Group' Designation Has Led to Dangerous Consequences

"SPLC's partisan tactics and slander have ruinous, real-world consequences for which they should not be excused; we are evaluating all our options to defend the good name of ADF, including possible legal action," Tedesco concluded.

Staver noted that the SPLC labels groups "in order to destroy them," and he pointed out that that characterization comes from the SPLC's own words. The Liberty Counsel chairman also referenced a terror attack inspired by SPLC and their "hate map." The SPLC publishes an annual report that includes a "hate map" which includes the locations of the groups it targets. That's proven to have dangerous consequences.

Case 1:12-cr-00182-RWR   Document 16-16   Filed 04/19/13   Page 3 of 5

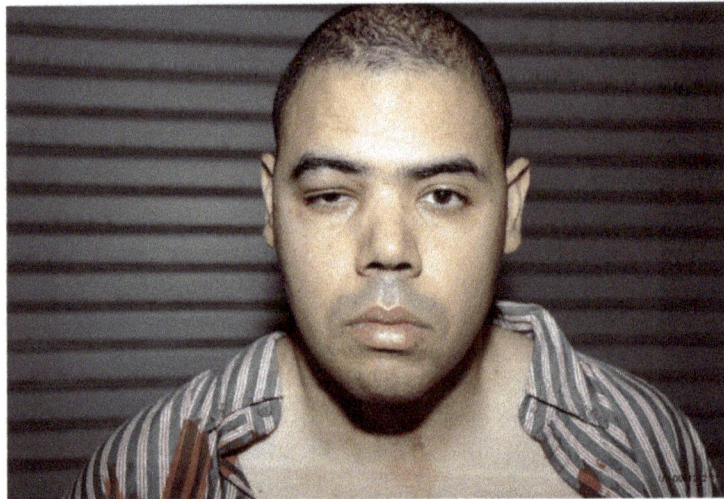

Credit: Mike Cernovich. Floyd Lee Corkins, convicted terrorist
serving a 25 year prison sentence.

In 2012, an LGBT activist by the name of Floyd Lee Corkins decided to invade Family Research Council's (RFC) premises in Washington, D.C. with a gun, in an attempt to murder as many employees as possible, while cramming Chick-fil-A sandwiches into the mouths of his victims. Only the heroic actions of the building manager/security guard, who was injured by a gunshot from the attacker in the lobby of FRC's building, prevented untold deaths at the hands of the perpetrator, who later admitted that he was motivated to target FRC because of the SPLC's "hate map."

In 2017, Congressman Steve Scalise and four others were shot and injured by James T. Hodgkinson, a deranged Facebook fan of the SPLC at a softball practice outside Washington, D.C. While no one was killed due to the quick response of security in the area, Scalise nearly died from his wounds and spent many months recovering. The SPLC, which had criticized and labeled Scalise for several years over his conservative views, denounced the shooting.

"There are people out there that are unhinged. They go out and take action. They assume that somebody hates them," the Liberty Counsel chairman explained. Due to these radical actors, "You have to be careful with your language. We can disagree but we can't demonize one another. Certainly, do not do anything that would put somebody that you disagree with in physical danger."

"The groups that we're talking to, that have approached us, all of them oppose violence," Staver said. "None of them advocate violence. They don't agree with the SPLC on certain issues, but they oppose violence. They have no reason to hate anyone."

PJ Media's coverage exposed the SPLC's complete lack of credibility when designating "hate" groups: "The SPLC's much-vaunted 'hate group' list includes mainstream Christian charities (like the law firm Alliance Defending Freedom (ADF) and the policy group Family Research Council) and conservative nonprofits like the Center for Security Policy, ACT for America, and the Center for Immigration Studies (CIS)."

So what makes a "hate group" earn that title according to the SPLC?

When discussing the nature of "hate groups" and how the SPLC determines that designation, the "Hate Free Philanthropy" document explained that "violence itself is not a requirement for being listed as a hate group. Because a group's ideology can inspire hate violence even when the group itself does not engage in violent activity, the SPLC concentrates its analysis on ideology." In other words, if the SPLC determines that a group's ideology could inspire hate violence, then that group could be classified as a hate group.

Under the guise of coming after violent extremists, the anti-Christian, anti-conservative Southern Poverty Law Center is coming after mainstream conservative organizations.

Using Donor-Advised Funds (DAFs) to Black List Conservative Groups

The SPLC has a history of sloppily categorizing mainstream conservative groups among violent fringe extremists in an attempt to silence opposition. Poynter had to scrap a blacklist of conservative sources created by SPLC producer Barrett Golding citing "weakness in the methodology."

As summarized in a piece by PJ Media, "Liberal activist groups are pressuring donor-advised funds (DAFs) to blacklist conservative and Christian organizations in the name of fighting white supremacy and 'hate.'" The PJ Media article explained how "the Southern Poverty Law Center (SPLC) and the Council on American-Islamic Relations (CAIR)," are calling for donors to stop donating to conservative organizations they deem hateful.

The massive "Hate Free Philanthropy" document claimed that "When hate groups that espouse and advance racism, sexism, xenophobia, and religious bigotry receive millions of dollars from charitable institutions, whether directly or indirectly, philanthropies are, in effect, funding hate."

Republicans Denounce Bigotry of the Southern Poverty Law Center

Leading up to the 2020 Republican National Convention, the Republican National Committee (RNC) has passed several resolutions, one of which directly addressed the oversized and negative influence of the Southern Poverty Law Center (SPLC) on government agencies. The RNC's criticism could also be extended to the SPLC's influence on social media and shopping sites.

As per The Daily Citizen post by Bruce Hausknecht in August 2020, the SPLC's radical agenda also plays out on social media and even shopping sites, where entities like Facebook, Twitter and Amazon censor messages or blackball charities based on the group's "hate" designations.

The group benefits from the loose legal rules involving slander and libel. In one case involving Coral Ridge Ministries, another Christian target of the SPLC, a federal judge dismissed such a case against the SPLC by ruling that the term "hate group" is an opinion, not a fact, and therefore not a defamatory statement.

The SPLC has, over the years, morphed into the very "hate group" that it was organized to expose. Only now it has targeted traditional religious values as "hate" and, by doing so, insidiously provides cover for government agencies, the mainstream news media, and other organizations to oppose and discriminate against religion in the name of fighting "hate." The RNC resolution is a necessary pushback against such tactics.

Nobody Expects the SPLC Inquisition!

Today's Left attempts to "completely destroy" its enemies by concocting outlandish guilt-by-association smears. In American politics, we don't expect the Spanish Inquisition—but it's here nonetheless states Mark Krikorian in November 2019 as follows:

Voltaire wrote that the Holy Roman Empire was neither holy, nor Roman, nor an empire. Something similar could be said of the Southern Poverty Law Center—if it ever had anything to do with helping poor people in the South with their legal problems, it doesn't any longer. (It is a center, though!)

Instead, it's turned into the Inquisition for the True Faith of today's leftism. It sniffs out heretics and blasphemers who are promoting the false doctrine they deem "hate" and uses smears to, in their own words, "completely destroy them." It even publishes a map to target the infidel.

This has proven an enormously lucrative enterprise for the SPLC. Rather than seizing the assets of its targets like the original Inquisition, the SPLC's fundraising feasts on the fear of gullible liberals, amassing a hoard of close to half a billion dollars, much of it stashed in offshore accounts.

The SPLC occasionally has paid a price for its promiscuous accusations of "hate" and "extremism", most notably in a court settlement of $3.375 million for smearing Muslim reformer Maajid Nawaz as an "anti-Muslim extremist".

But such settlements have not deterred the SPLC from its mission of cleansing society of heretics, the most notorious of which are designated as "hate groups." Krikorian's own organization, the Center for Immigration Studies (CIS), was placed on this list shortly after Donald Trump's election, and the list includes a host of other mainstream conservative groups, including the Alliance for Defending Freedom, the Family Research Council, the Federation for American Immigration Reform (FAIR), Liberty Counsel, The American Family Association, the Center for Security Policy, Act For America, the David Horowitz Freedom Center, and many others.

The point is to smear groups that disagree with the SPLC's radical-left politics by associating them with the hodgepodge of Klan factions, skinheads, and Neo-Nazis that are also on the list. As Krikorian wrote in the *Washington Post* after CIS was honored with the "hate group" tag, this is "an attempt to delegitimize and suppress views regarding immigration held by a large share of the American public." The "hate group" designation is a political weapon, wielded by the SPLC to gain power over its enemies.

SPLC Slams Trump's Terror Designation of Antifa as 'Dangerous and Unjust'

As rightful protests over George Floyd's death have devolved into looting, vandalism, and arson in cities across America, then President Donald Trump promised to hold the far-left agitators behind this violence accountable. He declared that America would designate Antifa a domestic terrorist group.

However, as noted in Tyler O'Neil's June 2020 PJ Media article "SPLC Slams Trump's Terror Designation of Antifa as 'Dangerous and Unjust' as America Burns," the far-left smear factory the Southern Poverty Law Center (SPLC) leaped into action, defending the agitators, and insisting that "right-wing" terrorism is the bigger threat. Worse, the group condemned police who are attempting to restore order for "punishing peaceful protest."

"Police are obligated to protect those in the community, and punishing peaceful protest is a gross abuse of human rights," the SPLC tweeted. Yet the far-left group went further, issuing a strong condemnation of Trump's domestic terrorism designation of Antifa.

"President Trump's tweet offers further criminalization as a response to mourners and protesters demonstrating against abuses of police power. It is dangerous and unjust," SPLC's Hatewatch declared in a June 2020 statement.

The SPLC statement minimized the looting and riots, admitting that "individuals loosely affiliated with Antifa are typically involved in skirmishes and property crimes at demonstrations across the country, but the threat of lethal violence pales in comparison to that posed by far-right extremists—a problem that, until the last year, federal authorities virtually ignored."

Nonetheless, the SPLC gave a very favorable definition for Antifa: Here it is below in their own words.

"Antifa, short for anti-fascist, is a broad, community-based movement composed of individuals organizing against racial and economic injustice," the statement read. "Those who identify with the label represent a large spectrum of the political left. The Trump administration frequently uses the term to describe any group or individual that demonstrates in opposition to its policies. Far-right extremists use similar tactics."

The "skirmishes" and "property crimes" have caused millions of dollars in damage—Sacramento's mayor estimated $10 million, damage in Atlanta has been estimated at between $10 and $15 million. An estimated 50 businesses and properties were damaged in Pittsburgh, with similar numbers in Seattle (50 businesses), Chicago (45 properties), and Madison, Wisconsin (75 businesses).

The SPLC is also wrong to downplay the "threat of lethal violence" from Antifa "skirmishes." These types of "skirmishes" in Portland left victims of Antifa violence with permanent scars. Journalist Andy Ngo has been hospitalized after receiving a beating. Local conservative Adam Kelly had his head busted open with a baton. He suffered a concussion and needed 25 stables to close the wounds. Gage Halupowski, an Antifa agitator, pled guilty to second-degree assault and was sentenced to 70 months in prison for the violence.

True, these "skirmishes" have not claimed the same kind of body count as racist terrorists like the man who shot up a black church in Charleston in 2015 or terrorists like the El Paso shooter—whose anti-immigrant hatred was matched by his own environmental extremism. Yet despite the SPLC's continual insistence that these terrorists are "right-wing," these terrorists have few to no connections with conservative groups.

While the SPLC often argues that its list of accused "hate groups" is a statistically-significant measure for the threat of white supremacist terrorism, it has failed to connect any such terrorist attack to the organizations it "monitors," especially mainstream conservative and Christian groups like the Family Research Council (FRC), Alliance Defending Freedom, ACT for America, or the Center for Security Policy.

The SPLC has continued its accusations despite facing multiple defamation lawsuits. The smear factory has also turned against Trump, mentioning the president no fewer than 66 times in its "hate group" report for 2019, released at the height of the coronavirus pandemic.

10 – Open Society Foundations (OSF) Are Sabotaging America's Laws & Criminal Justice

Credit: The Economist. George Soros interview.

George Soros is one of the United States' top political and advocacy donors, spending billions on campaigns, think tanks, start-ups, and nonprofits that promote his agenda. His principal philanthropic network centers on the Open Society Foundations (OSF) and Foundation to Promote Open Society (FPOS), two multi-billion-dollar left-of-center advocacy grantmaking foundations.

As you read through this chapter, you'll immediately notice organization after organization funded by George Soros. If you're not familiar with George Soros, and his philanthropic impact in the United States, your first reaction might be: This is a wonderful man donating $18 billion (yes, billion) to charities and philanthropies.

However, don't be fooled by the trojan horse of giving generosity by Soros because he's the godfather of the leftist causes and their primary funding source. Be aware, cautious, and concerned when you hear his name and the names of his foundations because they are connected to a number of publicly disclosed controversies—not conspiracy theories, as many of his supporters would argue.

Yes, there are deserving groups that the OSF supports—and there are controversial ones as well. This chapter focuses on the later but more importantly informs the reader how deep and wide Soros' funding is for the Democratic Party, 'so-called' progressive causes, and leftist movements undermining America.

For one man and his organizations to have that much influence, regardless of ideology, is very controversial as one would typically read about in the "Controversies" section of a typical Wikipedia article.

However, considering the left-leaning and factually handicapped Wikipedia accepted a $2 million gift to their Wikimedia Endowment from George Soros in 2018—it should come as no surprise they have no 'Controversies' section for their Open Society Foundations article (or for Antifa and SPLC for that matter and only a 'Criticisms' section for BLM).

George Soros: The Funding Father of Leftist, Socialist & Progressive Causes

The content for the next two chapter sections comes from the ongoing Influence Watch report on George Soros, his foundations, and controversial history. Through OSF and FPOS Soros has funded the vast majority of the most prominent left-progressive advocacy groups in the United States. He also created the Institute for New Economic Thinking to promote his unorthodox left-progressive economic policy viewpoints.

Now active in 70 countries, Open Society Foundations (OSF) was founded in the early 1980s and had the intention of propagating democracy and post-Communist prosperity in former Soviet-bloc states. Financial ties between the Black Lives Matter movement and Soros have been reported, as well as financial ties to Occupy Wall Street through intermediaries like the Tides Center. The network of Soros funded organizations indirectly touches 30 media organizations.

The day after the 2017 presidential inauguration, the "Women's March" took to the streets of Washington, D.C. Between 2000 and 2014, Soros donated to 40 of the groups affiliated with the march, his donations totaling at least $89.9 million.

George Soros spent over $18 million on political campaigns affiliated with the Democratic Party in 2016, $24 million on left-of-center Super PACs over the last few years—including $7 million on Hillary Clinton's primary PAC, Priorities USA—and partnered with other donors in a $15 million campaign to mobilize specific demographics.

In 2013, Soros had agreed to become co-chair for the Clinton-aligned Ready For Hillary Super PAC, as well as investing over $2 million in a left-of-center data analytics company, Catalist. After Hillary Clinton's defeat in the 2016 Presidential election, Soros met for three days with elite donors and Democrats to come up with new plans. Soros also spent $2 million in 2016 to help defeat then-Maricopa County Sheriff Joe Arpaio (R) as part of a nationwide push for criminal justice reform.

In the 2012 election, Soros announced that he would contribute $1 million each to the voter mobilization group America Votes and the Democratic super PAC American Bridge 21st Century. According to the Center for Responsive Politics, Soros gave American Bridge 21st Century $2 million in the 2015-2016 election cycle.

In the first three months of 2020, George Soros had put $28.3 million into various efforts to support the Democratic side in the 2020 election. Soros is using his Democracy PAC to distribute these payments, a new super PAC he launched in 2019 for the purpose of handing a victory to the Democrats in the upcoming presidential election.

Of the $28.3 million, $10 million went to Win Justice for its programs against voter disenfranchisement, namely, to mobilize "people of color and other infrequent voters" that might be affected by states choosing to suspend in-person voting come November due to the coronavirus pandemic. The voters that Win Justice talk to are "are among those who will most deeply and disproportionately affected by the upheaval the Covid-19 pandemic appears likely to cause in November," said a Soros spokesperson.

Soros also gave $5 million to left-of-center PAC Priorities USA and $7 million to the Democratic Senate Majority PAC. Soros' early 2020 giving also targeted several feminist groups, including EMILY's List and Supermajority.

In 2020, Soros funded political organizations that supported the campaigns of left-wing Illinois State Attorney Kimberly Foxx, Philadelphia District Attorney Larry Krasner, and Dallas County District Attorney John Creuzot. His contributions have supported these attorneys who seek to reduce theft-related prosecution. In 2017, State Attorney Kimberly Foxx was elected to office after receiving financial support from the Illinois Justice & Public Safety PAC that received $400,000 from Soros.

Foxx, whose jurisdiction includes Chicago, announced that her office sought to quit prosecuting shoplifters unless they possessed a record of over 10 previous felony convictions or had stolen more than $1,000 worth of goods. Similarly, Dallas County District Attorney John Creuzot announced in 2019 that his campaign received national funding through Soros and said that his office would no longer prosecute individuals for the theft of items valued under $750.

The office of Philadelphia District Attorney Larry Krasner states that refusing to prosecute certain crimes such as public camping, offering, or soliciting sex, and public urination is working to "decriminalize poverty and homelessness." Soros contributed $1.45 million to a super PAC that supported District Attorney Larry Krasner in the Democratic primary in May 2017.

Open Society Foundations (OSF)

The Open Society Foundations (OSF; formally Open Society Institute) is a private grantmaking foundation created and funded by billionaire financier and liberal philanthropist George Soros. OSF was founded in 1993 as the Open Society Institute (OSI), which remains the foundation's formal name; OSF has since become the main hub of a Soros-funded network of more than 20 national and regional foundations, making it one of the largest political philanthropies in the world.

Built on Soros' anti-capitalist, redistributionist political philosophy, the organization gives away nearly a billion dollars per year to left-wing organizations around the world to advance his vision of an "open society." Among those groups is the Foundation to Promote Open Society (FPOS), another foundation created after OSF which has since become the primary grant maker in the Soros network.

In 2018, OSF reported revenues of $376 million, expenditures of $215 million (including grants of $20.3 million), and assets of $3.7 billion.

In the United States, OSF's U.S. Programs have given hundreds of millions to left-wing political organizations, including multi-million dollar gifts to the American Civil Liberties Union (ACLU), Planned Parenthood, the Robin Hood Foundation, the Tides Foundation, the Brennan Center for Justice, and Alliance for Citizenship, among numerous others.

Confidential documents indicate that the OSF's U.S. Programs agenda prioritizes a number of liberal issue prerogatives and funds left-wing organizations to carry out these policies. Some of these prerogatives include enacting liberal comprehensive immigration reform (including a pathway to citizenship for illegal immigrants), cutting the number of prison inmates by 50 percent, increasing welfare handouts, and raising taxes to redistribute wealth. OSF has also been criticized for "compromising" American foreign policy.

George Soros and Open Society Foundations Controversies

OSF's operations are notoriously complex, and in 2016 the foundation was labeled the least transparent "think tank" in the United States reviewed by NGO Monitor, an OSF-funded transparency group. In spite of this, OSF maintains a position as a stalwart financier of left-wing nonprofits, financially supporting a large number of left-wing organizations in the U.S. and exporting leftist policies to countries across the world.

George Soros, a hedge-fund billionaire whose net worth was previously estimated at $26 billion, personally sets the budget of the Open Society Foundations and has contributed nearly $12 billion to a wide array of organizations since the late 1970s.

In his early life Soros was deeply influenced by philosopher Karl Popper's concept of the "open society." Based on Popper's philosophy, and despite having made his fortune in the financial markets, Soros argues, "the spread of market values into all areas of life is endangering our open and democratic society" and that "the main enemy of the open society," is no longer communism but rather capitalism.

U.S. Programs Budget

In 2017, Open Society Foundations plans to spend $100 million on grants and direct program costs for the United States, the largest budget amount for any single region amounting to 18% of the organization's total grant/program spending.

A leaked 2014 Open Society Foundations U.S. Programs budget indicated that the $125 million budget breaks down into five categories:

- $50.7 million (25% of U.S. Programs budget) for Core/New initiatives that included support for grantees, "social justice laboratories, a $25 million reserve fund, and "long-term idea generation" initiatives.

- $14.9 million (14.94%) for "Democracy" related initiatives

- $20.28 million (20.28%) for "Justice" related initiatives focused mainly on reducing incarceration, challenging punishments, police accountability in New York, and liberalizing drug laws.

- $22.95 million (22.65%) for "Equality" related initiatives namely focused on immigration reform, school discipline, "fiscal equity," and minority programs.

- $16.13 million (16.1%) for operations, admin, and program development.

U.S. Programs Agenda

An Open Society Foundations 2015-2018 U.S. Programs strategic plan that was taken from the group and leaked indicates that among other things, Open Society Foundations' U.S. Programs platform calls for:

- An economy governed by the "redistribution of resources;"

- A justice system that reduces incarceration, abolishes the death penalty, and promotes "health centered" drug use punishment.

- Enactment of comprehensive immigration reform, which gives "full political, economic, and civic participation" to illegal immigrants.

- A reduction in "the racial wealth gap" through income redistribution.

- and "Inclusive economic development" focused on raising the minimum wage and employment for ex-convict

Brett Kavanaugh Confirmation Protests

Following Justice Brett Kavanaugh's confirmation to the U.S. Supreme Court in October 2018, left-wing activists funded in part by OSF formed a protest outside the Supreme Court building in Washington, D.C. At least 50 of the left-wing groups sponsoring the protest had received funding from OSF or the Foundation to Promote Open Society, and included the:

George Floyd Protests

In July 2020, Open Society Foundations announced that it would be donating $150 million in 5-year grants to several racial justice groups, including Black Voters Matter Fund, Repairers of the Breach, and the Equal Justice Initiative. The group also announced a $70 million donation in local grants towards policing and criminal justice reform, civic engagement, and political training for younger demographics.

International Criticism

Open Society Foundations has offices in every region of the world and gives money to grantees in over 100 countries. As the publication NGO Monitor wrote, "the administrative and financial complexity of the global Open Society network cannot be overstated," because outside the U.S. "in most cases it is possible only to ascertain a basic outline of their activities."

Leadership

In September 2017, Patrick Gaspard was appointed president of Open Society Foundations, beginning in 2018. Gaspard previously served as a top aide to former President Barack Obama and as a national Democratic Party official.

Christopher Stone was interim president of Open Society Foundations through 2018. Before his current post, Stone spent most of career focused on U.S. criminal justice issues, most recently teaching at Harvard's Kennedy School. Stone's mission was to build Open Society Foundations into a more professional foundation "that didn't revolve around the combined institutional memory of [George] Soros and [previous President Aryeh] Neier."

In December 2020, Gaspard stepped down as president of Open Society Foundations. Mark Malloch-Brown, former UN deputy secretary-general, UK minister, and OSF Global Board member, succeeded him. Before becoming deputy secretary-general, Malloch-Brown was the administrator of the UN Development Program. As a UK minister, he worked in the UK's Foreign Office, presiding over Africa and Asia as minister of state. He was also once a World Bank vice president.

Soros Bankrolls a Broad Range of Political and Cultural Causes

Per Stefan Kanfer's Winter 2017 *City Journal* article "Connoisseur of Chaos: The dystopian vision of George Soros, billionaire funder of the Left" he observed the following:

In th United States, Soros bankrolls a broad range of political and cultural causes. One is to destabilize the Roman Catholic Church in the United States. In 2015, he dedicated $650,000 for the purpose of shaping Pope Francis's U.S. visit, using left-leaning Catholic groups to promote gay marriage, abortion, and physician-assisted suicide. Leading the effort was Hillary Clinton's campaign manager John Podesta, a self-professed Catholic.

Bill Donohue, outspoken president of the Catholic League, vainly called for Podesta's dismissal. "He is fomenting revolution in the Catholic Church, creating mutiny and is totally unethical," Donohue said. "He is the front man for George Soros to create a host of phony anti-Catholic groups. These are not just bad comments, as some have suggested. These words are orchestrated, calculated and designed to create fissures in the Catholic Church."

Another Soros favorite is Black Lives Matter, the radical protest group dedicated to the proposition that police are inherently racist. Working the streets with incendiary rhetoric, at odds with the truth about black-on-black crime, BLM has helped foster "depolicing," as Heather Mac Donald describes it, in high-crime urban areas.

In 2015, after days of rioting in Baltimore in response to the death of Freddie Gray in police custody, an Open Society Foundations memo excitedly commented that "recent events offer a unique opportunity to accelerate the dismantling of structural inequality generated and maintained by local law enforcement and to engage residents who have historically been disenfranchised in Baltimore City in shaping and monitoring reform."

Three straight acquittals of police officers involved in the matter left the prosecution's case in shreds but made no difference to the Open Society Foundations. It has donated at least $650,000 to Black Lives Matter and pledged more assistance to antipolice factions across the country. These activities prompted the father of one of the Dallas police officers killed during a Black Lives Matter protest to sue Soros (along with other individuals and groups) for inspiring a "war on police."

Soros's Open-Borders Obsessions

Soros's open-borders obsessions can be seen in the $2 million he gave to opponents of Maricopa County, Arizona, sheriff Joe Arpaio, an outspoken critic of illegal immigration. The sheriff's "influence on the national conversation about immigration has been poisonous," said a Soros spokesman. Arpaio fired back, calling the billionaire a "far-left globalist" who was trying to "buy a local race." The sheriff failed to ride in on Trump's November wagon, though, and Soros enjoyed one of his few election-night victories. Soros also spent millions backing liberal-minded district attorneys—they all opposed jail time for nonviolent drug offenders—in Louisiana, Mississippi, Florida, Illinois, New Mexico, and Texas. Some of these candidates won; most lost.

The emphasis on leniency for drug offenders is no accident. Two decades ago, Soros began an ardent campaign to decriminalize marijuana and other illegal drugs, which he promoted as an issue of fairness. Since then, Alaska, California, Colorado, Maine, Massachusetts, Nevada, Oregon, and Washington have all legalized marijuana, and Heads, a pro-drug magazine, enthusiastically dubbed Soros "Daddy Weedbucks." But data on the opioid epidemic confirms what skeptics had argued all along: that legalization serves as a forerunner to more drug use rather than less, more emergency-room visits rather than fewer, increased danger to the health of the young, and a consequent weakening of the social fabric.

As the 2016 post presidential fever abates, Soros's work carries on. In a New York City luxury hotel, Soros recently huddled with other devastated operatives in the so-called Democratic Alliance, including former House Democratic leader Nancy Pelosi, Massachusetts senator Elizabeth Warren, and Congressional Progressive Caucus cochairman Keith Ellison.

According to Politico, they discussed strategies to combat then President-elect Trump's "terrifying assault on President's Obama's achievements." Not all Democrats were pleased with the occasion. "The DA itself should be called into question," said one attendee. "You can make a very good case it's nothing more than a social club for a handful of wealthy white donors and labor union officials to drink wine and read memos, as the Democratic Party burns down around them."

Soros Indoctrinates Students Around the World

From the "Special Report: George Soros: Godfather of the Left" by the Media Research Center (MRC), left-wing donor George Soros spent more than $400 million world-wide to indoctrinate students and teach them to promote liberal, and in some cases extremist, causes. He has even funded his own university that promotes his own unique philosophy of open society. His reach and influence far surpasses that of the Koch brothers, who have been vilified by the left and the media for their grants to universities.

While the left shrivels at the thought of the Koch brother's donations to universities, their beloved Soros gave more than 50 times as much. Central European University and Bard College received the most from Soros. One professor at CEU praised the Occupy movement combining environmentalism, feminism, the labor movement, and social justice. Grants to Bard College for "community service and social action" included a Palestinian youth group and an initiative to educate prisoners across the country. To top it off, all of the Ivy League universities, along with a variety of state schools, private institutions, and even religiously-affiliated institutions, were also funded by Soros.

Soros funded programs and classes at universities around the world promote his radical ideology. Soros's Open Society Foundations granted $407,790,344 in gifts and commitments to higher education since the year 2000. The Koch brothers were vilified by the American political left for donating almost $7 million to universities while their beloved Soros gave more than 50 times that amount to the same type of groups. Alternet, funded by Soros complained about a "shady deal" that helped the Kochs fund Florida State University. Colorlines, also funded by Soros, said of the same donation: "FSU Trades Academic Freedom for Billionaire Charles Koch's Money."

David and Charles Koch are the libertarian businessmen in charge of Koch Industries. They have donated to libertarian and conservative groups along with medical research, the arts, and various other causes. Even with billions of dollars in funding from Soros, the left feels the need to criticize many of the Kochs much smaller endeavors.

Soros's Center for American Progress, which received $7.3 million from his foundations, posted a report on their Think Progress blog titled "Koch Fueling Far Right Academic Centers at Universities across the Country." In the article, the Koch-hating leftist Lee Fang lists universities that received money from the Kochs to include George Mason University, Utah State, and Brown. Totaling nearly $7 million, grants as small as $100,000 were criticized. A donation of $1.5 million to Florida State University supposedly gave the Kochs "a free hand in selecting professors and approving publications."

While Charles Koch is referred to as "a dominant player when it comes to meddling with academic integrity," Soros's name appears nowhere in the article. Giving 50 times the amount cited by the Center for American Progress is ignored by liberal bloggers that are funded by Soros.

Money from Soros goes to everything from general operating funds to specific pet projects that influence the local community and the world. Whether it's a top ranked university or a religiously-affiliated one, Soros has managed to find a left-wing cause to back with the help of his foundations.

There's no product the Soros family likes better than Obama. The Democratic president has received more money from Soros and his kin than any other political candidate in the last 11 years–$16,000 and counting. They gave an additional $250,000 to the inauguration fund, with five members of the family each giving the maximum contribution of $50,000.

Given limits on donations, that's an impressive amount of support. Obama leads a list of the most doctrinaire liberals running for office–all funded by Soros and his family. Those include former comic-turned Sen. Al Franken, lefty Calif. Sen. Barbara Boxer and new "progressive" darling and Massachusetts Senate candidate Elizabeth Warren.

Soros Outspent Koch Brothers in Individual Political Donations 8 to 1

To put that in perspective, he vastly outspent the libertarian Koch Brothers in individual political donations 8 to 1. Promoting left-wing ideology to include everything from electing judges to immigration reform, Soros has exerted his power over the nation's liberal political elite.

While Soros has been known worldwide for his investment skills, he hasn't always managed to stay clear of the authorities. He was found guilty in France of an insider trading case about 20 years ago and has repeatedly failed having it pulled from his record. According to The *New York Times*, in September 2011, a French panel upheld his conviction because "he had bought and sold shares of Société Générale in 1988 with the knowledge that the bank might be a takeover target." He was fined $3 million.

His fund ran into problems in Hungary, where Soros was born and lived till his late teen years. At issue was how he handled an investment into the "the country's largest bank," OTP. "His fund was fined $2 million by Hungarian regulators last week for having manipulated OTP's stock price," wrote the *New York Times* in 2009.

Soros has spread billions around the world–even to helpful projects. Some of that is true, even in the United States. Soros funds after-school programs, hospitals, and the arts. While some of organizations have a liberal spin, they aren't necessarily left-wing. However, his liberal and leftist views and aggressive undermining of criminal justice makes everything he does suspect.

But much of it flows to hardcore left-wing organizations. Eighty different liberal groups have received $1 million or more of Soros's charity in that time. Human Rights Watch, The Drug Policy Alliance, Tides Center and Foundation, National Public Radio (NPR), social justice initiatives and more all join the lefty millionaires club—thanks entirely to Soros.

The Drug Policy Alliance alone has received more than $31 million in those 10 years to oppose the "taboo associated with drug use." That commitment has earned Soros the title "sugar daddy of the legalization movement" from conservative columnist Charles Krauthammer. Prominent supporters of drug legalization - Sting, Soros himself, and former talk show host Montel Williams—are featured in a Drug Policy Alliance video that calls the drug war a "war on people."

Some of Soros's other donations go to fund his extensive network of liberal media outlets, which have received more than $52 million. Those operations include a wide range of liberal news operations as well as the infrastructure of news - journalism schools, investigative journalism and even industry organizations.

All of that is designed to create what Soros has been pushing for decades to achieve—what he calls an "open society." But what exactly is an open society? In "Open Society: Reforming Global Capitalism," he wrote that the concept is "an ideal to which our global society should aspire." But his influences are more complicated and more twisted.

Soros says he based the concept on works by philosopher Karl Popper, who Soros considers his mentor. "Popper proposed a form of social organization that starts with the recognition that no claim to the ultimate truth can be validated and therefore no group should be allowed to impose its views on all of the rest," Soros wrote in "The Age of Fallibility: Consequences of the War on Terror." "Open Society denotes freedom and the absence of repression," he summed up.

Where Does Other Soros Money Go?

Judicial Watch provides a detailed list below of groups receiving funds from OSF and they are universally "progressive" in their philosophy. Some recipients cover the full range of radical and progressive causes, including:

- The American Civil Liberties Union (ACLU).

- The Brookings Institution.

- The Center for American Progress.

- Common Cause.

- Planned Parenthood.

Other groups receiving financial support from the Soros network address specific issues. They include:

- Anti-Israel (Al-Haq, Amnesty International, Arab American Institute Foundation, New Israel Fund).

- Anti-conservative judicial appointments (Alliance for Justice).

- Anti-educational choice (American Federation of Teachers).

- Pro-abortion rights (Catholics for Choice, Center for Reproductive Rights, National Women's Law Center).

- Radical and LGBT agenda (Human Rights Campaign)

Soros' support also goes to groups involved in two issues that are extremely important to Judicial Watch: illegal immigration and honest elections. Here is a partial list of open-border and pro-amnesty groups that have received money from the OSF:

- America's Voice (pro-"comprehensive immigration reform").

- American Bar Association Commission on Immigration Policy ("opposes laws that require em-ployers and person providing education, health care or other social services to verify citizenship or immigration status").

- American Immigration Council (pro-amnesty).

- American Immigration Law Foundation (legal actions in support of amnesty).

- Brennan Center for Justice (legal actions, pro bono support to activists, media campaigns).

- Casa de Maryland (radical state lobbying organization for amnesty and expanded rights for illegal aliens living in Maryland).

- Center for Constitutional Rights (pro-open-borders).

- National Immigration Forum (pro-amnesty for illegal aliens and more visas for individuals wishing—to immigrate legally to the U.S.).

- National Immigration Law Center (pro-full access to government social welfare programs for illegal aliens).

- Unidos US (formerly National Council of La Raza) (pro-amnesty and expanded rights for illegal aliens).

Judicial Watch research has also identified Casa de Maryland, National Immigration Law Center and Unidos US as recipients of U.S. taxpayer dollars (through U.S. government grants).

The following groups have received Soros funding and are reportedly active in promoting, organizing, and supporting the "migrant caravans" from Central America which helped ignite the current unprecedented numbers of illegal aliens attempting to cross our border with Mexico.

- Amnesty International.

- The Catholic Legal Immigration Network (CLINIC) (the "largest network of nonprofit immigration legal services programs" in the country.

- The American Constitution Society (highly critical of Trump immigration policies).

- Center for Legal Action in Human Rights (active in OSF programs in Guatemala).

- Church World Service (compared Trump administration response to the migrant caravans to turning away Jewish refugees from Europe aboard the MS St. Louis in 1930).

- Human Rights First (actively opposes Trump administration immigration efforts).

- The Lawyers Committee for Civil Rights (sued Trump administration over his immigration executive order and the inclusion of a citizenship question on the 2020 Census form).

- The National Immigration Project of the National Lawyers Guild (provided legal assistance to caravan migrants);"

Judicial Watch research has also identified the Catholic Legal Immigration Network as a recipient of U.S. taxpayer dollars through grants from three U.S. government agencies.

Following is a partial list of Soros-funded groups determined to weaken ballot integrity, undermine election integrity laws, and make it easier for illegal aliens to vote in American elections.

- The Advancement Project (which advertises itself as "the next generation, multi-racial civil rights organization).

- Bend the Arc Jewish Action (condemns voter ID laws as barriers that make it harder for minorities to vote).

- Demos (whose board is now chaired by the daughter of radical U.S. Senator and Democratic presidential candidate Elizabeth Warren).

- Project Vote (the voter-mobilization arm of the discredited ACORN organization, which also received Soros support).

- Southern Coalition for Social Justice (involved in several challenges to voter ID and redistricting legal challenges in the South).

The Soros network clearly dwarfs both national political parties in its financial resources. Its impact on American public policies (both foreign and domestic) is only now beginning to be understood...thanks in large part of Judicial Watch's research, investigations and litigation, and other sapient organizations.

There is much more to be learned about the influence of the Soros network, and especially when U.S. taxpayer dollars are awarded to groups within the Soros network, therefore using public taxpayer funds to advance George Soros' radical left agenda.

11 – Black Lives Matter (BLM) Marxist Foundations & Anti-America Agenda

Credit: New York Post. Hawk Newsome, Greater NYC BLM chapter leader,
"If change doesn't happen, then 'we will burn down this system.'"

According to the Black Lives Matter website, their goal is to promote "Freedom, Liberation and Justice" and "to eradicate white supremacy and build local power to intervene in violence inflicted on Black communities by the state and vigilantes." The movement's ideological roots however, run deeper than bringing justice to victims of police brutality.

In a June 2020 interview with Fox News, Hawk Newsome, chairman of Black Lives Matter of Greater New York stated, "If this country doesn't give us what we want, then we will burn down this system and replace it. I could be speaking figuratively; I could be speaking literally. It's a matter of interpretation."

One of the BLM co-founders, Patrisse Khan-Cullors, explained the foundation of the movement, inspired by her and co-founders Alicia Garza and Opal Tometi, in an interview in 2015. "We actually do have an ideological frame," she told The Real News. "Myself and Alicia in particular are trained organizers. We are trained Marxists."

One click into the "What We Believe" portion of the BLM website reveals a far broader agenda for the organization. Stated goals include "disrupt the Western-prescribed nuclear family structure." Another mission statement refers to its members as "comrades" a common moniker used by communists.

In addition, the newest Black Lives Matter campaign, #WhatMatters2020, focused on highlighting certain political issues such as "racial injustice, police brutality, criminal justice reform, Black immigration, economic injustice, LGBTQIA+ and human rights, environmental injustice, access to healthcare, access to quality education, and voting rights and suppression" as well as "government corruption" and "commonsense gun laws" to emphasize and push in the 2020 election.

Using target goals, the organization hopes to increase the black voting demographic, educate, and amplify on the previously mentioned political goals, and increase voter registration for younger generations, the black demographic, and "allies." Using ActBlue, a platform dedicated to creating fundraising for "Democratic candidates and committees, progressive organizations, and nonprofits that share our values," Black Lives Matter solicits donations to further their goals.

Vision For Black Lives: End the War on Black People

The Movement for Black Lives (M4BL) launched the Vision for Black Lives, a comprehensive and visionary policy agenda for the post-Ferguson Black liberation movement, in August of 2016. The Vision, endorsed by over 50 Black-led organizations in the M4BL ecosystem and hundreds of allied organizations and individuals, has since inspired campaigns across the country to achieve its goals.

Per their website content and website link in the Appendix, after three years of consultations, writing retreats and Zoom sessions, research, and outreach, we are relaunching the Vision for Black Lives 2020. We will be rolling out revised, updated, and expanded policy briefs for each of the six planks of the platform over the coming months, leading up to a National Black Convention in August of 2020.

We begin with the first plank of our Vision: End the War on Black People, released on Juneteenth as we converge across the country in resistance to police and state sanctioned violence.

This document does not represent the entirety of our Vision–it is only the first section of six and focuses on state violence. We will be re-releasing revised and expanded policy briefs in each of the remaining sections of the Vision–Reparations, Economic Justice, Invest/Divest, Community Control and Political Power–over the course of 2020

Per M4BL there are many wars being waged against black people. However, any sapient being knows this is not the case, nonetheless, decide for yourself and critique their policy objectives below taken from their 2020 Policy Platform on their website (the caps are theirs):

- END THE WAR ON BLACK COMMUNITIES

- END THE WAR ON BLACK YOUTH

- END THE WAR ON BLACK WOMEN

- END THE WAR ON BLACK TRANS, QUEER, GENDER NONCONFORMING AND INTERSEX PEOPLE

- END THE WAR ON BLACK HEALTH AND BLACK DISABLED PEOPLE

- END THE WAR ON BLACK MIGRANTS

- END TO ALL JAILS, PRISONS, AND IMMIGRATION DETENTION

- END THE DEATH PENALTY

- END THE WAR ON DRUGS

- END THE SURVEILLANCE ON BLACK COMMUNITIES

- END TO PRETRIAL DETENTION AND MONEY BAIL

- THE DEMILITARIZATION OF LAW ENFORCEMENT

- END THE USE OF PAST CRIMINAL HISTORY

Support for Black Lives Matter Movement Has Decreased (For Now)

Pew Research Center surveys show public support for the Black Lives Matter movement surged in June amid worldwide protests after a white Minneapolis police officer knelt on George Floyd's neck and killed him. That increase included a swell in support among white people, according to Pew. But a few months later, support returned to its pre-June levels.

Per a detailed report in *The Dallas Morning News* by Jared Weber in November 2020 titled "Support for Black Lives Matter movement has decreased significantly since June, local and national polls agree" the article notes: In North Texas, Tramonica Brown said, the movement against racism and police violence is at a different point than a few months ago. Worries about the coronavirus and the election mean the protests occupy a smaller place in people's minds.

As a result, she said, major events such as a Kentucky grand jury's September decision to issue no charges in the March killing of Breonna Taylor didn't draw as much outrage as they would have a few months earlier.

Still, Brown said protesters' energy remains strong—with or without the massive support they appeared to have several months ago. "Those white allies were not allies that we had to begin with," Brown said. "They were just there as an extra body. They helped fill up space."

According to Pew, 55% of respondents supported Black Lives Matter in a 2017 phone poll conducted nationally. That figure rose to 67% at the height of protests in June. More white people than ever before—including 37% of white Republicans—said they at least somewhat supported the movement then.

But both of those figures dipped in Pew's most recent survey, released in September.

Support among whites dropped to 45% and as low as 16% among white Republicans. Support among Latinos also declined by 11 percentage points, and by six points among Asian Americans. Support among Black respondents rose to 87%—adding one percentage point since June.

Organizational Overview

Currently there is a "contentious distinction" over what Black Lives Matter is notes Weber. "There are at least two versions of BLM. There's the BLM network founded by the three black female activists who created the #BlackLivesMatter hashtag. Then there's the BLM Movement, a more amorphous collection of racial justice groups."

Where the BLM Network is structured and has 34 chapters, the BLM movement is decentralized and relies "almost solely on local, rather than national, leadership." The movement "eschews hierarchy and centralized leadership." According to one of the BLM originating activists, Patrisse Cullors, the movement's "organizing is often spontaneous and not directed by one person or group of people."

The Black Lives Matter Movement's collection of groups has come to take a variety of forms and political shapes, from groups that favor protest and have no intention of supporting candidates, to others that have begun lobbying candidates and elected officials on legislative issues, to others "hoping to use money to make a difference in elections."

In October 2020, activists from St. Louis created the Black Lives Matter PAC, a political action committee designed to endorse progressive, left-wing candidates and mobilize black voters. The Black Lives Matter movement leaders are not officially affiliated with Black Lives Matter PAC, but the Black Lives Matter Global Network Foundation does advertise the PAC to its email list.

Political Platform

In 2016, a coalition of over 50 organizations known as the Movement for Black Lives released a wide-reaching and in-depth platform detailing the coalition's policy demands. This platform was known as the "Vision 4 Black Lives" and laid out six far-left policy planks/demands pulled largely from the 1996 Black Panther Party ten-point program.

Per Weber, *The Atlantic* criticized the extremist parts of the platform as "elements unpalatable to most major politicians and people," such as extensive "reparations" that could "limit its potential to sway large audiences." The platform denounced the U.S. military, characterized Israel as an "apartheid state," demanded extensive redistribution of financial resources, and insisted upon the socialization of broad sectors of the American economy. It also demanded "special protections for trans, queer, and gender-nonconforming people … a call for free education for black people, and a proposal to implement black economic cooperatives."

Criticisms and Controversies

Weber notes that critics blame BLM for worsening race relations in America. Even family members of Jamar Clark, who was shot by police in 2015, have urged BLM to settle the protests because "there's a fine line between protesting a cause and hurting the community." One of

BLM's originating activists, Alicia Garza, has argued that black people cannot be racist, because "Racism is a system" rather than the act of merely judging people based on race.

Some commentators have argued that recent increases in crime and violence against police are the result of a so-called "Ferguson effect," named for the city that saw the first large Black Lives Matter demonstrations after the death of Michael Brown in 2014. In response to Federal Bureau of Investigation (FBI) findings that homicides of police officers have risen since then, some observers identified Black Lives Matter protests as a contributing cause to an anti-police environment.

The FBI released a report that found that 28 percent of those who used deadly force against police officers "were motivated by hatred of police and a desire to 'kill law enforcement,' in some cases fueled by social and political movements." The FBI reported that the perpetrators of attacks on police in Baton Rouge, Louisiana, and Dallas, Texas stated they were "influenced by the Black Lives Matter movement." The Dallas attack occurred at the end of a BLM protest "when a gunman who had a vendetta against white cops [killed] five and injured several other on-duty officers."

Barbara Reynolds, a veteran of the 1960s civil rights movement and an author, writes that many civil rights activists agree with BLM's goals but "fundamentally disagree with their approach." According to Reynolds, BLM uses "confrontational and divisive tactics" marked by boorish rhetoric and profanity, and rejects proven protest methods, which make it "difficult to distinguish legitimate activists from the mob actors who burn and loot." Reynolds argues that while 1960s-era civil rights activists used "loving" and "nonviolent" means to win allies and mollify enemies, the BLM Movement uses "rage and anger."

Reynolds argues that while "the civil rights movement valued all human lives, even those of people who worked against us," BLM focuses too narrowly on "black pain and suffering," shouting down "those who dare to utter 'all lives matter.'" She argued that in order to "win broader appeal [the BLM Movement] must work harder to acknowledge the humanity in the lives of others."

Black Lives Matter operations have been largely known for their extremism. Daunasia Yancey, a Black Lives Matter activist says, "We're a radical organization, with radical politics, and we have radical tactics. There's no way of softening that." BLM marches in Baltimore, Atlanta, Miami, Los Angeles, and Oakland took over interstates, forcing those cities to shut down roads. Numerous BLM demonstrators were arrested for chaining themselves to subway trains in San Francisco, to the irritation of otherwise-sympathetic locals.

The BLM Movement has also received wide coverage of its protestors interrupting and agitating 2016 Presidential candidates Hilary Clinton, Bernie Sanders, and Donald Trump. BLM originator Patrisse Cullors said the reasoning behind the protests of the Democratic Party is that the Democrats have "milked the Black vote while creating policies that completely decimate Black communities." Critics argue that Black Lives Matter "has become a movement about instilling fear—sometimes in politicians, sometimes in 'white people,' but mainly and most significantly in police."

Funding

It is estimated that groups associated with the BLM Movement have taken in $133 million since 2013. Organizations associated with liberal billionaire George Soros are said to have provided at least $33 million to various BLM movement groups since 2016, Weber reports.

In 2015, the fundraising club Democracy Alliance, led by liberal donors like George Soros and Taco Bell heir Rob McKay, recommended "its donors step up check writing to a handful of endorsed groups that have supported the Black Lives Matter movement." BLM Movement groups which received support from the Democracy Alliance were the Black Youth Project 100, the Center for Popular Democracy, the Black Civic Engagement Fund, Color of Change, and the Advancement Project.

Additionally, the Ford Foundation and the Borealis Philanthropy created the Black-led Movement Fund, a funding vehicle for the Movement for Black Lives, the coalition of groups responsible for the extremist "Vision 4 Black Lives." The fund has received "pledges of more than 100 million dollars from liberal foundations and others eager to contribute." So What is Black Lives Matter Really About?

The Hypocrisy of the BLM Movement

As reported in Diane Dimond's column in *The Winchester Star* in July 2020 that is syndicated by Creators with the heading of "The hypocrisy of the Black Lives Matter Movement," she notes that in New York, BLM organizers concentrate on painting their name on streets yet do nothing to help stop the ever-increasing civilian slaughter of mostly Black citizens.

Shootings during the first six months of this year are up 46%, and homicides increased more than 20%. Yet BLM's cries for defunding the police continue, and the mayor's response was to cut $1 billion from the NYPD budget. The department's anti-crime unit—focused on disarming criminals and curbing violent crime in mostly minority neighborhoods—was disbanded.

Dimond adds, "In what world does that make sense?"

In Chicago, where more than 100 mostly Black people were shot by civilians over a recent weekend, one local reverend said it's an "open season" killing field. Nearly 2,000 Chicagoans have been shot so far this year, hundreds fatally, and, yes, the majority of victims and known assailants are Black.

So, where is the Black Lives Matter movement in Chicago to try to curb this trend? Has BLM piled into the Windy City to marshal local ministers, community leaders and concerned citizens to try to combat the carnage against Black Americans? No.

In Atlanta, at the burned-out Wendy's restaurant where BLM gathered after police killed a Black man who shot at them with a Taser, another tragedy took place. An 8-year-old Black child was fatally shot as she rode by in a car. It was yet another mindless black-on-black shooting. Her father later told the criminals: "You killed a child. She didn't do nothing to nobody. Black Lives Matter? You killing your own."

The mantra of Black Lives Matter is now part of the American lexicon. All clear-thinking citizens embrace it and the idea that violent police tactics need to be abolished. Embracing those ideals and the BLM organization are two very different things.

**Political Violence, Demonstrations, & Strategic Developments in the US
(24 May - 22 August 2020)**

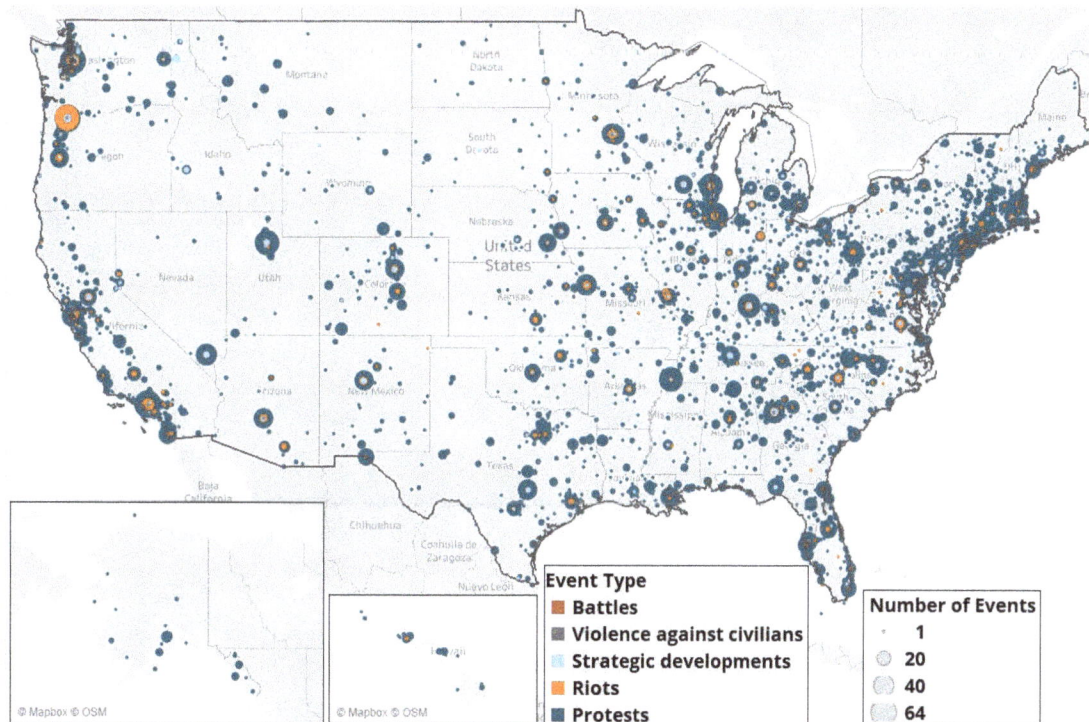

Credit: ACLED, US Crisis Monitor.

Top 10 Reasons Why Sapient Beings Do Not Support the BLM Movement

Ryan Bomberger has a rather unique perspective revealed in his Townhall post in June 2020 with the title of "Top 10 Reasons I Won't Support the #BlackLivesMatter Movement." Adopted into a large multi-racial family of 15 (Bomberger like Obama is bi-racial), he grew up in a Christian home that exuded compassion. Today he's an adoptee and adoptive father. As an Emmy Award-winning creative professional he is passionate about igniting, in people's hearts and minds, an awareness and a love of the intrinsic value we all possess.

In Bomberger's own words, here are his top ten reasons why he will never support the BLM movement:

1. **The premise isn't true.** I hate racism. And I hate when it's used as a political weapon. According to the FBI's latest homicide statistics, I'm 11 times more likely to be killed by someone of my own brown complexion than a white person. Also, a comprehensive

2019 study concluded: "White officers are not more likely to shoot minority civilians than non-White officers." Every loss of life is tragic, but *Washington Post*'s database on police-involved deaths puts things into further context. In 2020, among those killed were (all males): 2 Native Americans, 9 Asians, 46 Hispanics, 76 blacks, 149 unlabeled individuals and 149 whites (whose deaths don't get reported by national mainstream media). Only nine black individuals were actually unarmed.

2. **There is no goal of forgiveness or reconciliation**. None. It's never mentioned on their sites. You can't talk about the sins of the past and expect to move forward if there is no intention of forgiveness. I'm tired of the deeply prejudiced oppressed/oppressor critical race theory paradigm. It's not Gospel-centered. This should, immediately, be a deal-breaker for Christians.

3. **It's all about Black Power.** It's plastered all over the MFBL website. BLMF founders explain their "herstory": "It became clear that we needed to continue organizing and building Black power across the country." I don't promote a colorblind society; I love all of our diverse hues of skin. But I'm so much more than my pigmentation. Martin Luther King promoted "God's power and human power." I'm with him.

4. **They heavily promote homosexuality and transgenderism.** "We foster a queer-affirming network. When we gather, we do so with the intention of freeing ourselves from the tight grip of heteronormative thinking." I'm not embracing confusion. Loving every human being is not the same as loving every human doing.

5. **They completely ignore fatherhood.** From BLMF: "We disrupt the Western-prescribed nuclear family structure requirement by supporting each other as extended families and 'villages' that collectively care for one another, especially our children, to the degree that mothers, parents, and children are comfortable." Well, every "village" that has fatherless families is a village that suffers higher crime rates, higher drug usage, higher abortion rates, higher drop-out rates, higher poverty rates, and so much more. #DadsMatter.

6. **They demand reparations.** Ok. Sooooo, I guess the white half of me will have to pay the black half of me? If progressives want to push reparations, start with the Party of Slavery and Jim Crow—the Democrat Party! Let them ante up. But the #BlackLivesMatter movement bizarrely demands: "Reparations for...full and free access for all Black people (including undocumented and currently and formerly incarcerated people) to lifetime education...retroactive forgiveness of student loans, and support for lifetime learning programs." Uhhh, good luck with that.

7. **They want to abolish prisons and police forces.** And...cue utter chaos. MFBL asserts: "We believe that prisons, police and all other institutions that inflict violence on Black people must be abolished..." Defund and remove the police have been rallying cries. That would be anarchy in any community. I advocate some needed police reforms and better community/police relations, but this is just foolishness.

8. **They are anti-capitalism.** Oh the irony of this declaration made by a movement that is the result of capitalism: "We are anti-capitalist. We believe and understand that Black people will never achieve liberation under the current global racialized capitalist system." The videos that make us aware of police brutality are captured on phones that are a result of capitalism. The best way to elevate people out of material poverty. Capitalism. This system is why the United States is the most charitable nation.

9. **Colin Kaepernick supports it.** A "biracial" adoptee, Kaepernick is now obsessed with his "blackness." He idolizes the late murderous Fidel Castro and Che Guevara and worships Malcolm X (just see his social media feeds). Malcolm X was anti-integration, pro-violence, and a member of the virulently racist Nation of Islam (who forced him out). Kaepernick makes millions from Nike—a company whose entire Executive Leadership Team is white (isn't this white supremacy???)—that makes its shoes in the most murderous regime in the world. Kaepernick, of course, is completely silent on that. But you know, #SocialJusticeWarrior.

10. **Apparently, not all black lives matter.** Pro-abortion BLMF declared: "We deserve and thus we demand reproductive justice [aka abortion] that gives us autonomy over our bodies and our identities while ensuring that our children and families are supported, safe, and able to thrive." Aborted children don't thrive. BLM groups announced "solidarity" with "reproductive justice" groups back in February 2015. You cannot simultaneously fight violence while celebrating it.

Black Conservative's Counter Arguments to Identify Politics and BLM's False Narratives

Black conservatives typically oppose affirmative action, which is supported by the vast majority of African-American communities. They tend to argue that efforts to obtain reparations for slavery are either misguided or counter-productive. Black conservatives tend to be self-critical of aspects of African-American culture that they believe have created poverty and dependency. Moreover, black conservatives–especially black Republicans–are often accused of being Uncle Toms.

Three prominent black conservatives share their opinions on identity politics and false BLM narratives.

Journalist Larry Elder

The *Chicago Tribune's* John Kass, a political writer, wrote a piece headlined "What Frightens the American Left: Larry Elder's New Documentary 'Uncle Tom.'" Kass writes: "Is there anything more frightening to the American political left and their high media priests of the woke world than Black Americans who think for themselves and refuse to kneel? ...

And so, they are demeaned by Democratic politicians and either ignored outright or marginalized as race traitors, sellouts and 'Uncle Toms.' It's a way to humiliate them, shut them up, and cancel them. And the party's handmaidens of the media play along. But that's one reason why Larry Elder's stunning 2020 new film, 'Uncle Tom: An Oral History of the American Black Conservative,' is so important, especially now."

Each of the following three year-end lists of "best" documentary films of 2020 ignores "Uncle Tom," despite an IMDb viewer rating higher than any on the lists (8.9 out of 10!)—in most cases, far higher. (IMDb, the Internet Movie Database website, assigns films a rating, from one to 10, based on viewers' reviews.)

Finally, of the last 10 Oscar winners for Best Documentary, none has a higher IMDb rating than "Uncle Tom." None. Only one matched its 8.9 rating. See you at the Academy Awards?

Bishop E.W. Jackson Sr.

From Bishop E.W. Jackson Sr. for the Stand America PAC, in his own words:

As one of those black Americans who escaped the indoctrination process to think freely and independently, I see America for what she is: the greatest nation in the history of mankind; and the greatest place on earth to grow and thrive, obtain an education, raise a family, build a business, and fulfill your dreams. This is true for any American who is willing to work hard and do those things that lead to a stable, happy life.

When the Left says this is not available to black people, I am living proof that they are lying. I was born into poverty, raised in the ghetto, placed in foster care, became a juvenile delinquent and an academic failure. Yet here I am, a product of American freedom and opportunity: Marine Corps veteran, Summa Cum Laude college graduate, Harvard Law School graduate, former business owner, retired Attorney and married for fifty years with three beautiful children.

My black children—a son and two daughters—have never spent a day in jail, on drugs, collecting welfare, or fighting with police. We are Americans who embrace the legacy of freedom and prosperity which is the birthright of every citizen. For those who believe that they are victims of racism whose destinies are controlled by others, their lives are a self-fulfilling prophecy. They will descend to the level assigned them by the Left as perpetual members of the class of the downtrodden.

The Left today is inculcating in young and old alike that we are owed, entitled. My father taught me that nobody owes me anything, and that I should never ask others to do for me what I should do for myself. I was taught I have no right to what someone else has earned. I was taught that it is up to me to earn what I want out of life.

Dr. King said, "I have a dream. It is a dream deeply rooted in the American dream." So many have forgotten that Martin Luther King did not call for the overthrow of America, but the fulfillment of her promise. That is also my dream. It should be the dream of every American: to live in peace and harmony with our neighbors; to share the common hope that our nation offers; and to enjoy life, liberty, and the pursuit of happiness.

That is not the dream of the Left. They are determined to destroy the dream. We must defend it and defeat the forces that are trying to fundamentally transform our nation into a godless, secularist, socialist culture.

Attorney Leo Terrell

Leo Terrell is an author, commentator and civil rights attorney based in Los Angeles. He has served as an attorney for the NAACP, as former chairman of the Black-Korean Alliance, as an advisory board member for the Equal Employment Opportunity Commission and as a former member of California's Statewide Commission Against Hate Crimes.

He's spent over 20 years as a civil rights attorney in California and I'm known for not taking a back seat to anyone on police misconduct cases. And yet, my commitment to justice and my substantial track record of putting racially driven criminals behind bars should deserve special merit—considering Terrell is calling out the farce that is Black Lives Matter—and doing so loudly and proudly.

From his "Why Black Lives Don't Matter to 'Black Lives Matter'" *Newsweek* article in July 2020:

Why? In Terrell's own words: Because, this organization does not speak for me, as an African-American, and if you truly believe that Black lives DO matter, you should reconsider taking your cues from this group's self-serving agenda. Terrell continues:

In reality, Black Lives Matter is comprised of modern day-charlatans who learned the profitable way to protest from the Al Sharptons of the world. Style over substance. Chaos over real change. Some revealing questions about them are as follows:

- Is BLM setting up urban outreach and mentoring? No.

- Is BLM demanding better schools and safe community activities? No.

- Is BLM paying for the funerals of these Black babies killed by violence? No.

- Has BLM set up a GoFundMe or made donations to any of the destroyed—minority-owned—businesses in Minneapolis? Of course not.

To make it even worse, the Democratic Party is literally taking a pandering knee to them. What has Nancy Pelosi done for African-Americans? What has Joe Biden done? Nothing. In fact, the president they love to hate, Donald Trump, has done more in three years for Black Americans and police reform than Joe Biden has done in decades. With one recent executive order, President Trump accomplished more for police reform than the Obama/Biden administration did over all of its eight years in office.

Many do not like what I have to say. But enough is enough. I am being consistent in my beliefs by recognizing those who are actually helping, and those who are hurting the cause. It's not always the answer you want, but it's important to support those actually making a difference.

Naturally, you won't hear this frequently on media outlets because it's not profitable. It doesn't fit the approved narrative. And in an election year, it's always about the best narrative for your preferred candidate.

Yes, Black lives matter. They matter all the time and in every violent death—not just in the very few instances where a police officer is involved.

12 – Antifa's Anarcho-Communist Indoctrination & Fascist Insurrection

Credit: Epoch Times. Prepared and organized Antifa members ready for attack.

The origins of the group Antifa can be traced back to Germany's "anti-fascist" movement, which was part of the Soviet Union's front operations to incite a communist revolution in the European country.

Antifa–short for "anti-fascist" or "Anti-Fascist action"–is a left-wing extremist movement that violently opposes groups it considers "fascist," including democratic, center-right conservatives. Antifa lacks a known organizational structure or an official leader or headquarters, though individual groups in certain states reportedly hold regular meetings. Anyone can claim the title and set up a local branch.

The term Antifa is currently used to define a broad group of people whose political beliefs lean toward the left, often the extreme left, who engage in aggressive protests against right-wing and center-right political groups. Antifa's protest methods are often violent, and local leaders admit they're willing to physically attack anyone who employs violence against them or who "condones racism," as the Antifa demonstrators define it.

Antifa has reportedly grown rapidly and has become more active in the wake of Donald Trump's 2016 Presidential campaign. This surge of activity has been marked by more violent than traditional political protest movements. Though some decry their use of violence as a means of protest, Antifa's tactics have recently "elicited substantial support from the mainstream left."

In the United States, the group claims that its members are fighting fascism, but rarely do they confront actual fascists. Instead, their members, who are made up of communists, socialists, anarchists, and other hard-left radicals, label parties and individuals who don't align with their ideology as "fascists" to justify their use of violence against them.

The group has frequently made headlines for its violent attacks on opposing groups, particularly Trump supporters, whom they have branded as "fascists." Former President Donald Trump announced on May 31, 2020, that his administration would designate Antifa as a terrorist organization, which it did.

Antifa is a 'Revolutionary Group' Destabilizing America

Attorney General William Barr said federal authorities are conducting comprehensive investigations into certain individuals with ties to the extremist group Antifa. In a joint August 2020 report for *The Epoch Times* by Janita Kan, Bowen Xiao, Ivan Pentchoukov, and Jack Phillips: Barr said this is why the group Antifa hasn't been mentioned in criminal complaints related to the rioting amid protests following the death of George Floyd.

"We have some investigations underway and very focused investigations on certain individuals that relate to Antifa," Barr said during an interview with Fox News on June 8, 2020. "But in the ... initial phase of identifying people and arresting them, they were arrested for crimes that don't require us to identify a particular group or don't necessitate that."

He said these actors had "hijacked" the protests to "engage in lawlessness, violent rioting, arson, looting of businesses, and public property assaults on law enforcement officers and innocent people, and even the murder of a federal agent. Barr's comments were echoed by FBI Director Christopher Wray, who said these individuals have "set out to sow discord and upheaval rather than join in the righteous pursuit of equality and justice."

The government has made 51 arrests so far for federal crimes in connection with the rioting, according to the former Attorney General William Barr. However, the number of arrests and convictions of Antifa members have been few and far between amongst the various federal, state, and local law enforcement agencies, and cautioned it would take time (one to two years) to provide conclusive results

Despite this uncertain outcome, the tracking, observation, documentation, and infiltration of Portland's Antifa Rose City cell has been conclusive due to the extensive investigation and brave reporting by Andy Ngo, a Portland native. As you will see in this chapter, along with Project Veritas, they have been successful in illuminating the anarcho-communist group with RICO type attributes, which makes Antifa, their cells, and followers difficult to measure, quantify, and locate.

For the first time, the nation's top law enforcement officer has explicitly outlined the nature of far-left anarcho-communist group Antifa, describing it as a "revolutionary group" intent on establishing socialism or communism in the United States—and the experts agree.

Attorney General William Barr delivered a scathing critique of Antifa in an Aug. 9 interview with Mark Levin on Fox News, noting that the group's organization and tactics make it a difficult phenomenon to deal with. "They are a revolutionary group that is interested in some form of socialism, communism. They're essentially Bolsheviks. Their tactics are fascistic," Barr said.

Is There an Antifa's Connection to the 470 Unpeaceful Protests in 2020?

While Antifa publicly identifies with communist and socialist ideology, the interview marked the first time for Barr to go into such detail about the activities, involvement, and responsibility of the 470 unpeaceful protests that took place in 2020.

"The Attorney General's comments represent a significant improvement over previous government statements on Antifa, and he should be commended for his outspokenness," Kyle Shideler, director and senior analyst for Homeland Security and Counterterrorism at the Center for Security Policy, told the *Epoch Times*.

Shideler—who testified on Aug. 4, 2020, before the Senate Subcommittee on the Constitution about the structure and origin of Antifa—said he hopes Barr will direct the Justice Department to take Antifa's core mission to heart and begin "to treat the group as the subversive and insurrectionist force it is.

"Antifa's distributed and non-hierarchical network structure requires better intelligence to counter," he said, noting that the federal government has a unique responsibility to address this threat as local and state governments are unable or unwilling to do so.

Antifa is "fundamentally committed to the abolition of the U.S. government and the violent overthrow of the United States Constitution," Shideler said in his written testimony. To achieve that, it's committed to the use "of both subversion and violent extremism to enforce its political views by terrorizing American citizens."

"Antifa's activities clearly meet the definition of an organized criminal and conspiracy and terrorism established by federal law," he said in his testimony. The reality is that Antifa demonstrates "an elaborate and complex but non-hierarchical structure," Shideler said. He described how websites linked to the group attract users "who spend inordinate efforts discussing how Antifa groups can and should be organized."

The FBI has become increasingly concerned about violence perpetrated by Antifa at public events, according to a 2018 report by the Congressional Research Service, a public policy research arm of the U.S. Congress.

Barr: Antifa Wants 'Socialism, Communism' in America

Per another *Epoch Times* report by Ivan Pentchoukov in August 2020: Barr made the comments in response to a question about Antifa's apparent focus on removing the administration of President Donald Trump. He noted that the extremist group has been engaged with this goal since the first day of the Trump administration.

"They were trying to impeach him from day one. They have done everything they can. They have shredded the norms of our system to do what they can to drive him from office or to debilitate his administration, and I think that's because of the desire for power," Barr said.

"The left wants power because that is essentially their state of grace in their secular religion. They want to run people's lives so they can design utopia for all of us. That's what turns them on—it's the lust for power. "They weren't expecting Trump's victory and it outrages them," he added.

Barr had previously said that "the violence instigated and carried out by Antifa and other similar groups in connection with the rioting is domestic terrorism and will be treated accordingly." Antifa and other extremists groups hijacked peaceful protests in the wake of the police custody death of black American George Floyd. The extremists provoked violence, vandalism, and looting. Despite the apparently coordinated activity, the Department of Justice has been mum about whether many arrests made since the riots began are focused on Antifa as an enterprise.

Antifa's Tactics Make it a Difficult Phenomenon to Deal With

"It's a new form of urban guerrilla warfare," Barr said. "They are essentially shielding themselves or shrouding themselves in First Amendment activity. They go into the demonstrations, which are exercising First Amendment activity, and they insinuate themselves in there to shield themselves. That's where they swim. And what they do is they hijack these demonstrations, and they provoke violence, and they have various tiers of people from the sort of top provocateurs down through the people who are their minions and sort of run the violent missions."

"It's a difficult phenomenon to deal with," he added. "They're highly organized at these demonstrations."

Barr noted that legacy media outlets are lying to the American people by intentionally not showing the violence taking place at the riots.

I had the privilege of meeting in person Gabriel Nadales at a Leadership Institute meeting in Orange County, California in 2019. Nadales was a former Antifa protestor who shared why he got out, and interestingly, as adolescents, we both questioned our liberal and leftist ideologies (even when we're at least three decades apart in age) when we took economics classes in college.

Nadales, author of the book *Behind the Black Mask: My Time as an Antifa Activist*, shared his disturbing, yet all too common, story of why he joined Antifa. Nadales explained that growing up he had two main sources of anti-American propaganda: media (Spanish networks in particular) and school.

"A lot of [Spanish media] stories are uniquely targeted to make Hispanics feel marginalized, and make it seem like Hispanics against America. And in middle school and high school, I had several radical left-wing teachers who basically told me to hate America," Nadales said.

"When you're bombarded with so many anti-American beliefs and sentiments, it's easy for somebody growing up in this country to learn to hate America," he added. "Eventually I joined the Anti-fascist movement because I was preconditioned to hate America.

Nadales went on to explain that he believed "America and Neo-Nazis were one and the same" and how even concepts such as freedom of speech were conflated with fascism because of teachers who see themselves as "activists first and educators second."

Structure

Antifa's lack of centralized structure make it difficult to calculate the movement's size and membership or verify and prosecute. While interest has spiked since the 2016 presidential election, it remains virtually impossible to quantify how many people are active members or supporters of Antifa.

The chapters of Antifa are loosely connected and highly secretive and organize mostly on message boards such as Reddit and over social networks like Twitter and Facebook. Liberal commentator Peter Beinart reported, "According to NYC Antifa, the group's Twitter following nearly quadrupled in the first three weeks of January 2017 alone.

Similarly, Antifa's decentralized character makes it difficult to pin down what exactly it is they oppose and who are their members and followers. Moreover, this lack of national organization, combined with the group's secrecy and cloak of anonymity, make the group almost "impossible to track."

Activities and Expectations

While the decentralized nature of Antifa makes it difficult to identify how they operate, an excerpt from a widely disseminated guide for new Antifa organizations published by It's Going Down describes Antifa operations and expectations Antifa members are obliged to meet.

Antifa's "obligations" include:

- "Track white nationalist, Far Right, and fascist activity. Your group will be expected to document fascist groups and organizing in your area. This means gathering information on who is doing what and knowing the makeup and key players of the various groups that are active. Once information is verified, Antifa groups periodically release this information in a publicly available format. It is also crucial to alert any intended targets about specific threats you [encounter] while doing research."

- "Oppose public Far Right organizing. If the Klan or the National Socialist Movement hold a public rally, if Alt Right speakers come to town, or if the Daily Stormer holds a meet up, you will be expected to organize a counter-demonstration. If they hold postering or sticker campaigns, you should not only take down their materials but also put up your own; public outreach campaigns should likewise be countered."

- "Support other anti-fascists who are targeted by fascists or arrested for Antifa-related activities. This could include supporting regional groups or organizing benefits and fundraisers for prisoners and injured comrades."

- "Build a culture of non-cooperation with law enforcement. If you have any intention of working with the police, FBI, or other agencies; or if you publicly condemn anti-fascists who break the law: don't call yourself an anti-fascist. The cops will be Trump supporters; do not collaborate with them."

Additionally the Antifa guide lays out a number of other suggestions/best practices including:

- "We strongly recommend against Antifa groups being organized using the open, public model of most contemporary activism because of the risk of infiltration ... a traditional mass organizing activist model ... should be kept separate from the long-term group structure."

- "Take photos with Antifa banners, blur the faces, and put them on social media."

- "Carefully manage your online presence" using only Twitter; new members are urged to "leave social media," ... "Individual members, when possible, should get off social media, especially Facebook, altogether. Where they don't, they should maintain strictly separate personal and political accounts."

- "Websites imply that your group is more legitimate, and should be used especially if you want to doxx local fascists"

- "Consider using a cell model ... in which one member meets with others when required" and where "one person is designated as the semi-public face, even if they never admit they are a group member." Thus limiting the overall group's exposure.

- Doxx identified opponents and make their personal contact information widely available in order to encourage harassment.

- "Regular marshal [sic] arts' training" is recommended.

- "Find out what the laws are in your city and state about a variety of self-defense weapons and make sure to practice with, and carry, everything that is legal."

- Pressure venues to cancel racist or fascist events.

Ideology and Collaboration

The anti-fascist movement has come from multiple theoretical currents; Antifa is based on an agreement on tactics—not ideological uniformity. In the U.S., most activists are anarchist, although a few are Maoist or anti-state Marxists. (In other countries, the movement is predominately Marxist.)

Antifa groups have one unifying feature, "tracking and countering fascists and white supremacists." Otherwise, the lack of hierarchy means that each local Antifa chapter decides what causes they choose to fight against. These include, but are by no means limited to:

- "Other Radical right-wing forces"

- Anti-immigrant movements

- The Patriot movement

- The militia movement

- Islamophobes

- Men's Rights Activists

The Antifa organizing guide states, "Antifascism is not a stand-alone ideology; it is a piece of a whole." Antifa operations are therefore seen as "a certain set of practices within the broader radical movement against white supremacy … hierarchy and oppression in general." As such, Antifa members are encouraged to organize mass demonstrations against opponents with allied groups who are willing to work with them or to join demonstrations by other groups such as Black Lives Matter or for immigrants and refugees, all the while carrying Antifa flags and banners.

Yet again the decentralized nature of Antifa allows each individual chapter to decide what other "radical movements" they choose to align themselves with. These include, but are by no means limited to:

- Immigrant movements

- Refugee movements

- Work with prisoners

- Rojava solidarity work

- Anti-Racist Action

- Showing Up for Racial Justice

- Violent Activism

Black Lives Matter is the group Antifa collaborates with the most frequently.

Antifa groups directly advocate violence and "don't apologize" when violence breaks out at their rallies. "Their methods are often violent and Antifa leaders admit they're willing to physically attack anyone who employs violence against them or who condones racism–as long as force is used in the name of eradicating hatred." As one Antifa leader explained, "You have to put your body in the way … and you have to make it speak in the language that they understand. And sometimes that is violence."

Antifascists rationalize their violent actions as "defensive." They argue, "Hate speech against vulnerable minorities … leads to violence against vulnerable minorities." However, there is little to no documented, scientific, and/or statistical evidence during Trump's term that can qualify as hate speech against vulnerable minorities. Against principles, policies, and actions—yes and could conservatives these days be considered "vulnerable minorities?"

Hate speech is defined by the Cambridge Dictionary as "public speech that expresses hate or encourages violence towards a person or group based on something such as race, religion, sex, or sexual orientation". Hate speech is "usually thought to include communications of animosity or disparagement of an individual or a group on account of a group characteristic such as race, color, national origin, sex, disability, religion, or sexual orientation".

Without any tangible proof of the above requirements necessary for hate speech, today's progressives seem to construe disagreement as their litmus test of "hate" and Antifa is no exception. Furthermore, if these definitions above are applied to Antifa's platform, statements, and actions—would Antifa provide a more evident case of being guilty of the sins they state they're fighting against? As you read on—you be the judge.

Nonetheless, the subjective topic of hate can cover a chapter by itself and will be set aside and explored in more detail in *Progressivism Madness*. In the meantime, consider these actions by Antifa and if they meet any of the qualifications of hate speech or inherent hatred.

Trump's Inauguration Saw More than 200 Antifa Members Formed a "Black Bloc"

On January 20, 2017, the day of President Trump's inauguration, more than 200 Antifa members formed a "black bloc" in which members wearing black or dark clothes and other riot gear armed with hammers, crowbars, wooden sticks, and other weapons marched through downtown Washington, D.C., and "within minutes" began vandalizing public and private property. They smashed storefront windows, trashed the streets, confronted peaceful inauguration and parade attendees, lit a limousine on fire, and set several other fires across the downtown area.

At one point the group of more than 200 participants charged at a police line and approximately 50 individuals broke through, some of whom continued to engage in violence. In one detailed court account, Dane Powell admitted that he and others threw approximately 16 bricks, rocks, or pieces of concrete at uniformed officers, one of whom was knocked unconscious.

More than 230 people were arrested in the aftermath of the incidents on January 20, 2017. Powell was the first to plead guilty to felony charges. He was among 212 defendants named in a superseding indictment, all charged with felonies.

Despite wielding weapons, damaging property, and lighting a limousine on fire, some members of the group thought that there was not enough violence. "I think there should have been more violence yesterday ... there were some rocks thrown ... the police stopped me," said Tom Massey of Philadelphia.

Portland, Oregon: Antifa Central and Hotbed of Their Activities and Resistance

In Portland, Oregon, Antifa has been involved in at least 10 recent protests ending in violence. In May 2017, 25 anarchists were arrested in Portland for rioting, random acts of vandalism to public and private property, and for throwing incendiary devices, including fireworks and Molotov cocktails, at police.

Then in August, police in Portland again geared up for the tenth protest since Election Day involving extremist nationalist and extreme-left street demonstrators. In the days leading up to the planned protests, the Portland police said they "saw on social media that there was a lot of threats being put back and forth" that caused "concern about physical violence." The police created a human barricade, with officers standing shoulder to shoulder between two city squares—one filled with extremist nationalist groups, the other with Antifa activists. That strategy worked for a few hours, but police caught word that Antifa members were planning to push past police into the opposing extremists' rally square.

Police gathered the masked Antifa activists and detained them. In the process, they seized a large number of weapons from Antifa protestors that day. "Everything from knives to brass knuckles to poles and sticks and bricks and bottles and road flares and chains." According to Portland's Police Spokesmen, "One hundred percent, they came geared up to fight if it would be allowed."

Perhaps a more fitting acronym for Antifa should be Anarchy Now Today Is Fighting America?

Antifa Investigations Will Take Time to Be Effective

While Attorney General William Barr revealed that there are multiple investigations into the anarcho-communist group Antifa underway, that doesn't necessarily mean arrests are imminent. These kinds of investigations, if done right, usually take a long time, according to a former FBI special agent.

In an *Epoch Times* report by Petr Svab in June 2020: Barr and FBI Director Christopher Wray singled out Antifa as one of the culprits behind the instigation of violence during recent protests sparked by the death of George Floyd during an arrest in Minneapolis.

Yet, for such an investigation, "in order to be effective, it has to be long-term," Ruskin told The Epoch Times.

The advantage of a "thorough, long-term investigation" is that "the organization can essentially be dismantled," according to Marc Ruskin, a 27-year FBI veteran and contributor to the *Epoch Times*.

"If there's a two-year investigation or one-year investigation and results in the arrest of 30 members or high-level members, then it can … really be very effective," he said.

One particular approach that came to mind, he said, was charging Antifa members under the Racketeer Influenced and Corrupt Organizations Act (RICO), which allows for longer sentences for people involved in a criminal organization. "RICO penalties are significant. People go to jail for decades for RICO violations," Ruskin said.

Putting important members behind bars for decades not only cripples the organization, but also deters others who may have thought it "was a lot of fun to destroy the system," but may reconsider when they see that their "buddies are now serving 28-year prison terms."

Barr acknowledged that Antifa is "very loosely organized," but said "there are people who can be characterized as leaders in any given situation." At least some parts of the group are highly organized, including initiation procedures, security protocols, and "lectures" on violent action, according to an undercover reporter who infiltrated the Antifa cell in Portland, Oregon, on behalf of Project Veritas, an investigative journalism nonprofit.

Undercover Videos Show Antifa Members' Combat Training

A series of surreptitiously recorded videos show Antifa members training for combat, including sessions at an anarchist center known as "The Base," according to a watchdog group. The videos were recorded by people who infiltrated different groups and shared footage with the watchdog, Project Veritas.

Per the *Epoch Times* report by Zachary Stieber in June 2020: Footage published Friday shows people said to be Antifa members learning intense hand-to-hand combat moves in an undisclosed year.

"You're trying to basically cut off both, both arteries," a man identified as a fight instructor tells attendees in one video that Project Veritas says is from "The Base."

The person who filmed the videos said in a video released by the watchdog group that Antifa's goals include abolishing the state, shutting down prisons, defunding police departments, and abolishing the U.S. government.

The videos came after a Project Veritas operative appeared to infiltrate Rose City Antifa in Portland, Oregon, one of the most prominent Antifa cells in the country.

Antifa is an Organized 'Revolutionary Group' That Thrives on Anarchy

Yes, Antifa is an 'Organized' Terrorist Organization No Matter What Fake News Tries to Say Otherwise and this chapter will provide overwhelming evidence to prove that.

Independent journalist Andy Ngo and his family have been so threatened by the "violent, insurrectionary" group Antifa that he feared testifying before Congress, but he said he was even more afraid "of remaining silent."

In an *Epoch Times* report by Mark Tapscott in August 2020: Ngo, who has covered Antifa since 2016, told a hearing on Aug. 4, 2020, of the Senate Judiciary Committee's Subcommittee on the Constitution that "unless we take action, what is happening in Portland today will soon be happening in cities across the country."

That's because, Ngo said, "what we have witnessed are almost daily violent protests and riots led by Antifa. Even when they aren't starting fires, using explosives, and trying to maim officers, they leave threatening messages like decapitated pig heads outside the courthouse.

Ngo was referring to the more than two months of nightly destructive rioting seen in the Oregon city organized and led by the radical left-wing group, using as its pretext the nation's outrage over the May 25, 2020 death of George Floyd in the custody of Minneapolis police.

As editor-at-large of The Post Millennial digital news site, Ngo's highly detailed and well-sourced reporting has exposed Antifa's decentralized organizational structure, fundraising methods, recruitment of new members, training in violent tactics, and insurrectionary plans to destroy the United States and replace it with a totalitarian regime.

"Antifa is not a myth. I have been reporting on its activities since 2016. Its threats to me and my family have proven all too real. As any good journalist knows, the most important stories are often those that are not being told. This story is not being told," Ngo told the panel

"The American public knows little about this violent insurrectionary group and its radical ideology," Ngo testified. "I made Antifa my beat, and that makes me a target. Its followers regard my reporting as a threat to their mission, so they use violence and intimidation to try to frighten me into silence."

When Antifa's attempts in 2018 to discredit him as a "white supremacist" failed (Ngo is Asian), he said the group turned to direct threats to kill him and hurt his family. "They almost succeeded last year when they surrounded me in the middle of downtown Portland. I was beaten so badly that I was hospitalized with a [brain hemorrhage]," he said. Ngo said he still suffers from the aftereffects of his beating, and he said local authorities have yet to arrest and charge anybody in connection with the assault.

"Unfortunately, too many in the media have chosen to ignore or downplay this extremism masquerading as demands for racial justice," he told the subcommittee. The Portland violence has been organized and led by the Youth Liberation Front (YLF), which he described as "a shadowy Antifa organization with secret membership." The YLF has "fronts across the U.S., organized on social media sites like Twitter. They openly advocate for violent uprisings in Portland and elsewhere," Ngo said.

On July 25, 2020, for example, Ngo said the YLF issued "calls for national action" that were followed by riots in Seattle, Portland, Oakland, Austin, Atlanta, and Richmond, among others. "There were multiple shootings, dozens of officers injured, and even a homicide," he said. "I have seen with my own eyes how hundreds of so-called protestors work together to carry out acts of organized criminality against government and civilians."

Antifa Seizes Seattle Police Department and Sets Up 'Autonomous Zone'

Just as the Islamic State (ISIS) claimed territory in Iraq and Syria, Antifa militants have claimed territory in Seattle, Wash. According to reports on the ground from The Post Millennial's Andy Ngo and Townhall's Julio Rosas, protesters and Antifa instigators have seized land in the Capitol Hill area around the Seattle Police East Precinct. Like ISIS, the rioters appear to have decided on setting up a government in their occupied territory, naming it "Free Capitol Hill."

"Seattle [Mayor Jenny Durkan] is allowing a dangerous situation to fester. [Antifa] militants have taken over & created an 'autonomous zone' in city w/their own rules. Police precinct abandoned. Antifa set up barricades to create a border. Calling for volunteers to provide armed guard," Ngo tweeted.

His message included tweets from rioters and pictures of the "Free Capitol Hill" poster on the side of a barricade, along with a map of the area Antifa had taken over. "The Capitol Hill Autonomous Zone (CHAZ) folks in Seattle have secured six block of city [at the moment], barricaded it, and gotten local businesses and residents to agree to, well, disaffiliate from Seattle basically. It's a flux state in the making," Alex Humva tweeted.

"Speaker at the autonomous zones advocating folks with firearms take shifts defend the barricades. Sh*t is getting organized," another inside the barricades tweeted.

The map Ngo tweeted claims to represent Seattle on the night of June 8. Antifa rioters claim to have taken over the "Capitol Hill Free Zone (Protester Occupied Seattle)" in yellow. The zone includes the "Captured Regime East Precinct (Abandoned Police Station with doors left unlocked lol)," along with areas marked "Commune Food Stations," "CHAZ Commune Barricades," "Relaxation & Dining Field (food regularly handed out + coffee bar)," and a "Stoa (Informal Congregational Area)."

Ngo compared the situation to Portland in 2018 when Mayor Ted Wheeler allowed a similar Antifa "zone" to exist inside that city for five weeks. "Not only did it become a biohazard site w/intravenous drug abuse, the local businesses & residents were terrorized. Tax payers had to pay for the extensive cleanup."

Naturally, the mayor made tremendous concessions to the rioters even while claiming she would keep the area safe. But Ngo has made no concession with his reporting, and because of he has been forced to leave the United States after enduring credible death threats from Antifa domestic terrorists over the course of many months.

Ngo made the shocking announcement that he has relocated to London on Jan 27, 2021 during a recent appearance on Sky News. He explained how Antifa's reign of terror forced him to leave his home of Portland, Oregon and then the country to protect his safely.

"For a number of months now there's just been increasing threats of violence against me, promises by Antifa extremists to kill me," Ngo said about his ordeal.

Credit: Politico. Journalist Al Letson jumps on and protects a Trump supporter pleading with Antifa to stop beating him.

13 – Democratic Controlled Cities, Riots, Chaos & Radical Mayhem

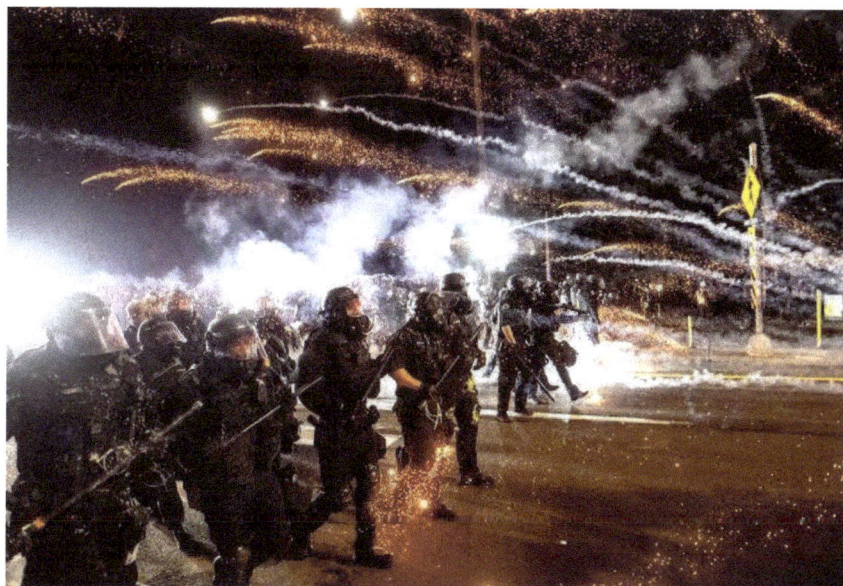

Credit: Noah Berger/AP. Police use chemical irritants and crowd control munitions to disperse protesters during ongoing demonstrations in Portland 2020.

The majority of murders in the U.S. occur in only a small percentage of counties across the country. The Crime Prevention Research Center (CPRC) said in a new report that there is a "geographical concentration" of murders, with 68 percent of killings occurring in just 5 percent of the nation's counties. The homicides also tend to be concentrated to relatively small pockets of those counties, the report said.

In a report titled "US murders concentrated in 5 percent of counties" by Perry Chiaramonte of Fox News in April 2017, her guest John Lott, president of the CPRC said to Fox News states: "It is stunning how concentrated murders are in the U.S. And we show that even within these counties, with all these high rates, murders are very concentrated." "These high [rate] counties have very large areas where there are no murders."

In 2014, the U.S. murder rate was 4.4 per 100,000 people, according to the data of the report. If the deadliest 5 percent of the counties were removed, the U.S. murder rate would be 2.56 per 100,000 people, the report showed. More than half of last year's murders occurred in only 2 percent of the nation's counties. If these counties were removed from the totals, the US murder rate would drop by almost half!

Looking at the historical data, the CPRC said that murders were even more geographically concentrated in decades past. On average, 73 percent of counties in any given year had zero murders from 1977 to 2000. The majority of counties with zero murder rates were in the suburbs or rural areas. However, dissecting the counties with a high number of murders, the data revealed the following:

- Los Angeles County, which had 526 murders in 2014—the most of any other county in the U.S. But parts of L.A. County, including Beverly Hills, Hawthorne, and Van Nuys, had virtually no murders that year.

- Indianapolis, Indiana had 135 murders but only four occurred outside of the 465 highway loop that encircles the downtown area.

- Washington, D.C. has large swaths without a single recorded murder. The study found that murders were overwhelmingly limited to the eastern half of Washington, D.C.

One of the most interesting findings in the report is that areas with the highest gun ownership rates have low murder rates. "While many factors explain these concentrated murders, it is also striking that the counties with zero murders are the counties with by far the highest gun ownership rates," Lott said.

The report's authors also looked at numbers from a 2013 Pew Research Center survey, which found that the household gun ownership rate in rural areas was over two times greater than in urban areas. That study also found that suburban homeowners are 28 percent more likely to own guns than urban dwellers.

Liberal Cities, Radical Mayhem

The Editorial Board of *The Wall Street Journal* reported in June 2020: Many 2020 Democratic mayors and governors seem unable to stop the destruction of their own cities when they allowed rioters exploiting the memory of George Floyd run wild in the streets. Even after nearly a week of violence, they let lawless radicals harass and plunder almost at will.

In downtown St. Louis, four police officers were shot after midnight. "I believe some coward randomly shot at the police line," said police chief John Hayden. A 7-Eleven was looted and set afire, but firefighters were deliberately slowed by protesters in responding. "We had people lying down in the street" and trash cans were placed as obstacles to block fire trucks, said fire chief Dennis Jenkerson.

In Philadelphia, city of brotherly vandals, gangs of rioters rolled through several neighborhoods Sunday burning businesses and cars. They returned for more the next day, shutting down the highway that bisects the city at evening rush hour.

Police Commissioner Danielle Outlaw said a crowd of more than 100 surrounded a lone state trooper inside a vehicle and began rocking it. When two SWAT teams arrived, the crowd pelted them with rocks from the road and above. Police had to fire spray pellets, bean bags and tear gas to escape.

At first Mayor Jim Kenney backed the police. But days later was tweeting that "there may have been additional uses of tear gas. I am deeply concerned by this development. All of these incidents will be investigated by Internal Affairs." Police are threatened by a mob, the officers defend themselves by non-lethal means, and the mayor wants to investigate the police. No wonder rioters feel they can do whatever they want.

In New York City, hoodlums rampaged through Herald Square and the flagship Macy's store, Fordham Road in the Bronx, Times Square and SoHo, among other places. Nearly every storefront on lower Fifth Avenue was vandalized. A cop was struck and injured by a hit-and-run driver in the Bronx. This isn't protest. It's anarchy.

Gov. Andrew Cuomo had set an 11 p.m. curfew but somehow managed not to enforce it. TV cameras showed gangs of youths working as teams to loot one store, then move on to another. Overwhelmed police could do little more than wave their clubs and hope to catch one or two as they sprinted past on their way to their next target.

The NYPD has some 36,000 officers. How could they not be deployed in enough numbers to contain this rampage? And how can these public officials not deploy the National Guard to assist the police in restoring public order and protecting the innocent? This wasn't the first night of mayhem. It was the fourth in a row, and the police clearly knew what could happen. The only explanation is that Cuomo and Bill de Blasio lack the political will to stop it.

This isn't merely about damage to property. It's about destroying the order required for city life. Non-criminals are afraid to go into these cities to make a living. The police pull back from active policing, which creates more opportunity for criminals, especially in poor and minority neighborhoods. Businesses that are finally starting to emerge from government lockdowns have new costs to absorb and more reasons for customers not to return.

What Do These Cities Have in Common?

What all these cities have in common is that they are led by Democrats who seem to have bought into the belief that the police are a bigger problem than rampant disorder. They are either cowed by their party's left, or they agree that America is systemically racist, and rioting is a justified expression of anger against it. They offer pro forma disapproval of law breakers but refuse to act to stop them.

They should recognize that widespread lawlessness is not helping their cause. Americans have the right to protest, peacefully, and the killing of George Floyd in police custody is cause for anger and grief. But as the violence continues, Americans of goodwill will support the police and a return to safe streets as the highest priority. Police reform and social injustice will get a smaller hearing.

Public officials need to deploy enough police and National Guard to stop the mayhem. They need to channel the peaceful demonstrations by time and place, as American law allows, so agitators can't use them to attack police to create violent confrontations. If they can't or won't do that, these Democrats will be complicit in destroying their own cities and harming the very people they claim to speak for.

And of those cities, which ones are the deadliest for blacks? The Trace, an independent nonprofit news organization, answers that question. Using 2017 data from the FBI's Uniform Crime Reporting program, The Trace listed the 20 major U.S. cities with the highest homicide rates—factoring in both the number of people murdered in cities and their populations. Chicago, with 589 murders in 2018—one murder every 15 hours—is often called the nation's murder capital. In 2017, the top three were:

- In 2017, St. Louis had the nation's highest murder rate, at 66.1 homicides per 100,000 residents.

- Baltimore came in second, with 55.8 murders per 100,000 people.

- Detroit was third, with 39.8 murders per 100,000 people.

Other cities with high murder rates included New Orleans; Kansas City, Missouri; Cleveland; Memphis, Tennessee; and Newark, New Jersey. With 24.1 murders per 100,000 residents, Chicago ranked ninth in the nation. It was followed by Cincinnati and Philadelphia, and Washington, D.C., was 17th.

Now here's the kicker. Of the 20 most dangerous major cities, all but one had a Democratic mayor. In many of these cities, the Democratic Party has ruled for a half-century or more. Only Tulsa, Oklahoma, with 17.3 murders per 100,000 residents, had a Republican mayor.

Who knows what conclusion can be drawn from the finding that the most murderous cities have been controlled by Democrats—and often black Democrats? The Editorial Board of *The Wall Street Journal* is not suggesting that Democratic control causes murder and mayhem. What they're saying is that murder, mayhem, and other violent crime are not reduced by the election of black or white Democrats to run our cities.

Violent Crime is Not the Only Problem In Our Major Cities

Mostly because of high crime, poor schools, and a less pleasant environment, cities are losing their economic base and their most productive people (of all colors) in droves. Below is a list of major American cities and their population decline:

- When World War II ended, Washington, D.C.'s population was about 900,000; today it's about 694,000.

- In 1950, Baltimore's population was almost 950,000; today it's around 612,000.

- Detroit's 1950 population was close to 1.85 million; today it's down to 673,000.

- Camden, New Jersey's 1950 population was nearly 125,000; today it has fallen to 75,000.

- St. Louis' 1950 population was more than 856,000; today it's less than 309,000.

A similar story of population decline can be found in most of our formerly large and prosperous cities. In some cities, the population decline since 1950 is well over 50 percent. In addition to Detroit and St. Louis, those would include Cleveland and Pittsburgh.

During the 1960s and '70s, academic liberals, civil rights advocates and others blamed the exodus on racism—"white flight" to the suburbs to avoid blacks. And more recently, the same "white" flight argument was expounded by Michelle Obama. However, since the '70s, blacks have been fleeing some cities at higher rates than whites.

The five cities whose suburbs have the fastest-growing black populations are Miami, Dallas, Washington, Houston, and Atlanta. It turns out—and reasonably so—that blacks, like whites, want better and safer schools for their kids and don't like to be mugged or have their property vandalized. And just like the case with white people, if they have the means, black people can't wait to leave troubled cities.

It's a Mayor's Policies, Not Politics—That Influence Crime Rates

Despite former President Trump's assertions, a mayor's political affiliation has nothing to do with a city's crime rate. But experts say crime trends are not beyond mayoral control. Homicides are up 29% in cities with Democratic mayors, and 26% in cities with Republican mayors compared to the same time frame in 2019, according to one analysis.

Trump's claims tying a crime spike in cities to Democratic leadership have become commonplace during the election season. But experts say political affiliation does not matter when it comes to crime "trends" anyway, and data backs this up. Analysis by Jeff Asher, a crime analyst and *New York Times* contributor, shows that while the homicide rate is spiking in the U.S., it's rising similarly in both Democrat and Republican led cities.

But while experts say that pinning a spike (i.e., crime trend) in violence on a mayor's political affiliation is wrong, they do agree that mayors have the power to institute policies that can control crime rates. The key is to better understand why violent crime is increasing–which it appears to be doing in much of the country.

Trump added, "We have a record positive rating on crime, a record positive rating on crime this year. The best. You hear about certain places like Chicago and you hear about what's going on in Detroit and other cities, all Democrat-run. Every one of them is Democrat-run. The 20 worst, the 20 most dangerous are Democrat-run."

A quick fact check shows that Trump is at least mostly correct. One ranking says the top 20 most dangerous cities are run by 18 Democrat mayors and two mayors who were elected in nonpartisan races. According to the website Neighborhood Scout, which in January published a list of the 100 most dangerous cities in America, heavily Democrat Detroit tops the list. At No. 20 is Chester, Pennsylvania, also with a Democrat mayor.

Trump went on to refer to the so-called autonomous zone in central Seattle, where extremists have taken over six city blocks. "We have one city, two cities in particular, worse than Honduras, worse than Afghanistan. These are cities within the United States, Democrat-run. Radical left-run. You see what's going on in Seattle. Seattle of all places, who would even think that's possible," he said.

"The Democrats want to weaken very substantially our law enforcement, our police," Trump added. "Frankly, they want to defund [police departments], at least largely. Some want to defund and abolish our police. If nothing happens with [police reform], it's one of those things. We had different philosophies. They want open borders. They want sanctuary cities. We don't.

Minneapolis Effect?

A September 2020 report for the Council on Criminal Justice, for example, found that homicides and aggravated assaults started to rise in late May 2020 after the tragic death of George Floyd in Minneapolis. Homicide rates specifically increased by more than 50% between June and August compared to the same period last year. The report studied crime data between January 2017 and August 2020 from 27 cities with populations greater than 250,000—20 of which provided statistics on homicides.

For many mayors, however, discovering why violent crime is spiking can prove challenging. However, cities with larger than average gang populations seem to be more prone. Furthermore, "The root causes of violence tend to happen in cities where there's issues of poverty and education systems," says Kirby Gaherty, a program manager for justice reform and youth engagement at the National League of Cities, an advocacy organization representing cities, towns, and villages.

Neighborhood Scout Ranking of the Most Crime-Ridden Cities and Their Mayors

Credit: Reddit. Camden, New Jersey.

NeighborhoodScout.com puts out a yearly report of the 100 most dangerous cities in America with populations of 25,000 or more, based on the number of violent crimes per 1,000 residents. Violent crimes include murder, rape, armed robbery, and aggravated assault. The data used for this research are the number of violent crimes reported to have occurred in each city, and the population of each city.

There are some newcomers to the list in 2020. Atlantic City, New Jersey creeps back into the list at ninety-nine with a 16% year-over-year increase in its violent crime rate. Dallas, TX, the 9th largest city in the U.S., appears on the list for the first time at number eighty-nine with a violent crime rate of 8.7 per 1,000. This is an increase of 13% compared to the previous year. Spartanburg, South Carolina a historic Revolutionary War city, is the newcomer with the highest violent crime rate of 12.0 per 1,000 population.

See the complete dangerous U.S. cities list in the Appendix link. For the 20 most crime-ridden cities and their mayors the list is below from worst to least-worst:

1. Detroit: Violent crime rate (per 1,000 residents): 20.0 Odds of being a victim: 1 in 50 Mayor: Michael Edward Duggan, Democrat.

2. Memphis, Tennessee: Violent crime rate (per 1,000 residents): 19.5 Odds of being a victim: 1 in 51 Mayor: Jim Strickland, Democrat.

3. Birmingham, Alabama: Violent crime rate (per 1,000 residents): 19.3 Odds of being a victim: 1 in 52 Mayor: Randall Woodfin, Democrat.

4. Baltimore: Violent crime rate (per 1,000 residents): 18.5 Odds of being a victim: 1 in 54 Mayor: Jack Young, Democrat.

5. Flint, Michigan: Violent crime rate (per 1,000 residents): 18.3 Odds of being a victim: 1 in 55 Mayor: Sheldon Neely, Democrat.

6. St. Louis: Violent crime rate (per 1,000 residents): 18.2 Odds of being a victim: 1 in 55 Mayor: Lyda Krewson, Democrat.

7. Danville, Illinois: Violent crime rate (per 1,000 residents): 18.0 Odds of being a victim: 1 in 55 Mayor: Ricky Williams Jr. (nonpartisan election).

8. Saginaw, Michigan: Violent crime rate (per 1,000 residents): 16.7 Odds of being a victim: 1 in 60 Mayor: Floyd Kloc (nonpartisan election).

9. Wilmington, Delaware: Violent crime rate (per 1,000 residents): 16.3 Odds of being a victim: 1 in 61 Mayor: Mike Purzycki, Democrat.

10. Camden, New Jersey: Violent crime rate (per 1,000 residents): 16.2 Odds of being a victim: 1 in 62 Mayor: Francisco Moran, Democrat.

11. Pine Bluff, Arkansas: Violent crime rate (per 1,000 residents): 16.0 Odds of being a victim: 1 in 62 Mayor: Shirley Washington, Democrat.

12. Kansas City, Missouri: Violent crime rate (per 1,000 residents): 15.9 Odds of being a victim: 1 in 63 Mayor: Quinton Lucas, Democrat.

13. San Bernardino, California: Violent crime rate (per 1,000 residents): 15.3 Odds of being a victim: 1 in 65 Mayor: John Valdivia, Democrat.

14. Alexandria, Louisiana: Violent crime rate (per 1,000 residents): 14.6 Odds of being a victim: 1 in 68 Mayor: Jeffrey Hall, Democrat.

15. Little Rock, Arkansas: Violent crime rate (per 1,000 residents): 14.6 Odds of being a victim: 1 in 68 Mayor: Frank Scott Jr., Democrat.

16. Cleveland: Violent crime rate (per 1,000 residents): 14.5 Odds of being a victim: 1 in 69 Mayor: Frank Jackson, Democrat.

17. Milwaukee: Violent crime rate (per 1,000 residents): 14.3 Odds of being a victim: 1 in 70 Mayor: Tom Barrett, Democrat.

18. Stockton, California: Violent crime rate (per 1,000 residents): 14.2 Odds of being a victim: 1 in 70 Mayor: Michael Tubbs, Democrat.

19. Monroe, Louisiana: Violent crime rate (per 1,000 residents): 14.1 Odds of being a victim: 1 in 71 Mayor: James Earl Mayo, Democrat.

20. Chester, Pennsylvania: Violent crime rate (per 1,000 residents): 14.0 Odds of being a victim: 1 in 71 Mayor: Thaddeus Kirkland, Democrat.

Chaos: Three Dem Controlled Cities As "Anarchist Jurisdictions'

Maybe the word chaos can represent a new acronym: Cities Having Abusive & Obsolete Security? Regardless, Chris Donaldson's September 2020 article "AG Barr To Designate Three Dem Controlled Cities As "Anarchist Jurisdictions'" adds more fuel to the fire of anarchist jurisdictions.

Per Donaldson, in an effort to quell the violence and rioting that erupted this summer {2020} and which has been tacitly sanctioned by Democrats and the media, Attorney General William Barr is preparing to focus efforts on major hot spots. According to a bombshell report, the nation's top law enforcement official is designating three Democrat-controlled cities as "anarchist jurisdictions" for the failure of their elected leaders to protect citizens and property and to stop rioting.

The cities that are set to be branded as "anarchist jurisdictions" are Bill de Blasio's New York City, Ted Wheeler's Portland, and Jenny Durkan's Seattle, all of which have failed to bring a halt to the mayhem. The designation would result in the loss of federal money at a time when the rioting and lockdowns imposed using the coronavirus as an excuse have decimated their economies and blown holes in city budgets.

"When state and local leaders impede their own law-enforcement officers and agencies from doing their jobs, it endangers innocent citizens who deserve to be protected, including those who are trying to peacefully assemble and protest," Barr said in a statement to the press.

"We cannot allow federal tax dollars to be wasted when the safety of the citizenry hangs in the balance," the AG added. "It is my hope that the cities identified by the Department of Justice today will reverse course and become serious about performing the basic function of government and start protecting their own citizens."

President Trump requested that Barr review the cities' status and apply the designation in a memo that was issued earlier in September. A statement from the Justice Department is expected will send a strong message to Dem mayors who refuse to enforce the law. In Ted Wheeler's case, Portland has all but given the key to the city to Antifa, a brutal pack of organized goons that serve as the Democratic party's paramilitary wing.

Barr has been increasingly critical of the ongoing violence and lack of response and has singled out Antifa who he referred to as a "ramrod of violence" during an interview with CNN's Wolf Blitzer.

U.S. Attorney General William Barr said the Justice Department was monitoring the protest movement Antifa, saying that it is at the heart of violence in cities around the country. "I've talked to every police chief in every city where there has been major violence and they all have identified Antifa as the ramrod for the violence," Barr said in an interview with CNN's Wolf Blitzer. "They are flying around the country. We know people who are flying around the country."

"We see some of the purchases they are making before the riots of weapons to use in those riots," Barr added. "So, we are following them." President Trump and federal law enforcement have repeatedly offered carrots to the Democrat mayors to get the violence under control, but they refused—now it is time for the stick.

Worst Mayors in America Demand Congress Stop Trump From Ruining Their Riots

Driving this point home, PJ Media reporter Victoria Taft's incendiary July 2020 report "Worst Mayors in America Demand Congress Stop Trump From Ruining Their Riots" cannot be understated as follows:

The nation's worst mayors, who oversee the nation's most violent cities, sent a letter to Congress complaining that President Trump is ruining their election-year riots. They're calling for an investigation into federal officers arresting rioters for attacking federal buildings.

The mayors of Portland, Seattle, Chicago, D.C., Atlanta, and Kansas City wrote to the leaders of Congress arguing that their nightly riots and bloodshed are made worse by President Trump because federal police aren't nice to the rioters.

Whereas the mayor of Portland, who's also the police commissioner, orders his kneeling officers to spectate the violence, the federal police used tear gas to back the rioters away from federal property, investigate, arrest, and charge the perpetrators of the violence.

As you know, Portland is in its 8th straight week of rioting. Antifa and Black Lives Matter groups, comprised of devoutly anti-American, communist and anarchist militants, hold nightly riots to burn, vandalize and terrorize Portlanders. It's a low-level war on civil society by groups that are revealed as the shock troops of the Democratic Party. No high-profile Democrats condemn their actions. In fact, Nancy Pelosi dismisses the attacks on statues as "people are going to do what they do."

During the sixth week, as Antifa and BLM terrorists continued their attacks on the Mark O. Hatfield United States Courthouse in downtown Portland, federal officers were called in to protect the building and arrest rioters. Now Mayor Ted Wheeler blames President Trump for all the riots.

Democrat Mayors Say Riots Are Trump's Fault

Taft continues with her satire: While the riots continue, instead of catching, releasing, and dropping charges against rioters, as Multnomah County prosecutors do, federal authorities have brought federal charges against the terrorists, who have come from all over the country to riot and attack police.

In their complaint letter to Congress, Mayors Muriel Bowser (D.C.), Jenny Durkan (Seattle), Keisha Lance Bottoms (Atlanta), Lori Lightfoot (Chicago), Quinton D. Lucas (Kanas City) and Ted Wheeler (Portland) accuse President Trump of abuse of power because he's "creating an environment of fear and mistrust."

The murder of George Floyd in Minneapolis sparked a national uprising and reckoning. Millions have joined protests and exercised their constitutional rights. The majority of the protests have been peaceful and are aimed at improving our communities. Even in circumstances where this is not the case, it is still a matter for local law enforcement.

The President's decision to unilaterally deploy these paramilitary type forces into our cities mirrors the very tyranny our country has fought against and is wholly inconsistent with our democracy.

Instead, he is politicizing conflict, creating an environment of fear and mistrust, and raising the prospect of more deployments of federal forces in cities like Seattle, Chicago, and other American communities. This abuse of power cannot continue.

The letter does not address the "fear and mistrust" that the lack of leadership from the above-stated mayors have caused in law-abiding people who hate the nightly riots by domestic terrorists and who do not consider professional rioters creating havoc as a "reckoning."

The letter never refers to the federal officers as police, but calls them "forces," "agents," and "paramilitary," in an effort to cast them as something other than police officers. In a gobsmacking tweet, Senator Ron Wyden called the police from DHS and Border Patrol "secret police" in order to smear the officers enforcing the law.

The computer hacking arm of the Antifa terror group has outed the names and addresses of federal officers responding to the riots to encourage violence and intimidation against them. Federal Protective Service (FPS) Deputy Director of Operations Richard Cline said at a press conference that approximately 38 law enforcement officers had been doxed as he explained why officers had had name badges removed.

"We are going to convert their name [tags] to their badge number as about 38 of our officers that are out there have been doxed and their personal information has been put online," he said. The Antifa computer hackers also previously outed local police officers on a spreadsheet. This occurred before federal officers arrived.

Taft's satirical—but logical parody continues:

Chicago Mayor Lori Lightfoot who, as PJ Media colleague Megan Fox calls "the world's worst mayor," presides over a city in which there are hot-and-cold-running shootings on a daily basis.

PJ Media's Rick Moran writes about the latest attack in which 15 people were shot while attending a funeral for a shooting victim. But Lightfoot vows never-will-she-ever allow Donald Trump to send federal "troops" to her fair and peaceful city to "terrorize" citizens. Apparently, she doesn't want the competition.

Seattle Mayor Jenny Durkan, who allowed a "summer of love" occupation to be set up in the swanky Capitol Hill section of her city that ended with two murders and multiple shootings, believes President Trump is the big problem. While the mayors try to sell the idea that President Trump has no standing to send in troops, I explain over here that, naturally, the feds have every right to plus-up police to protect, defend and investigate federal crimes.

Washington, D.C., Mayor Muriel Bowser, who literally presides over a city that is explicitly federal property says, "All extraordinary federal law enforcement and military presence needs to be withdrawn from American cities @realDonaldTrump." Apparently, stopping rioters from destroying federal property is considered "extraordinary."

And on it goes. The letter has gained a few more signatories, such as L.A. Mayor Eric Garcetti, who presided over coronavirus-exploding riots himself. The message from these mayors is: President Trump, don't interrupt our riots. Our base will get mad at us.

14 – Gangs, Sanctuary Cities, States & Sympathizers vs. Federal Laws

Credit: FBI. NY FBI SWAT with MS-13 suspects in custody.

Gangs in the United States include several types of groups, including national street gangs, local street gangs, prison gangs, motorcycle clubs, and ethnic and organized crime gangs. Approximately 1.4 million people were part of gangs as of 2011, and more than 33,000 gangs were active in the United States.

As of 2011, the National Gang Intelligence Center found that American gangs were found to be responsible for "an average of 48% of violent crime in most jurisdictions and up to 90% in several others." Major urban areas and their suburban surroundings experience the majority of gang activity, particularly gang-related violent crime. Gangs are known to engage in traditionally gang-related gambling, drug trafficking, and arms trafficking, white collar crime such as counterfeiting, identity theft, and fraud, and non-traditional activity of human trafficking and prostitution.

Many American gangs began in major cities such as New York City (Bronx), Detroit and Chicago but they later grew in other American cities like Albuquerque and Washington, D.C. The earliest

American street gangs emerged at the end of the American Revolutionary War in the early 1780s. However, these early street gangs had questionable legitimacy, and more serious gangs did not form until at least the early 1800s. and the earliest of these serious gangs formed, particularly in New York.

Youth gang members often are actively involved in drug use, drug trafficking, and violence. Although drug use is strongly associated with drug trafficking and drug selling is strongly associated with other serious and violent crimes, gang drug trafficking does not necessarily cause more frequent violent offending. Rather, gang participation, drug trafficking, and violence occur together.

Gangs Are a Key Element in Crime in the United States

Gangs can be categorized based on their ethnic affiliation, their structure, or their membership. Many of these gangs are highly sophisticated and organized, using violence for control. Illegal moneymaking activities include robbery, gun and drug trafficking, fraud, white-collar crime, extortion, and prostitution. Gangs also exploit the most advanced technologies and social media for recruitment, communication, targeting enemies, and advancing criminal activities.

The National Gang Intelligence Center on the FBI site states:

- Gangs are responsible for about 48 percent of violent crime in most jurisdictions and up to 90 percent in others.

- Gangs are increasingly becoming engaged in alien smuggling, human trafficking, and prostitution as well as counterfeiting, identity theft, and mortgage fraud.

- Family members assist with gang activities during a gang member's incarceration.

- Gang infiltration of the U.S. military involves at least 53 gangs identified on domestic and international installations.

- Gang members often acquire high-powered, military-style weapons, posing serious threats to law enforcement and communities.

- Gangs encourage members, associates, and relatives to obtain law enforcement, judiciary, or legal employment in order to gather information on rival gangs and law enforcement operations.

Gang Activity is an Epicenter of Violence in America

Tracking gang statistics and trends can help to assess the demographics of gangs in the U.S., including age range, prevalence, location, and types of crime associated with gangs. This information can help to target prevention initiatives and interventions and determine youth at risk for gang involvement. Some compelling gang statistics are:

- Although gang activity in the U.S. showed a decline in the mid 1990's to 2000, it increased from 2001 to 2005 and has since remained constant. Over the past decade, annual estimates of the number of gangs have averaged about 25,000 nationally and the number of gang members has been about 750,000.2

- In 2009, larger cities and suburban counties accounted for the majority of gang-related violence and more than 96 percent of all gang homicides.3

- During 2009-2012, cities with 100,000 or more persons saw gang-related homicides increase by 13 percent.4

- In Chicago and Los Angeles, nearly half of all homicides were attributed to gang violence from 2009-2012.5

The demographic characteristics of gang members are typically:

- Between 1998 and 2009, gang members were overwhelmingly male with less than ten percent of total gang members being female. Learn more about the involvement of girls in gangs and juvenile delinquency.

- While the majority of gang members are adults, as of 2008, two out every five gang members are under 18, as reported by law enforcement.6

- The prevalence of youth under 18 in gangs is higher in smaller cities and rural communities where gang problems are less established, compared to larger cities.7

Between 1996 and 2008, gang members were more likely to be Hispanic/Latino and African-American/black than other race/ethnicities. Specifically they reported gang members were 50 percent Hispanic or Latino, 32 percent African American, 10 percent Caucasian, and 8 percent identifying as another race or ethnicity. In the early 19th century, U.S. gangs were primarily Irish, Jewish, and Italian.

The Sanctuary City Debate

The election of Donald Trump as President in 2016 reignited a key debate about American immigration policy. Do illegal aliens commit crimes at a higher rate than native-born U.S. citizens and lawful immigrants? And, if so, how should that influence any proposed changes to our immigration system?

Advocates of open borders are fond of claiming that illegal aliens commit fewer crimes than native-born U.S. citizens and cite many reports and studies backing this claim. That makes perfect sense, they assert, because illegal aliens do not wish to be brought to the attention of law enforcement and risk deportation from the United States. In reality, however, this is a weak argument, and the studies are questionable.

While the Trump administration has taken unlawful migration seriously, most illegal aliens still have little to fear. The vast majority of recent enforcement efforts have been directed at narrow groups of individuals who fit a specific profile, e.g. gang members, those working without authorization, etc. And, as the protests following President Trump's rescission of the Deferred Action for Childhood Arrivals (DACA) program clearly demonstrate, many illegal aliens feel perfectly comfortable announcing their unlawful status and making demands of the United States government. Hence, their motto, "Undocumented and unafraid!"

Nevertheless, despite evidence to the contrary, open-borders advocates have persisted in their claims that fear of deportation means illegal aliens are inherently pre-disposed to avoiding criminal behavior. (This argument conveniently ignores the fact that improper entry by an alien is, in and of itself, a federal crime). Are these assertions legitimate?

Hard data indicate that they are not. Research conducted by the Federation for American Immigration Reform (FAIR) strongly suggests all claims that illegal aliens commit crimes at a lower rate than native-born U.S. citizens, or lawfully-present immigrants, are a myth. In fact, the February 2019 FAIR report by Matt O'Brien, Spencer Raley and Casey Ryan, titled "SCAAP Data Suggest Illegal Aliens Commit Crime at a Much Higher Rate Than Citizens and Lawful Immigrants" finds that in the states examined, illegal aliens are incarcerated up to five and a half times as frequently as citizens and legal immigrants.

A False Narrative, Based on Bad Data From Multiple Sources

As noted above, for decades, open-borders proponents have parroted the same narrative: "Illegal aliens commit less crime than native-born citizens." However, this claim typically rests on studies that manipulate data in order to support the fictitious "illegal aliens = less crime" narrative.

Why are the majority of studies of illegal alien criminality so flawed? First, as Peter Kirsanow, of *National Review* notes, "Illegal-immigrant crime calculations conveniently and invariably steal a base by leaving out the millions of crimes committed by illegal immigrants related to procuring fraudulent social security numbers, obtaining false drivers' licenses, using fraudulent green cards, and improperly accessing public benefits." That error is then compounded when researchers intentionally elect to leave out broad classes of crimes for example, drug offenses—as the Cato Institute frequently does.

Secondly, most federal, state, and local government agencies do not collect data on the rates at which illegal aliens are convicted of crimes. Most likely, this is due to political correctness, and a desire to keep the truth about the number of crimes committed by illegal aliens from coming to light.

Kirsanow is one of the few who has commented openly on this tendency. He states, "Unfortunately, almost every public official not named (former Trump Attorney General) Jeff Sessions guards against disclosure of illegal-immigrant crime data more tenaciously than disclosure of nuclear launch codes." Regardless of why this information is not collected, the end result is that there are a limited number of sources for obtaining data on crimes committed by known illegal aliens.

Finally, most researchers tend to ignore the few established sources that provide data on criminal acts by known illegal aliens. They point to all types of alleged, and typically baseless, "flaws" in this data, ranging from "limited sample size" to an inability to determine whether illegal aliens are being counted more than once. In actuality, however, the only real flaw, from the perspective of mainstream research organizations, is that examinations of data on criminal activity by known illegal aliens tend to establish that those who enter the U.S. in violation of our immigration laws also commit other crimes at a higher rate.

Per the FAIR report, this should not be surprising to anyone. The simple fact that illegal aliens violated American immigration laws—and must continuously violate other federal, state, and local laws in order to mask their ongoing illegal presence in this country—demonstrates a blatant lack of respect for the rule of law.

Sanctuary cities can be defined as municipal jurisdictions that limit their cooperation with the federal government's effort to enforce America's immigration laws. Implemented and defended by leading Democratic policy makers, open border advocates, and immigration attorneys, they provide safe harbor that prevents deportation for those in the country illegally.

Sanctuary policies contribute to the terrorization of immigrant communities by depriving the police of what on occasion may be their only immediate tool to remove a psychopathic gangster from the streets, sanctuary policies leave law-abiding immigrants defenseless against the social and financial devastation of crime and handicapped in the march up the economic ladder.

Taking immigration law seriously may make a start in combating these worrisome trends. The police should be given the option of reporting and acting on immigration violations, where doing so would contribute to public safety. The decision about when to use immigration rules will be a matter of discretion, but discretion is at the heart of all wise policing.

Sanctuary Cities Put Law-Abiding Citizens at Risk

Hans von Spakovsky of The Heritage Foundation is an authority on a wide range of issues— including civil rights, civil justice, the First Amendment, and immigration and his December 2015 report, "Sanctuary Cities Put Law-Abiding Citizens at Risk" as noted below:

San Francisco and other cities across the United States have created so-called "sanctuaries" for illegal aliens. These municipalities are defying federal immigration law, just like some Southern jurisdictions that defied federal civil rights laws in the 1960s. But unlike that earlier era, today's sanctuary cities are also creating safe havens for known criminals. Their policies have victimized innocent Americans, enabling illegal aliens to commit thousands of crimes that would not otherwise have occurred.

There is no question that sanctuary policies violate federal immigration law. One provision of the law (8 U.S.C. 1373) bans local governments from preventing law enforcement or other government officials from sharing information with the federal government on the "citizenship or immigration status, lawful or unlawful, of any individual."

So sanctuary policies such as those in San Francisco that ban local police officers from notifying the Department of Homeland Security when they arrest a criminal alien—or release him after he has served his sentence—are plainly illegal. Unfortunately, in keeping with its general non-enforcement policy regarding immigration law, the Obama administration announced in 2010 that it would not sue sanctuary cities for flouting the law.

Sanctuary Laws Defy the Will of the American People

Brian Lonergan is director of communications at the Immigration Reform Law Institute (IRLI), a public interest law firm working to defend the rights and interests of the American people from the negative effects. His December 2019 report "Sanctuary laws defy the will of the American people" raises a number of serious concerns as follows:

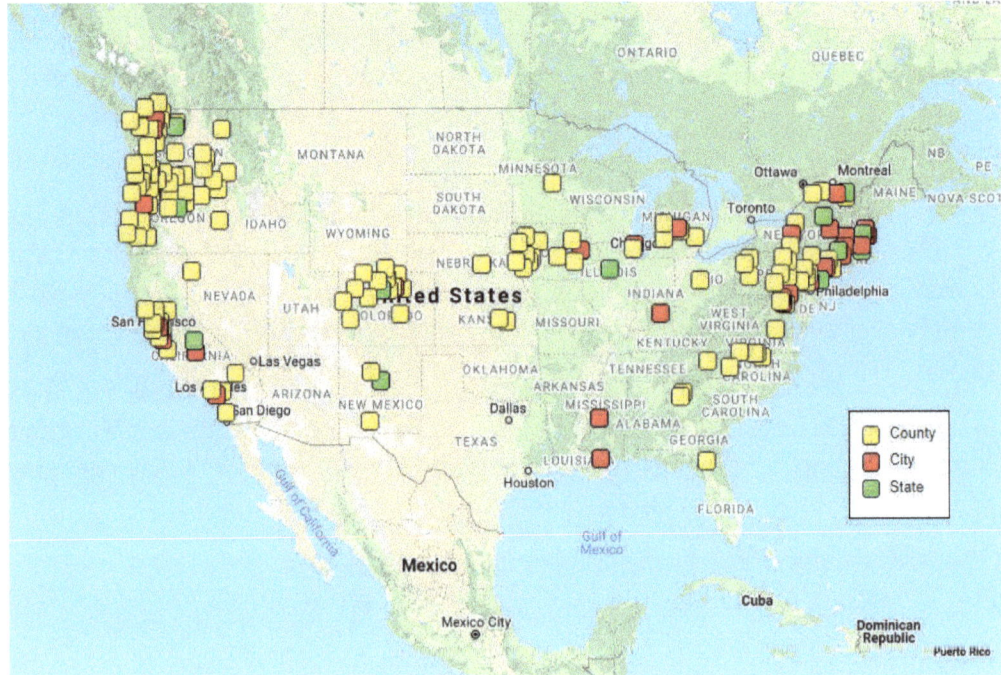

Credit: Center for Immigration Studies, Immigration and Customs Enforcement Data.

With a few exceptions, successful attempts to impose sanctuary laws on a community have largely come from the stroke of a pen by a governor, city council or county commissioner. Rarely is it from a groundswell of support from the voters, and for good reason.

Every selling point of sanctuary laws crumbles in the face of reality. We have been told that sanctuary laws make a community safer because illegal aliens will be unafraid to report crimes and cooperate with police investigations. Yet there is an abundance of cases where illegal aliens are arrested in sanctuary communities for shockingly violent crimes.

The very same month sanctuary laws were implemented in Montgomery County, Maryland, this summer, illegal aliens were arrested for a spree of sexual assault crimes. After a public uproar that included a vocal rally against the laws in the left-leaning Washington, D.C., suburb, the county announced it would reverse its anti-ICE policy.

Pro-sanctuary politicians talk about how the "welcoming" posture will encourage more aliens to speak to law enforcement about crimes. This is just more upside-down thinking. Instead of waiting for horrific crimes to occur and then hoping to get cooperation, the obvious and better alternative would be to simply prevent more violent aliens from settling in the community in the first place. That's not cruel, it's being a smart and effective public servant by acting in the best interests of your community.

The idea that sanctuary laws are fair and compassionate to aliens has also been exposed as fraudulent. Such laws attract more aliens, and they tend to cluster in dense communities. Inevitably, that population includes drug traffickers, sexual predators, and members of violent gangs like MS-13 who gravitate to the lenient law enforcement atmosphere. Those miscreants prey on the nearest available victims, most often nonviolent aliens living among them.

How Our Suburbs Are Under Attack From Illegal Immigrant 'Sanctuary' Laws

The rationale for cities and counties to provide "sanctuary" for illegal aliens falls apart under closer examination. Dale L. Wilcox is executive director and general counsel at the Washington, D.C.-based Immigration Reform Law Institute, a public interest law firm, tells us why:

Liberal politicians sell sanctuary laws to the public as a great benefit to their communities. If we obstruct federal immigration authorities in their mission to deport those here illegally, they say, we will have a safer, more welcoming community. They also say that immigrants will have less fear of law enforcement and, therefore, will be more willing to alert police and act as witnesses to criminal acts.

All of those claims are demonstrably false as noted by Wilcox in his September 2020 report in The Daily Signal titled "How Our Suburbs Are Under Attack From Illegal Immigrant 'Sanctuary' Laws."

Sanctuary laws serve as a beacon to attract aliens with criminal records and violent tendencies. Jose Inez Garcia Zarate, the five-times deported Mexican national whose actions resulted in the death of Kate Steinle on a San Francisco pier in 2015, told authorities he settled in the city because he was aware of its permissive sanctuary laws.

Others with bad intentions have similarly taken notice. America's worst sanctuary communities have a growing presence of violent gangs, such as MS-13, which recruit heavily among immigrant populations. Did the gangs select those communities by coincidence, or did they realize that sanctuary laws would allow them to commit rape, murder, drug trafficking, and other crimes with a buffer of protection from immigration enforcement?

Aside from the fact that many victims of crimes committed by illegal aliens are other illegal aliens, the claim that sanctuary laws breed greater immigrant cooperation with police is faulty. Immigration and Customs Enforcement (ICE) simply does not apprehend or deport anyone who gives it a tip on a criminal alien.

Nonetheless, county and city officials around the country have resorted to creative tactics to thwart ICE while denying they are sanctuary communities. In Fairfax County, officials require ICE to produce a criminal warrant signed by a judge or else they will not honor ICE detainer requests. There's one problem there. Immigration is a civil, not criminal, matter. Our immigration law provides no process for ICE to obtain a criminal warrant and Fairfax County knows it.

America's Ten Worst Sanctuary Communities

Calling attention to a grave threat to our country, the Immigration Reform Law Institute (IRLI) has released its list of America's Ten Worst Sanctuary Communities. Home cities of Reps. Pelosi, AOC, and Omar rank 1-2-3 on "List of Shame." Per the September 2019 report authored by Brian Lonergan:

Sanctuary policies often prohibit local law enforcement personnel from cooperating with requests from ICE to hold illegal aliens in police custody for possible deportation. These policies release dangerous foreign nationals into communities, often resulting in violence and even death.

"Sanctuary policies are absolute poison for America," said Dale L. Wilcox, executive director, and general counsel of IRLI. "They are unconstitutional—a violation of the Supremacy Clause—and threaten the integrity of our republic. More importantly, sanctuary policies bring violent crime and murder that is entirely preventable.

"Political leaders who advocate for and defend sanctuary policies are directly responsible for the lawlessness and human suffering they have inflicted on their communities. The law-abiding, legal residents of these communities need to know that their leaders have prioritized the interests of often violent illegal aliens over them."

"This is a list of shame," he added, and is shown below:

1 – San Francisco, California: Mayor: London Breed (Democrat)

2 – New York City, New York: Mayor: Bill de Blasio (Democrat)

3 – Minneapolis, Minnesota: Mayor: Jacob Frey (Democrat)

4 – Philadelphia, Pennsylvania: Mayor: Jim Kenney (Democrat)

5 – Seattle, Washington: Mayor: Jenny Durkan (Democrat)

6 – Chicago, Illinois: Mayor: Lori Lightfoot (Democrat)

7 – TIE: Montgomery County, Maryland and Fairfax County, Virginia:

- Montgomery County, Maryland: County Executive: Marc Elrich
- Fairfax County, Virginia: County Chair: Sharon Bulova; County Executive: Bryan Hill

8 – Prince George's County, Maryland: County Executive: Angela Alsobrooks

9 – Boston, Massachusetts: Mayor: Marty Walsh (Democrat)

10 – Santa Clara County, California: Board of Supervisors

Note: The data used for this report are the results of Freedom of Information Act (FOIA) requests by IRLI to ICE for records regarding the number of ICE detainers for criminal and illegal aliens ignored by law enforcement agencies for a 27-month period ending on December 31, 2017.

ICE classifies each detainer request as threat levels 1, 2, or 3 offenses. Threat level 1 and 2 offenses include but are not limited to, homicide, kidnapping, sexual assault, robbery, aggravated assault, drugs, burglary, fraud, and larceny. Level 3 offenses are other crimes, primarily misdemeanors.

'Sanctuary' California Failed to Honor Over 5,600 ICE Detainers

IRLI investigation shows state released detained aliens with previous convictions or pending criminal charges. Per another disturbing report by Brian Lonergan in February 2019, "'Sanctuary' California Failed to Honor Over 5,600 ICE Detainers" he notes the following:

An investigation by the Immigration Reform Law Institute (IRLI) has revealed that California law enforcement agencies have refused to honor a shocking number of immigration detainer requests for illegal aliens charged with serious felonies, an indictment of the state's deadly and unconstitutional sanctuary laws.

In response to a Freedom of Information Act lawsuit filed by IRLI, U.S. Immigration and Customs Enforcement (ICE) released records regarding law enforcement agencies that failed to honor ICE detainer requests. For a 27 month period ending on December 31, 2017, many California police and sheriff's departments refused to honor over 5,600 immigration holds, of which over 3,400 were classified by ICE as threat level 1 and 2 offenses. These included, but were not limited to, homicide, kidnapping, sexual assault, robbery, aggravated assault, drugs, burglary, and fraud.

IRLI is awaiting additional data from ICE, which would show how many illegal aliens charged with serious felonies were released from jail and later charged with additional crimes.

The California Values Act, Also Known as SB 54

The release of these illegal aliens came before passage of The California Values Act, also known as SB 54, which limits law enforcement's ability to cooperate and share immigration information with ICE. It is logical to conclude that refusals of ICE detainer requests and the release of aliens previously convicted of crimes or have pending criminal charges from police custody will only rise now that sanctuary policies are state law in California.

Per Lonergan: There is growing evidence that violent crime by illegal aliens is prevalent in jurisdictions with sanctuary policies. A recent example occurred recently during a routine traffic stop by Napa County Deputy Sheriff Riley Jarecki in which Javier Hernandez-Morales, a Mexican national and criminal alien, pulled a revolver and shot at the deputy at point-blank range. After Hernandez-Morales's bullet narrowly missed her, Deputy Sheriff Jarecki returned fire and killed him.

ICE confirmed that they had lodged four separate ICE detainer requests for Hernandez-Morales, three with the Napa County Sheriff's Office and the other with the Sonoma County Sheriff's Office after he had been arrested for battery on a peace officer, probation violations, driving under the influence, and selling liquor to a minor. ICE also confirmed that Hernandez-Morales had been deported three times.

Moreover, of the 5,600 immigration detainers placed against criminal and illegal aliens with California law enforcement agencies, 250 of those detainers were not honored by the Napa and

Sonoma County Sheriff's Offices and the aliens were released back into the community. Napa and Sonoma counties had been sanctuary counties prior to the passing of SB 54.

ICE further commented that this incident might had been prevented if ICE had been notified about any of the multiple times Hernandez-Morales was released from local custody over the last few years. This is an impactful, scary example of how public safety is affected by laws or policies limiting local law enforcement agencies' ability to cooperate with ICE.

The California Sheriffs' Association opposed SB 54 and issued a press release stating that the bill restricts communications with federal law enforcement about the release of wanted, illegal alien criminals from jails, including known gang members, repeat drunk drivers, persons who assault peace officers, serial thieves, animal abusers, and other serious offenders.

Sanctuary Cities Are Breaking Federal Laws

On January 25, 2017, Donald Trump carried through on a campaign promise and signed Executive Order 13768 which declared sanctuary jurisdictions across the United States to be in willful violation of Federal law. Attorney General Jeff Sessions promised to enforce it. Section 2(c) of the Order sets out to "ensure that jurisdictions that fail to comply with applicable Federal law do not receive Federal funds, except as mandated by law."

The Order also contained a list of types of illegal aliens that are to be "promptly" deported. These include aliens who:

- Have been convicted of any criminal offense.

- Have been charged with any criminal offense, where such charge has not been resolved.

- Have committed acts that constitute a chargeable criminal offense.

- Have engaged in fraud or willful misrepresentation in connection with any official matter or application before a governmental agency.

- Have abused any program related to receipt of public benefits.

- Are subject to a final order of removal, but who have not complied with their legal obligation to depart the United States; or

- In the judgment of an immigration officer, otherwise pose a risk to public safety or national security.

In response, the list of U.S. cities declaring that they are sanctuaries, which began growing even during the Obama administration, increased dramatically. There are now estimated to be nearly 300 such cities, counties and even states that have made such declarations. Several states are offering illegal aliens state driver's licenses. Going one step further, Chicago offered "undocumented" immigrants money for legal fees to fight federal deportation.

To see if your locality is a sanctuary, check the Appendix under Sanctuary Cities, Counties, and States—Center for Immigration Studies.

California Becomes a Sanctuary State

There is nothing unlawful in a city declaring itself a sanctuary city; the declaration is not the problem, the actions which may follow are. Usually, all a sanctuary city is asserting is that their city's resources will not be utilized in helping the federal government enforce federal law, something the Supreme Court has said the federal government cannot force a state or city to do (refusing to cooperate is called "anti-commandeering").

However, it is a federal felony, punishable by five years in prison for each violation, for any person to conceal, harbor, or shield from detection any illegal alien. The word "harbor" is defined as any conduct that tends to substantially facilitate an alien's remaining in the U.S. illegally.

The Supreme Court rejected arguments (in *Reno v. Condon*) that a state or local government's refusal to supply information requested by the federal government should be protected. Providing requested information was not seen by the court as "enforcing" a federal statute.

Furthermore, the 1996 Illegal Immigration Reform and Immigrant Responsibility Act prohibited any Federal, State, or local government entity or official from restricting any other government entity or official from sending to, or receiving from, the [Department of Homeland Security] information regarding the citizenship or immigration status, lawful or unlawful, of any individual." To get around this, sanctuary localities make it a point not to determine an apprehended person's immigrant status; they can't provide information they don't have, right? Sort of "Don't ask, don't ... ask?"

So it appears the sanctuary cities do not have much legal "wiggle room." They can't be forced to detain individuals at Immigration and Naturalization Services (INS) request; they can't be forced to apprehend illegal immigrants who have committed no other crime, but that's about it. They can be prosecuted for refusing to provide information on aliens in their custody, and they can be prosecuted for shielding aliens they do apprehend, provided they know the alien's status. But can the federal government withhold funds solely on the basis of a sanctuary declaration?

Trump DOJ Sues California Over Its Immigration and Sanctuary Policies

As reported by Warren Mass in *The New American* in March 2018: Attorney General Jeff Sessions delivered a speech at a gathering of the California Peace Officers Association in Sacramento in March 2018, during which he denounced officials who support so-called sanctuary city policies, describing them as "extremists" promoting "open borders.

Sessions had harsh words in particular for Oakland Mayor Libby Schaaf, who issued a public warning on Twitter on the night of February 24 that immigration raids in her city were upcoming. "[Schaaf's] actions support those who flout our laws and boldly validates illegality," Sessions said. "There's no other way to interpret those remarks."

"So here's my message to Mayor Schaaf: How dare you?" Sessions continued. "How dare you needlessly endanger the lives of law enforcement to promote an open borders agenda."

Sanctuary Schools Defy Immigration Enforcement

A growing number of school systems in multiple states are passing resolutions, declaring themselves "safe zones" for illegal-immigrant children, adding to the mounting, sanctuary-style resistance from scores of cities and counties to the enforcement of U.S. immigration law.

Outlined in the May 2017 *Newsmax* article "Sanctuary Schools Defy Immigration Enforcement by Jane Blakemore: As a matter of policy, many U.S. public-school systems only ask students for proof of residency, not for proof of citizenship.

The school systems' resistance to enforcement of federal immigration law appears to be taking a variety of forms. Some of the resolutions voice support for the Deferred Action for Childhood Arrivals (DACA), the de facto amnesty program advanced by the Obama administration. Others stipulate that schools will not permit.

Immigration and Customs Enforcement (ICE) officers on school premises unless they serve a warrant. Still other proposals restrict any response to ICE information requests regarding students or parents. Taken as a whole, the measures could complicate federal efforts to deport illegals with criminal backgrounds.

The organizations lobbying school boards to adopt the measures include Service Employees International Union (SEIU) union locals, teachers' unions, pro-immigrant coalitions, and local activist organizations.

According to the Center for Immigration Studies, immigrants are transforming U.S. public schools in several respects:

- In 2015, about 1 in 4 U.S. public school students came from an immigrant household, compared to 11 percent in 1990 and 7 percent in 1980.

- About 1 out of 4 student-immigrants has undocumented parents.

- Because immigrants tend to concentrate in certain areas, a typical immigrant student will live in an area where over 40 percent of their fellow public-school students also live in immigrant households.

- In 1980 , 9 percent of students spoke a language other than English at home. By 1990, that number raised to 14 percent, and in 2015 it reached 23 percent.

Furthermore, as reported in the August 2018 "Sanctuary Schools" Defy Immigration Crackdown" article by Colton R. Overcash in FAIR:

Public school districts are the latest group to join the sanctuary madness in America. (The school districts' actions are going beyond the law's requirement to educate all students regardless of their immigration status.) In a resounding rebuke of the Trump Administration and its immigration agenda, several school boards have recently declared their districts "safe havens" or "sanctuaries," meaning they offer protections to illegal aliens residing in the districts against deportation by Immigration and Customs Enforcement (ICE).

In California alone—where about 250,000 illegal alien children are enrolled in public schools and 750,000 have at least one illegal parent—over 113 school districts and county offices of education have declared themselves sanctuaries or safe havens for illegal aliens. Unfortunately, a majority of these districts have gone to extreme lengths with their sanctuary policies. Some districts will even "spread the word" to illegal aliens if ICE personnel are in the area, potentially inviting federal criminal charges against the school district under the alien smuggling/harboring statute (8 U.S. Code § 1324).

Educators, like everyone else, are of course entitled to their own opinions about the immigration laws of this country, but do not have the right to disregard them. They need to be cognizant of the message they are sending their students. Do school districts really have the authority to decide which federal laws they're going to obey and which ones they're going to ignore? Can the nation expect the next generation of Americans to follow its laws if those who are shaping their minds willfully ignore them?

15 – Illegal Immigrants vs. Crime Rates, Asylum & Birth Tourism

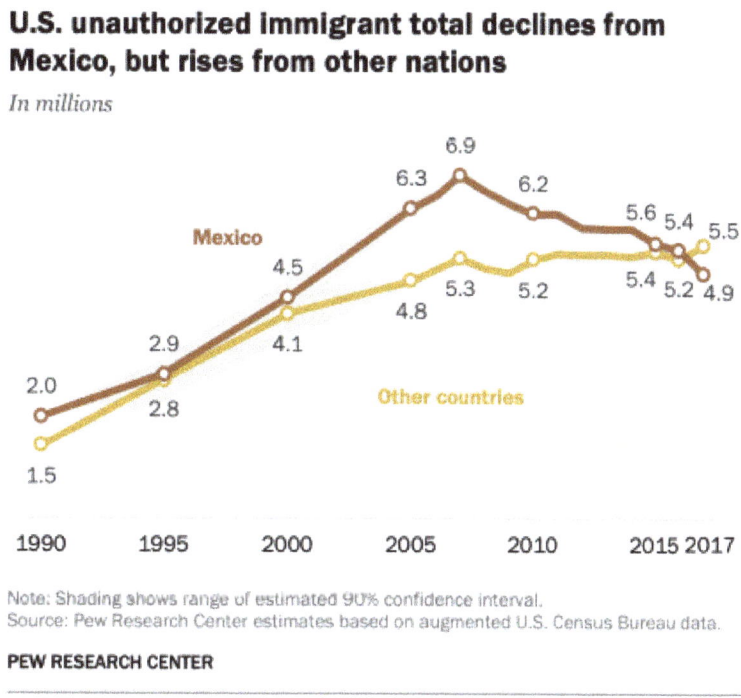

U.S. unauthorized immigrant total declines from Mexico, but rises from other nations

In millions

Mexico: 2.0 (1990), 2.9 (1995), 4.5 (2000), 6.3 (2005), 6.9, 6.2 (2010), 5.6, 5.4, 5.5, 4.9 (2017)

Other countries: 1.5 (1990), 2.8 (1995), 4.1 (2000), 4.8, 5.3 (2005), 5.2 (2010), 5.4, 5.2, 5.5 (2017)

1990   1995   2000   2005   2010   2015 2017

Note: Shading shows range of estimated 90% confidence interval.
Source: Pew Research Center estimates based on augmented U.S. Census Bureau data.

PEW RESEARCH CENTER

The Center for Immigration Studies (CIS) is an independent, non-partisan, non-profit research organization founded in 1985. It is the nation's only think tank devoted exclusively to research and policy analysis of the economic, social, demographic, fiscal, and other impacts of immigration on the United States.

In June 2004, the CIS website published a leading article from law enforcement expert Heather Mac Donald, a John M. Olin fellow at the Manhattan Institute and a contributing editor *to City Journal* titled "Crime and the Illegal Alien: The Fallout from Crippled Immigration Enforcement." Amongst her many findings and conclusions that cover the beginning of this chapter are as follows:

Prisons can easily determine the race and ethnicity of inmates but determining immigration status is harder because it is generally based on self-reporting. Convicted felons are not eager to admit they are not citizens because they could be deported after they are released. So-called sanctuary cities forbid local police departments even from asking prisoners about immigration status.

Despite the difficulty in determining immigrant crime rates, Hispanics have higher crime rates than the majority white population, and many immigrants are Hispanic. Legal immigrants are people whom the United States chooses to admit to its territory. If the selection process were perfect, no criminals would be admitted, and the immigrant crime rate would be zero. For immigrants to have even low crime rates reflects poorly on immigration policy.

Illegal immigrants are, by definition, not even selected, and there are only partial data on illegal immigrants, the crimes they commit, and where they are from. And speaking of definitions, the terms illegal alien, illegal immigrant, undocumented immigrant, unauthorized immigrant, are all used in this chapter.

The Department of Justice's State Criminal Alien Assistance Program (SCAAP) reimburses prisons and jails for the costs of holding illegal aliens. Prison systems must document the immigration status of inmates to get SCAAP payments—sanctuary jurisdictions choose to forego this subsidy. For this reason, and because the SCAAP data provides the most accurate statistical database for illegal aliens, it is used in the reports highlighted in this chapter.

Crime and Illegal Aliens

In a 2011 report, "Criminal Alien Statistics," the Government Accountability Office (GAO) studied the 249,000 illegal aliens for whom SCAAP funds were paid in 2009. It found that this group of aliens had been arrested a total of 1.7 million times— an average of roughly seven arrests per illegal alien inmate—and had been charged with 2.9 million separate offenses, or roughly 12 offenses each.

All told, these criminal aliens accounted for the following numbers of arrests for the following crimes:

- Homicides: 25,064
- Sex offenses: 69,929
- Assaults: 213,047

GAO found that about 66 percent of the SCAAP criminal illegal aliens in state prisons were born in Mexico and another 17 percent were born in the Dominican Republic, Guatemala, Honduras, El Salvador, Cuba, or Jamaica. Local jail inmates were even more heavily Mexican. Seventy percent were born in Mexico, while another 13 percent were from other Latin American countries.

The operating costs (prison staff salaries, medical care, food, utilities) of incarcerating these criminal illegal aliens in state prison systems totaled $7 billion for fiscal years 2003 through 2009. This figure obviously does not include the costs of incarcerating illegal aliens in sanctuary jurisdictions because those costs are unknown.

Per Mac Donald's report, in Los Angeles for example, dozens of gang members from a ruthless Salvadoran prison gang have snuck back into town after having been deported for such crimes as murder, shootings, and drug trafficking. Police officers know who they are and know that their mere presence in the country is a felony. Yet should an LAPD officer arrest an illegal gangbanger for felonious reentry, it is the officer who will be treated as a criminal by his own department—for violating the LAPD's rule against enforcing immigration law.

The LAPD's ban on immigration enforcement is replicated in immigrant-heavy localities across the country—in New York, Chicago, Austin, San Diego, and Houston, for example. These so-called "sanctuary policies" generally prohibit a city's employees, including the police, from reporting immigration violations to federal authorities.

Sanctuary laws are a testament to the political power of immigrant lobbies. So powerful is this demographic clout that police officials shrink from even mentioning the illegal alien crime wave. "We can't even talk about it," says a frustrated LAPD captain. "People are afraid of a backlash from Hispanics." Another LAPD commander in a predominantly Hispanic, gang-infested district sighs: "I would get a firestorm of criticism if I talked about [enforcing the immigration law against illegals]." Neither captain would speak Mac Donald, for attribution.

In 2003, the Immigration and Naturalization Service (INS) was broken up into three bureaus in the Department of Homeland Security (DHS): the Bureau of Immigration and Customs Enforcement (ICE); the Bureau of Customs and Border Protection (CBP); and U.S. Citizenship and Immigration Services (USCIS). Mac Donald's backgrounder report focuses on ICE, which is responsible for, among other things, enforcement of federal immigration laws in the interior of the United States.

A Safe Haven

The ordinarily tough-as-nails former LAPD Chief Daryl Gates enacted Special Order 40 in 1979—in response to the city's burgeoning population of illegal aliens—showing that even the most unapologetic law-and-order cop is no match for immigration demographics. The order prohibits officers from "initiating police action where the objective is to discover the alien status of a person."

In practice, this means that the police may not even ask someone they have arrested about his immigration status until after criminal charges have been entered. They may not arrest someone for immigration violations. Officers certainly may not check a suspect's immigration status prior to arrest, nor may they notify ICE about an illegal alien picked up for minor violations.

Per Mac Donald, only if an illegal alien has already been booked for a felony or multiple misdemeanors may they inquire into his status or report him to immigration authorities.

Los Angeles' sanctuary law, and all others like it, contradicts everything that has been learned about public safety in the 1990s. A key policing discovery of the last decade was the "great chain of being" in criminal behavior. Pick up a law-violator for a "minor" crime, and you'll likely prevent a major crime. Enforcing graffiti and turnstile-jumping laws nabs you murderers and robbers. Enforcing known immigration violations, such as reentry following deportation, against known felons would be even more productive.

LAPD officers recognize illegal deported gang members all the time—flashing gang signs at court hearings for rival gangbangers, hanging out on the corner, or casing a target. These illegal returnees are, simply by being in the country after deportation, committing a felony. "But if I see a deportee from the Mara Salvatrucha [Salvadoran prison] gang crossing the street, I know I can't touch him," laments a Los Angeles gang officer. Only if the deported felon has given the officer some other reason to stop him—such as an observed narcotics sale—can the officer accost him, and only for that non-immigration-related reason. The officer cannot arrest him for the immigration felony. Madness!

And no one has ever suggested not enforcing drug laws, say, for fear of intimidating drug-using crime victims. But in any case, the official rationale for sanctuary rules could be honored by limiting police utilization of immigration laws to some subset of immigration violators: deported felons, say, or repeat criminal offenders whose immigration status is already known to the police.

The real reason why cities prohibit their police officers and other employees from immigration reporting and enforcement is, like nearly everything else in immigration policy, the numbers. The population of illegal aliens and their legal brethren has grown so large that public officials are terrified of alienating them, even at the expense of annulling the law and tolerating avoidable violence.

Criminal Aliens Are Victimizing Americans

In 2011, the Government Accountability Office released a study on approximately 250,000 illegal aliens locked up in our federal, state, and local prisons. Those prisoners had been arrested nearly 1.7 million times and committed 3 million offenses, averaging about seven arrests and 12 offenses each. Their convictions ran the gamut from drug-dealing and sex crimes to kidnapping and murder.

Mac Donald, reports: California, Texas, and Arizona, which have large numbers of illegal aliens, have significant problems due to those aliens breaking the law. Indeed, an unreleased internal report by the Texas Department of Public Safety indicates that from 2008 to 2014, illegal aliens committed over 600,000 crimes—including nearly 3,000 homicides and almost 8,000 sexual assaults—in that state alone. No wonder Texas is leading 26 states in a lawsuit against the federal government that has so far successfully blocked Obama from implementing his 2014 immigration amnesty plan.

When local jurisdictions protect illegal aliens from law enforcement, they enable them to commit more crimes. Kathryn Steinle, a 32-year-old resident of San Francisco, would be alive today but for that city's sanctuary policy, she was murdered by an illegal alien who had previously committed seven felonies. The man who shot her in the back, Juan Francisco Lopez-Sanchez, had been released from custody by San Francisco after city officials decided not to prosecute him on a drug charge. They did not hand him over to U.S. Immigration and Customs Enforcement, even though the agency had filed an immigration detainer on him. Lopez-Sanchez stated in an interview that "he knew San Francisco was a sanctuary city where he would not be pursued by immigration officials."

It was an all-too-familiar story. In 2008, an illegal alien gang member murdered a father and his two teenage sons as they returned to their San Francisco home from a family barbecue. The killer had been convicted of two violent felonies as a juvenile: a gang-related assault and the attempted robbery of a pregnant woman. But because San Francisco's policy is to ignore immigration status, federal authorities were never informed that the two-time felon was in the country illegally.

Every day, thousands of innocent Americans are victimized by sanctuary policies that allow dangerous predators to roam their cities. Local officials are putting the welfare of criminals who have no right to be in our country above the welfare of their law-abiding citizens. These policies must be changed.

But the same reality that drives cities to enact sanctuary policies—the growing numbers of legal and illegal immigrants—also cripples federal authorities' own ability to enforce the immigration law against criminals. Even if immigrant-saturated cities were to discard their sanctuary policies and start enforcing immigration violations where public safety demands it, it is hard to believe that ICE could handle the additional workload.

Perennially starved for resources by Congress and the executive branch, ICE lacks the detention space to house the massive criminal alien population and the manpower to manage it. In fact, little the Immigration and Naturalization Service (INS) and its successors have done over the last 45 years—above all its numerous displays of managerial incompetence—can be understood outside of the sheer overmatch between the agency and the size of the population it theoretically oversees.

Illegal Immigrant Crime (More Than Unsapient Studies Suggest) Isn't Being Reported

State	% of Citizens/Lawful Immigrants Incarcerated	% of Illegal Aliens Incarcerated	% More Likely Than Citizens/Lawful Immigrants to be Incarcerated	Total Number of Illegal Aliens Incarcerated	Total Illegal Alien Population
California	0.482%	1.594%	231%	42,188	2,646,000
Texas	0.754%	1.210%	60%	22,477	1,858,000
Florida	0.732%	1.303%	78%	12,475	957,000
New York	0.354%	1.017%	187%	8,877	873,000
New Jersey	0.322%	1.738%	440%	9,783	563,000
Arizona	0.702%	2.815%	301%	10,300	366,000
Washington	0.395%	1.373%	248%	3,866	282,000
Nevada	0.595%	1.552%	161%	3,671	236,000
Oregon	0.454%	1.667%	267%	2,440	146,000
New Mexico	0.667%	0.948%	42%	907	96,000
		*		**	8,023,000**

*Based on data reported by states to the State Criminal Alien Assistance Program

**As reported by FAIR

Anecdotes, though numerous and damning, can explain only so much in an attempt to deny conflicting illegal immigrant crime studies as noted in May 2001 by Carl F. Horowitz's "An Examination of U.S. Immigration Policy and Serious Crime" for Center for Immigration Studies. Per his report:

Supporters of keeping U.S. immigration at high levels argue, with apparently convincing evidence, that immigrants as a whole are no more crime-prone than the native-born. Yet such an appraisal invites an age-old question: What's wrong with this picture? How is that the foreign-born as a whole, according to several studies, represent no statistical anomaly, yet so much other evidence indicates they are responsible for a wave of individual and organized crime? The explanation, this report argues, is that much of the crime, a lot more than structured studies would suggest, isn't being reported.

For one thing, immigrants are victims of crimes committed by fellow immigrants (all the more likely to be hidden from view if the assailant is a family member or close relative), and are often too scared, bound by custom, or fearful of deportation. This tendency may be heightened by the insularity of certain immigrant cultures, especially where concentrated in low-income neighborhoods. Many foreign-born criminals either hide within our nation's borders or operate outside of them. And the FBI's crime figures reflect state and local crime reports, which often omit any mention of an offender's national identity.

But this reality should not undercut concern over the crimes immigrants commit. States with large immigrant populations, such as California and New York, have had to devote an enormous portion of their law enforcement and criminal justice budgets to investigating, apprehending, and incarcerating immigrants to ensure safety for the law-abiding. The federal government since the mid-1990s has stepped up funding of state and local efforts for this purpose. That many of the immigrants committing crimes entered here illegally (or overstayed their visas) adds fuel to the fire.

Given that the flow of illegal immigration shows little or no sign of slowing, further federalization of crime control, for better or worse, appears to be a fixture on the long-term horizon. As such, proposals for reforming the Immigration and Naturalization Service may be at best of limited benefit. In the final analysis, the most effective way of controlling immigrant crime is to better enforce entry and visa time limits, alter the main basis for legal entry from family reunification to employment skills, and lower the overall immigration ceiling.

Getting a Realistic Portrait of Illegal Alien Crime

Horowitz's report examines the rate at which illegal aliens are incarcerated in state and local correctional facilities after being convicted of a crime. To determine that rate:

- He and his team analyzed incarceration data from the federal government's State Criminal Alien Assistance Program (SCAAP) and compared it to the public records of state and local prisons.

- Via SCAAP, state entities apply to U.S. Immigration and Customs Enforcement (ICE) to obtain reimbursement for the costs associated with incarcerating illegal aliens.

- Accordingly, the rate at which a state seeks reimbursement provides a good snapshot of the number of illegal aliens in its criminal justice system.

- In order to estimate how many illegal aliens are currently incarcerated in a given state, we relied on data from the most recent SCAAP report published by the Department of Justice's (DOJ) Bureau of Justice Assistance (BJA).

- Our other calculations are based on commonly available state corrections/criminal justice reports and other non-SCAPP federal data.

The Data They Used

The Horowitz report for CIS focuses on Arizona, California, Florida, Nevada, New Jersey, New Mexico, New York, Oregon, Texas, and Washington because:

- The majority of the illegal population in the United States lives within these states.

- Individually, they all have significant, dense illegal alien populations.

- They consistently report to SCAAP, and therefore have the most reliable and complete data.

- The majority of the population in these states lives within a SCAAP-reporting district.

There is little to suggest that our conclusions would be significantly different were we somehow able to obtain valid data for those jurisdictions that either do not participate in SCAAP or that do not produce enough SCAAP data to reliably estimate their total numbers of incarcerated illegal aliens.

Taken together, these ten reporting states represent a statistically significant sample. Although the calculations in this report are specific to those states, they include 65 percent of the total illegal alien population in the U.S. Therefore, even if the majority of unlawfully-present foreigners in the states not covered were never arrested, the rate at which illegal aliens are incarcerated would not change appreciably.

This report does not cover illegal aliens who have been convicted of federal criminal charges and are serving time in a Federal Bureau of Prisons (BOP) facility. Therefore, it does not include those illegal aliens incarcerated for committing immigration-related crimes such as illegal re-entry, welfare fraud, or identity theft.

Summary of Findings

FAIR found that in all SCAAP-reporting states along the Southern Border, and in SCAAP-reporting interior states that are preferred destinations for unlawful migrants, illegal aliens are incarcerated at a much higher rate than citizens and lawfully-present aliens.

SCAAP data indicate that illegal aliens are typically at least three times as likely to be incarcerated than citizens and lawfully-present aliens. Since the SCAAP program only includes those illegal aliens who have, at some point, been convicted of a crime, the only reasonable conclusion is that illegal aliens must commit crimes at a higher rate than citizens or lawfully-present aliens in order to be incarcerated at such high rates.

These findings stand in stark contrast to the narrative pushed by the open-borders lobby that illegal aliens are less likely to commit crimes compared to citizens or lawfully-present aliens.

Why They Used SCAAP Data for Their Study

SCAAP is governed by Section 241(i) of the Immigration and Nationality Act, 8 U.S.C. 1231(i), as amended, and Title II, Subtitle C, Section 20301, Violent Crime Control and Law Enforcement Act of 1994, Public Law 103-322.

SCAAP provides federal cash assistance to states and localities that incurred correctional officer salary costs for incarcerating criminal illegal aliens. The program will reimburse state and local correctional authorities for "Verified Illegal Aliens"—foreign nationals who have been determined by ICE to be in the United States illegally.

Illegal aliens for whom reimbursement is sought must have at least one felony or two misdemeanor convictions. And they must have been incarcerated for at least four consecutive days during the reporting period. These requirements mean that SCAAP reporting provides the best data currently available on illegal alien rates of incarceration because it furnishes information on individuals who are both convicted criminals and known illegal aliens.

As such, more accurate conclusions can be drawn from the analysis of SCAAP data than can be drawn from other available sources of information on illegal aliens and crime (used by open-border proponents) for these reasons:

- Researchers using SCAAP data need not apply subjective criteria in an effort to make educated guesses about which foreign nationals in a given sample might be illegal aliens.

- Similarly, researchers examining SCAAP data do not need to rely on notoriously inaccurate self-reported information about an individual's immigration status.

Methodology

As previously noted, SCAAP reimbursement is provided only for those illegal aliens who have sustained "at least one felony or two misdemeanor convictions for violations of state or local law," and who have been "incarcerated for at least 4 consecutive days during the reporting period."

Because the program covers only those illegal aliens who have had more than just a brief brush with the law, Horowitz's team of researchers believe (as listed below) that the SCAAP data provide the most accurate snapshot currently available of the rate at which illegal aliens commit crimes for these logical reasons:

- To determine the total number of citizens and lawfully-present aliens who are incarcerated, they took the overall population of each referenced state and subtracted the estimated total number of illegal alien residents.

- They then took the number of incarcerated individuals and subtracted SCAAP-reported illegal aliens from that total. This allowed them to distinguish illegal aliens from citizens and those aliens who are lawfully present in the United States.

- They then determined incarceration rates by comparing the total number of illegal aliens in each state to the total reported by SCAAP as incarcerated in that state.

- Using population data from the Census Bureau and overall prison population data aggregated by the Prison Policy Initiative, they then performed similar calculations to determine incarceration rates for U.S. citizens and lawfully-present aliens.

'Illegal' Aliens Commit Crime at a Far Higher Rate Than Citizens and 'Legal' Immigrants

When making immigration policy, it is important that we be honest about the facts. In this case, the available facts appear to show that illegal aliens (primarily Mexican and Central American) commit crimes at a much higher rate than the rest of the population. But, as noted above, much of the research on illegal aliens and crimes is marked by a deliberate attempt to ignore such data.

From the Statista Research Department, December 2020 update, the "World's most dangerous cities, by murder rate 2020" found from their crime statistics that rank the 50 most dangerous cities of 2020, by murder rate per 100,000 inhabitants, in the world—most of the world's most dangerous cities are located in Latin America. The murder rate of Los Cabos in Mexico was 138.26 for every 100,000 people living in the city. The highest ranked city outside of Latin America is St. Louis in the United States, which is ranked thirteenth with a murder rate of 60.59 in 2018. Detroit, with a murder rate of 39.7, came in at forty-second place.

Violence in Latin America is caused in great part by drug trafficking, weapons trafficking, and gang wars. Between 2007 and 2012, it was estimated that there were nearly 38,000 drug-related fatalities in Mexico alone. Though rates of gang and drug-related activities in Mexico reportedly fell from 2007 to 2012 due to a government squeeze, traffickers have gone elsewhere, and violence surged in other regions.

Meanwhile, violence in Latin America has influenced immigration from affected areas into the United States. Migration from Mexico to the U.S. is considered the largest migration flow in the world, with 11.6 million migrants by 2010.

As noted in the January 2019 City Journal article by Barry Latzer titled "Do Illegal Aliens Have High Crime Rates?" Per Latzer: No amount of crime by those who enter this country unlawfully should be acceptable because it is "extra" crime that wouldn't occur if our border security were effective. Crime by illegal aliens is costly.

The real issue underlying the current public debate is whether the crimes of illegal immigrants are so numerous that they provide a compelling reason, or at least a powerful supporting argument, for urgent spending to secure our southern border. To answer that question, the simple fact of the matter is that an examination of SCAAP reporting that relies on tested methods of statistical analysis clearly demonstrates that:

- In states with significant illegal alien populations, illegal aliens are incarcerated at a much higher rate than citizens and lawfully-present aliens.

- Illegal aliens commit crimes at a higher rate than U.S. citizens and lawfully-present aliens.

Until lawmakers in the United States are able to review accurate, transparent data regarding the rate at which illegal aliens commit criminal offenses, they will, inevitably, continue making bad immigration policy. As a result, too many Americans will continue becoming victims of preventable crimes, and the terrible stories that occupy our news cycles all too often will remain a regular part of daily life in this country.

Hopefully, this study (and chapter content and conclusions) represents a step in the right direction, and will encourage legislators, the media, and academic researchers to demand better information on illegal aliens and crime.

Non-Citizens Committed a Disproportionate Share of Federal Crimes, 2011-16

The Center for Immigration Studies is an independent, non-partisan, non-profit research organization founded in 1985, and per Steven A. Camarota's January 2018 report from The Center for Immigration Studies titled "Non-Citizens Committed a Disproportionate Share of Federal Crimes, 2011-16" the findings show that in 2018, 21% of those convicted of non-immigration crimes were non-citizens—2.5 times their share of the population. Among the findings of the new data:

Areas where non-citizens account for a much larger share of convictions than their 8.4 percent share of the adult population include:

- 42.4 percent of kidnapping convictions.

- 31.5 percent of drug convictions.

- 22.9 percent of money laundering convictions.

- 13.4 percent of administration of justice offenses (e.g. witness tampering, obstruction, and contempt).

- 17.8 percent of economic crimes (e.g. larceny, embezzlement, and fraud).

- 13 percent of other convictions (e.g. bribery, civil rights, environmental, and prison offenses); and

- 12.8 percent of auto thefts.

Areas where non-citizens account for a share of convictions roughly equal to their share of the adult population include:

- 9.6 percent of assaults.

- 8.9 percent of homicides; and

- 7.5 percent of firearm crimes.

Areas where non-citizens account for a share of convictions lower than their share of the adult population include:

- 4.1 percent of sex crimes.

- 3.3 percent of robberies.

- 4.5 percent of arsons; and

- 0 percent of burglaries.

These tables showing convictions were compiled by the Government Accountability Office (GAO) at the request of the Senate Judicatory Committee based on data from the U.S. Sentencing Commission "Interactive Sourcebook of Federal Sentencing Statistics". Convictions are in the federal courts for felonies and class A misdemeanors. Death penalty cases and petty offenses are not included. The non-citizen share of the overall adult population comes from the public-use data file of the 2011-2016 American Community Survey collected by the U.S. Census Bureau.

Working to End the Great Asylum Hustle

Advocates for illegal immigrant amnesty argue that it is the only solution to the illegal alien crisis because enforcement clearly has not worked. As noted by Dale Wilcox in July 2018 *The Hill* article titled "The Sessions DOJ is working to end the great asylum hustle" and they are wrong in their key assumption:

Full enforcement has never been tried. Amnesty, however, has been tried—in both an industrial-strength version in 1986, and in more limited doses ever since—and it was a clear failure. Before we proceed again to the ultimate suspension of the nation's self-definition, it is long past time to make immigration law a reality, not a charade.

President Trump often talked about the loopholes in our immigration laws, and there is no better example than asylum laws. Unlike others seeking entry into the United States, those requesting asylum do so based on the honor system. The applicant need only assert persecution or a well-founded fear of future persecution in their homeland by the government (or a non-governmental actor that the government is unwilling or unable to control) based on race, religion, nationality, membership in a particular social group, or political opinion.

No proof of persecution is required and would be nearly impossible to acquire if it even existed. This "credible fear" standard is easily met and has allowed many illegitimate claimants to remain in the country. So the United States is expected to accept people about whom little is known and based on claims that may or may not be true.

It gets worse. Asylum seekers are, by definition, those who have already entered the United States to request protection. The law of the land states that all asylum petitioners, the merits of their claims notwithstanding, must have their cases adjudicated. As the system has been overwhelmed with more applicants than it can detain, the overflow are released within the United States.

Back in 2018, the Executive Office for Immigration Review currently had over 312,000 cases with pending asylum applications. Those applicants are expected, again on the honor system, to appear at a future date for their hearing. Is it a shock to anyone that few ever show up?

This inept process has created a back door into the United States, and the world has taken notice. Seven years ago the number of arriving aliens claiming credible fear was one out every 100. Today it is one out of every ten. The backlog in the U.S. Citizenship and Immigration Services affirmative asylum process has grown by more than 1,900 percent since the end of fiscal year 2012.

Did the world get exponentially crueler and more dangerous in just the last few years? More likely is that groups seeking a borderless United States discovered a loophole ripe for exploitation and have been coaching waves of foreigners on how to game the system.

Is America still a compassionate nation? Of course it is, and we should continue to be a safe haven to those who legitimately meet the conditions for asylum. Allowing widespread fraud and exploitation of our asylum process, however, serves neither the new asylum arrivals nor the American citizens who welcome them.

Stopping the Practice of Citizenship for Sale

Citizenship for sale? Such an idea may seem ridiculous to most Americans. Nevertheless, this concept is not a mere abstract hypothetical, but rather a reality in the United States as the Kevin Berghuis report in August 2020 "Stopping the Practice of Citizenship for Sale Birth tourism in the United States and Canada" points out:

As one of the only developed countries in the world to adopt jus soli—Latin for "right of soil"— the United States guarantees citizenship to every child born within its territory. Birthright citizenship has been a fixture in the United States for over a century. However, in modern times, the policy has been exploited and has evolved into a magnet for birth tourism: the practice of pregnant foreign mothers travelling to the United States with the sole intention of delivering their children on American soil in order to secure U.S. citizenship for their newborns.

As American citizens, birth tourism babies go on to possess one of the world's most powerful passports, are eligible for federal education scholarships, and are guaranteed access to the U.S. job market. After turning 21, they are eligible to sponsor their foreign parents to become American citizens through chain migration. Through birth tourism, any foreigner with enough resources to travel to the United States can deliver an American baby. This is nothing more than citizenship for sale.

Appendix

50 *MADNESS* Textbook Titles: https://www.fratirepublishing.com/madnessbooks
- *Fake News Madness*

Adversity & Less Privilege Rankings Survey For Townhall Scoring & Discussion:
https://www.fratirepublishing.com/post/adversity-less-privilege-rankings-survey-for-townhall-scoring-discussion

Criminal Justice Information Services (CJIS): https://www.fbi.gov/services/cjis/ucr/

FBI: UCR - Crime in the United States: Table 21 Arrests by Race and Ethnicity, 2016:
https://ucr.fbi.gov/crime-in-the-u.s/2016/crime-in-the-u.s.-2016/topic-pages/tables/table-21

FBI: UCR - Race, Ethnicity, and Sex of Victim by Race, Ethnicity, and Sex of Offender, 2016
https://ucr.fbi.gov/crime-in-the-u.s/2016/crime-in-the-u.s.-2016/tables/expanded-homicide-data-table-3.xls

Map of Sanctuary Cities, Counties, and States—Center for Immigration Studies: https://cis.org/Map-Sanctuary-Cities-Counties-and-States

Movement For Black Lives: End the War on Black People: https://m4bl.org/policy-platforms/

NeighborhoodScout's Most Dangerous Cities—2021:
https://www.neighborhoodscout.com/blog/top100dangerous

PRAGER U: IS AMERICA RACIST? – WHAT IS SYSTEMPIC RACISM?
https://www.prageru.com/search/?refinementList%5Btopics%5D=&page=1&query=rac&gclid=Cj0KCQiAoab_BRCxARIsANMx4S7Nxpom-c109v7erAfBhTF6DRM8f8hOMiXaZC0OGaWANx2EeyT2vbQaAnVCEALw_wcB
- **Racism Is Not in America's DNA**
- **Is Harvard Racist?**
- **Is America Racist?**
- **Values Matter. Race Doesn't.**
- **Does Systemic Racism Exist?**
- **Who Are the Racists?**
- **Calling Good People "Racist" Isn't New: The Case of Ty Cobb**
- **Are the Police Racist?**

SPLC – The Biggest Lie in the White Supremacist Propaganda Playbook: Unraveling the Truth About 'Black-on-White Crime: https://www.splcenter.org/20180614/biggest-lie-white-supremacist-propaganda-playbook-unraveling-truth-about-%E2%80%98black-white-crime

The Color of Crime 2016: https://www.amren.com/wp-content/uploads/2016/03/Color-Of-Crime-2016.pdf

The Execution Style Murder of the Interracial Pietrzak Newlyweds:
https://www.cbsnews.com/news/execution-style-slayings-of-marine-sergeant-wife-involved-torture-greed-double-lives/

The National Crime Information Center (NCIC): https://www.fbi.gov/services/cjis/ncic

SAPIENT BEING PROGRAMS:
- **Make Free Speech Again On Campus (MFSAOC) Program:** https://www.sapientbeing.org/programs
- **World Of Writing Warriors (WOWW) Program:** https://www.sapientbeing.org/programs
- **World Of Writing Warriors (WOWW) Journalism Code of Ethics, Practical Logic & Sapience Guidelines:** https://www.sapientbeing.org/resources

The S.A.P.I.E.N.T. Being: https://www.fratirepublishing.com/books

Glossary

Arson – Intentionally damaging a building with fire or explosives.

Assault – An unlawful physical attack or threat of attack. Assaults may be classified as aggravated or simple. Rape, attempted rape, and sexual assaults are excluded from this category, as well as robbery and attempted robbery. The severity of assaults ranges from minor threats to nearly fatal incidents.

Burglary – The crime of breaking into a house with intent to commit theft. Until some time ago this charge occurred only if the felon broke into the house at night.

Contextual Factors – Are factors, particularly in statistical analysis, which reflect a particular context, characteristics unique to a particular group, community, society and individual.

Correlation Coefficients – Are used to measure how strong a relationship is between two variables. There are several types of correlation coefficient, but the most popular is Pearson's. Pearson's correlation (also called Pearson's R) is a correlation coefficient commonly used in linear regression.

Crime – An act punishable by law, as being forbidden by statute or injurious to the public welfare. Legally, a crime consists of two parts: actus rea, the criminal action, and mens rea, the criminal intention.

Crime Classification – Victimizations and incidents are classified based on detailed characteristics of the event provided by the respondent. Neither victims nor interviewers classify crimes at the time of interview. During data processing, a computer program classifies each event into one type of crime, based on the entries on a number of items on the survey questionnaire. This ensures that similar events will be classified using a standard procedure.

Critical Race Theory - Programs, based on a neo-Marxist ideology that originated in law schools a generation ago, purport to expose and correct "unconscious racial bias" and "white privilege" among their employees. Critical race theory treats "whiteness" as a moral blight and maligns all members of that racial group as complicit in oppression.

Domestic Violence – Refers to violence between spouses, or spousal abuse but can also include cohabitants and non-married intimate partners.

Drug Possession – Includes possession of an illegal drug but excludes possession with intent to sell.

Ecological Fallacy – Also known as ecological inference fallacy or population fallacy is a formal fallacy in the interpretation of statistical data that occurs when inferences about the nature of individuals are deduced from inferences about the group to which those individuals belong.

Equality of Outcomes – It means that given the same opportunity and privileges two people should end up in the same position or at least equal position. But equality of opportunity does not promise equality in the outcome. People have different levels of skill and put different amounts of effort into work they do.

Ethnicity – A classification based on Hispanic culture and origin, regardless of race. Persons are asked directly if they are Spanish, Hispanic, or Latino before being asked about their racial category.

Fake News – A broad term that collectively includes media bias manifested in many different ways in mainstream journalism, social media, and illiberal establishments that in principle and practice are antithetical to an intellectually vibrant and viewpoint diverse sapient being mindset. Per Andrew Klavan's edited definition at: https://www.youtube.com/watch?v=FOZ0irgLwxU.

Felony – An offense, as murder or burglary, of graver character than those called misdemeanors, especially those commonly punished in the U.S. by imprisonment for more than a year.

Ferguson Effect – Refers to an increase in violent crime rates in a community caused by reduced proactive policing due to the community's distrust and hostility towards police.

Forgery – The creation of a false written document or alteration of a genuine one, with the intent to defraud.

Hispanic – A person who describes himself or herself as Mexican American, Chicano, Mexican, Mexicano, Puerto Rican, Cuban, Central American, South American, or from some other Spanish culture or origin, regardless of race.

Human Trafficking – Is the crime of displacing people with a view to exploiting them.

Identity Theft – Includes one or more of three types of incidents: (1) unauthorized use or attempted use of an existing account, (2) unauthorized use or attempted use of personal information to open a new account, or (3) misuse of personal information for a fraudulent purpose. Person level identity theft is captured in the Identity Theft Supplement (ITS) to the National Crime Victimization Survey (NCVS). Household level identity theft is captured by the main NCVS.

Idiocracy – An idiocracy is a disparaging term for a society run by or made up of idiots (or people perceived as such). Idiocracy is also the title of 2006 satirical film that depicts a future in which humanity has become dumb.

Illegal Immigration – Refers to the migration of people into a country in violation of the immigration laws of that country, or the continued residence without the legal right to live in that country.

Illiberalism – In popular usage, the word is used to describe an attitude that is close-minded, intolerant, and bigoted.

Incident – A specific criminal act involving one or more victims and offenders. For example, if two people are robbed at the same time and place, this is classified as two robbery victimizations but only one robbery incident.

Intellectual Humility – A mindset that encompasses empathy, trust, and curiosity, viewpoint diversity gives rise to engaged and civil debate, constructive disagreement, and shared progress towards truth.

Intersectionality – A theoretical framework for understanding how aspects of one's social and political identities might combine to create unique modes of discrimination.

Kidnapping – In current usage, the crime of kidnapping is the abduction of a person of any age with the intention of holding the person for ransom or for some other purpose.

Locke, John – An English philosopher and physician, widely regarded as one of the most influential of Enlightenment thinkers and commonly known as the "Father of Liberalism." Considered one of the first of the British empiricists, following the tradition of Sir Francis Bacon, Locke is equally important to social contract theory. His work greatly affected the development of epistemology and political philosophy. His writings influenced Voltaire and Jean-Jacques Rousseau, and many Scottish Enlightenment thinkers, as well as the American Revolutionaries. His contributions to classical republicanism and liberal theory are reflected in the United States Declaration of Independence.

Mainstream Media (MSM) – Traditional forms of mass media, as television, radio, magazines, and newspapers, as opposed to online means of mass communication.

Marcuse, Herbert – A German-American philosopher, sociologist, and political theorist, associated with the Frankfurt School of Critical Theory. Author of the *One-Dimensional Man: Studies in the Ideology of Advanced Industrial Society*, a 1964 best seller primarily known by the "power of negative thinking" became the standard for revolutionary speech in the movement he called the "Great Refusal." Marcuse distinguished between repressive tolerance, a form of tolerance that favors the already powerful and suppresses the less powerful, and a liberating tolerance, a form of tolerance that discriminates in favor of the weak and restrains the strong.

Marxism – The political, economic, and social principles and policies advocated by Marx and a theory and practice of socialism including the labor theory of value, dialectical materialism, the class struggle, and dictatorship of the proletariat until the establishment of a classless society.

Murder – Is intentionally causing the death of another, either through premeditation focused on a particular individual, or by extreme indifference to human life. First degree murder is defined by federal and state laws, which vary.

Non-Hispanic – Persons who report their culture or origin as something other than "Hispanic" as defined above. This distinction is made regardless of race.

Progressivism – A political philosophy in support of social reform based on the idea of progress in which advancements in science, technology, economic development, and social organization are vital to improve the human condition.

Property Crime – Burglary/trespassing, motor-vehicle theft, and theft. This category includes both attempted and completed crimes.

Race – For the National Crime Victimization Survey, respondents self-identify with one or more racial categories. Racial categories defined by the Office of Management and Budget are American Indian or Alaska Native; Asian; black or African American; Native Hawaiian or other Pacific Islander; and white. The race of the head of household is used in determining the race of the household for computing household crime demographics.

Rape – Forced sexual intercourse including both psychological coercion and physical force. Forced sexual intercourse means vaginal, anal, or oral penetration by the offender(s). This category also includes incidents where the penetration is from a foreign object, such as a bottle. Includes attempted rape, male and female victims, and both heterosexual and same sex rape. Attempted rape includes verbal threats of rape.

Robbery – Is theft committed openly and with force.

Sapience – Also known as wisdom, is the ability to think and act using knowledge, experience, understanding, common sense and insight. Sapience is associated with attributes such as intelligence, enlightenment, and unbiased judgement and also recognizes the humanistic concepts of Western European culture, American exceptionalism, and conservative values.

Scientific Method – A way of investigating a phenomenon that's based on the collective analysis and into interpretation of evidence to determine the most probable explanation. The five basic steps in scientific method: 1) statement of the problem, 2) collection of facts, 3) formulating a hypothesis, 4) making further inferences, and 5) verifying the inferences.

Social Justice – A political and philosophical theory which asserts that there are dimensions to the concept of justice beyond those embodied in the principles of civil or criminal law, economic supply and demand, or traditional moral frameworks.

Social Media – Websites and other online means of communication that are used by large groups of people to share information and to develop social and professional contacts.

Theft – Implies subterfuge, while robbery is the open taking of property. Burglary is committed when the thief breaks into a building.

Trespass – Is entering another's property without permission. If it is with an illegal intent, it's a crime. Illegal dumping is a form of trespass.

Viewpoint Diversity – Viewpoint diversity occurs when members of a group or community approach problems or questions from a range of perspectives.

White Privilege – The set of social and economic advantages that white people have by virtue of their race in a culture characterized by racial inequality.

Woke – Having or marked by an active awareness of systemic injustices and prejudices, especially those related to civil and human rights.

References

Antifa. Influence Watch. https://www.influencewatch.org/movement/antifa/.

Auster, Lawrence. "The Truth Of Interracial Rape In The United States." Front Page Magazine. May 3, 2007. https://www.amren.com/news/2007/05/the_truth_of_in/.

Baker, Gerard. "The Often Distorted Reality of Hate Crime in America." *Wall Street Journal*. May 15, 2020. https://www.wsj.com/articles/the-often-distorted-reality-of-hate-crime-in-america-11589562033.

Beanz, Tracy. "UC Berkeley History Professor's Open Letter Against BLM, Police Brutality and Cultural Orthodoxy." www.UncoverDC.com. June 12, 2020. https://uncoverdc.com/2020/06/12/uc-berkeley-history-professors-open-letter-against-blm-police-brutality-and-cultural-orthodoxy/.

Berghuis, Kevin. "Stopping the Practice of Citizenship for Sale Birth tourism in the United States and Canada." Center for Immigration Studies (CIS). August 10, 2020. https://cis.org/Report/Stopping-Practice-Citizenship-Sale.

Blakemore, Jane. "Sanctuary Schools Defy Immigration Enforcement." *Newsmax*. May 2017.

Bomberger, Ryan. "Top 10 Reasons I Won't Support the #BlackLivesMatter Movement." Townhall. June 05, 2020. https://townhall.com/columnists/ryanbomberger/2020/06/05/top-10-reasons-i-reject-the-blm-n2570105.

Camarota, Steven A. "Non-Citizens Committed a Disproportionate Share of Federal Crimes, 2011-16." Center for Immigration Studies (CIS). January 10, 2018. https://cis.org/Camarota/NonCitizens-Committed-Disproportionate-Share-Federal-Crimes-201116.

Chiaramonte, Perry. "US murders concentrated in 5 percent of counties." Fox News. April 27, 2017. https://www.foxnews.com/us/us-murders-concentrated-in-5-percent-of-counties.

Constitutional Corner–Sanctuary Cities and the Constitution. Constitutional Leadership Initiative. April 9, 2017. https://constitutionleadership.org/2017/04/09/constitutional-corner-sanctuary-cities-and-the-constitution/.

D'Souza, Dinesh. "The Philosopher of Antifa." *Epoch Times*. June 23, 2020. https://www.theepochtimes.com/the-philosopher-of-antifa_3380743.html.

Davidson, Jordan. "New Documentary Examines The Death Of Michael Brown And Race In America." The Federalist. Sept. 17, 2020. https://thefederalist.com/2020/09/17/new-documentary-examines-the-death-of-michael-brown-and-race-in-america/.

Davis, Elliott. "Experts: It's a Mayor's Policies, Not Politics, That Influence Crime Rates." *US News & World Report*. Nov. 3, 2020. https://www.usnews.com/news/cities/articles/2020-11-03/how-mayors-democrat-or-republican-can-address-a-recent-spike-in-violent-crime.

Dimond, Diane. "The Hypocrisy of the Black Lives Matter Movement." *The Winchester Star*. July 18, 2020. https://www.winchesterstar.com/winchester_star/dimond-the-hypocrisy-of-the-black-lives-matter-movement/article_52c889fb-a67c-5376-9181-7da5496a2f35.html.

Donaldson, Chris. "AG Barr To Designate Three Dem Controlled Cities As 'Anarchist Jurisdictions.'" Trending Politics. September 21, 2020. https://trendingpolitics.com/ag-barr-to-designate-three-dem-controlled-cities-as-anarchist-jurisdictions-report/.

Elder, Larry. "'Uncle Tom' blacklisted by Hollywood." Standard-Examiner. Jan. 22, 2021. https://www.standard.net/opinion/national-commentary/elder-uncle-tom-blacklisted-by-hollywood/article_aa26cf9f-a65c-5780-b849-48655b449fa1.html.

George Soros. Influence Watch. https://www.influencewatch.org/person/george-soros/.

George Soros: Godfather of the Left. Media Research Center. https://www.mrc.org/special-reports/special-report-george-soros-godfather-left.

Hanson, Victor Davis. "Opportunists Fan the Flames of Racial Unrest." Townhall. Aug. 21, 2014. https://townhall.com/columnists/victordavishanson/2014/08/21/untitled-n1881023.

Hausknecht, Bruce. "Republicans Denounce Bigotry of the Southern Poverty Law Center." The Daily Citizen. Aug. 25, 2020. https://dailycitizen.focusonthefamily.com/republicans-denounce-bigotry-of-the-southern-poverty-law-center/.

Higgins, Jeffrey James. "Enough of the lying—just look at the data. There's no epidemic of racist police officers killing black Americans." Citizens Journal. July 2, 2020. https://www.citizensjournal.us/higgins-enough-of-the-lying-just-look-at-the-data-theres-no-epidemic-of-racist-police-officers-killing-black-americans/.

Hutchinson, Bill. "Police officers killed surge 28% this year and some point to civil unrest and those looking to exploit it." July 22, 2020. https://abcnews.go.com/US/police-officers-killed-surge-28-year-point-civil/story?id=71773405.

I was preconditioned to HATE America: Ex-Antifa activist shares DISTURBING story of why he joined Antifa. Blaze TV. Oct. 29, 2020. https://www.theblaze.com/wilkow/i-was-preconditioned-to-hate-america-ex-antifa-activist-shares-disturbing-story-of-joining-antifa?rebelltitem=1#rebelltitem1.

Jackson Sr., Bishop E.W. Stand America PAC. https://www.standamerica.us/.

Johnson, Rose. "Obligations & Job Duties of Police Officers." Officers Chron. June 27, 2018. https://work.chron.com/obligations-job-duties-police-officers-24841.html.

Kan, Janita, Bowen Xiao, Ivan Pentchoukov, and Jack Phillips. "DOJ Is Conducting 'Very Focused Investigations' on Individuals Linked to Antifa, Barr Says." June 13, 2020. https://www.theepochtimes.com/doj-is-conducting-very-focused-investigations-on-individuals-linked-to-antifa-barr-says_3381409.html.

Kanfer, Stefan. "Connoisseur of Chaos The dystopian vision of George Soros, billionaire funder of the Left." City Journal. Winter 2017. https://www.city-journal.org/html/connoisseur-chaos-14954.html.

Krikorian, Mark. "Nobody Expects the SPLC Inquisition!" Center for Immigration Studies (CIS). November 22, 2019. https://cis.org/Oped/Nobody-Expects-SPLC-Inquisition.

Latzer, Barry. "Do Illegal Aliens Have High Crime Rates?" City Journal. January 24, 2019. https://www.city-journal.org/illegal-alien-crime-rate-data.

Latzer, Barry. "The Facts on Race, Crime, and Policing in America." Law & Liberty. June 18, 2020. https://lawliberty.org/the-facts-on-race-crime-and-policing-in-america/.

Latzer, Barry. "The Need to Discuss Black-on-Black Crime." National Review. December 5, 2019. https://www.nationalreview.com/magazine/2019/12/22/the-need-to-discuss-black-on-black-crime/.

Terrell, Leo. "Why Black Lives Don't Matter to 'Black Lives Matter.'" Newsweek. July 3, 2020. https://www.newsweek.com/why-black-lives-dont-matter-black-lives-matter-opinion-1515183.

Lewis, Jason. "Black-on-white crime in America." Star Tribune. Sept. 14, 2013. https://www.startribune.com/black-on-white-crime-in-america/223696071/.

Liberal Cities, Radical Mayhem. *Wall Street Journal*. June 2, 2020. https://www.wsj.com/articles/liberal-cities-radical-mayhem-11591140986.

Lonergan, Brian. "Meet America's Ten Worst Sanctuary Communities." Immigration Reform Law Institute (IRLI). September 24, 2019. https://www.irli.org/meet-americas-ten-worst-sanctuary-communities/.

Lonergan, Brian. "Sanctuary California Failed to Honor Over 5,600 ICE Detainers." February 28, 2019. https://www.irli.org/sanctuary-california-failed-to-honor-over-5600-ice-detainers/.

Lonergan, Brian. "Sanctuary laws defy the will of the American people." Immigration Reform Law Institute (IRLI), December 31, 2019. https://www.irli.org/sanctuary-laws-defy-the-will-of-the-american-people/.

Mac Donald, Heather. "Crime and the Illegal Alien: The Fallout from Crippled Immigration Enforcement." Center for Immigration Studies (CIS). June 1, 2004. https://cis.org/Report/Crime-and-Illegal-Alien.

Mac Donald, Heather. "The Myth of Systemic Police Racism." *Wall Street Journal*. June 3, 2020. https://www.manhattan-institute.org/the-myth-of-systemic-police-racism.

Mac Donald, Heather. "There Is No Epidemic of Racist Police Shootings." Manhattan Institute. July 31, 2019. https://www.manhattan-institute.org/white-cops-dont-commit-more-shootings.

Mac Donald, Heather. *The War on Cops: How the New Attack on Law and Order Makes Everyone Less Safe*. Encounter Books: New York. 2017.

Margolis, Matt. "Is There Really an 'Epidemic' of Racist Police Shootings? Several Studies Say No." June 7, 2020. PJ Media. https://pjmedia.com/news-and-politics/matt-margolis/2020/06/07/is-there-really-an-epidemic-of-racist-police-shootings-several-studies-say-no-n484099.

Mass, Warren. "Trump DOJ Sues California Over Its Immigration and Sanctuary Policies." The New American. March 8, 2018. https://thenewamerican.com/trump-doj-sues-california-over-its-immigration-and-sanctuary-policies/.

Mock, Brentin. "What New Research Says About Race and Police Shootings." Bloomberg CityLab. August 6, 2019. https://www.bloomberg.com/news/articles/2019-08-06/race-and-police-shootings-what-new-research-says.

Movement For Black Lives: Vision For Black Lives. https://m4bl.org/policy-platforms/.

Ngo, Andy. "My terrifying five-day stay inside Seattle's cop-free CHAZ." *New York Post*. June 20, 2020. https://nypost.com/2020/06/20/my-terrifying-5-day-stay-inside-seattles-autonomous-zone/.

O'Neil, Tyler. "About 60 Organizations Are Considering a Lawsuit Against the SPLC Following $3M Nawaz Settlement." June 19, 2018. PJ Media. https://pjmedia.com/news-and-politics/tyler-o-neil/2018/06/19/about-60-organizations-are-considering-a-lawsuit-against-the-splc-following-3m-nawaz-settlement-n58792.

O'Neil, Tyler. "SPLC Slams Trump's Terror Designation of Antifa as 'Dangerous and Unjust' as America Burns." PJ Media. June 02, 2020. https://pjmedia.com/news-and-politics/tyler-o-neil/2020/06/02/splc-carries-water-for-antifa-condemns-police-for-punishing-peaceful-protest-amid-riots-n483010.

O'Brien, Matt, Spencer Raley and Casey Ryan. "SCAAP Data Suggest Illegal Aliens Commit Crime at a Much Higher Rate Than Citizens and Lawful Immigrants." Feb. 3, 2019. Federation for American Immigration Reform (FAIR). https://www.fairus.org/issue/illegal-immigration/scaap-data-suggest-illegal-aliens-commit-crime-much-higher-rate-citizens?gclid=Cj0KCQiA6Or_BRC_ARIsAPzuer-vK4V5r1bsQz2Mya_wV3yS6wqzv0KP_FF07xyMI2WLY3s3FaX3XEcaAsgbEALw_wcB.

Open Society Foundations (OSF). Influence Watch. https://www.influencewatch.org/non-profit/open-society-foundations/.

Overcash, Colton R. "Sanctuary Schools Defy Immigration Crackdown." Federation for American Immigration Reform (FAIR). August 23, 2018. https://www.fairus.org/legislation/state-local-legislation/sanctuary-schools-defy-immigration-crackdown.

Ozimek, Tom. "Majority of Americans Support Use of National Guard, Military to Help Address Riots." *Epoch Times.* June 3, 2020. https://www.theepochtimes.com/majority-of-americans-support-use-of-national-guard-military-to-help-address-riots_3374980.html.

Pan, GQ. "Law Professor at Senate Hearing: Antifa Is Winning on College Campuses." August 9, 2020. https://www.theepochtimes.com/law-professor-on-senate-hearing-antifa-is-winning-on-college-campuses_3452769.html.

Pentchoukov, Ivan. "Barr: Antifa Wants 'Socialism, Communism' in America." August 10, 2020. https://www.theepochtimes.com/barr-antifa-wants-socialism-communism-in-america_3455777.html.

Polumbo, Brad. "65% of College Students Say Rioting and Looting is 'Justified,' New Poll Finds." Foundation for Economic Education (FEE). October 29, 2020. https://fee.org/articles/65-of-college-students-say-rioting-and-looting-is-justified-new-poll-finds/.

Polumbo, Brad. "George Floyd Riots Caused Record-Setting $2 Billion in Damage New Report Says. Here's Why the True Cost Is Even Higher." Foundation for Economic Education (FEE). Sep. 16, 2020. https://fee.org/articles/george-floyd-riots-caused-record-setting-2-billion-in-damage-new-report-says-here-s-why-the-true-cost-is-even-higher/#:~:text=New%20reporting%20from%20Axios%20reveals,%241%20billion%20to%20%242%20billion.&text=%E2%80%9CThe%20arson%2C%20vandalism%20and%20looting,insurance%20claims%2C%E2%80%9D%20Axios%20reports.

Roos, Meghan. "BLM Leader: We'll 'Burn' the System Down If U.S. Won't Give Us What We Want." *Newsweek.* June 25, 2020. https://www.newsweek.com/blm-leader-well-burn-system-down-if-us-wont-give-us-what-we-want-1513422.

Rubenstein, Edwin S. "The Color of Crime 2016: Race, Crime, and Justice in America." 2016 Revised Edition. New Century Foundation. http://2kpcwh2r7phz1nq4jj237m22.wpengine.netdna-cdn.com/wp-content/uploads/2016/03/The-Color-of-Crime-2016.pdf.

Schiller, Dr. Andrew. "NeighborhoodScout's Most Dangerous Cities–2021." NeighborhoodScout.com. Jan. 2, 2021. https://www.neighborhoodscout.com/blog/top100dangerous.

Simpson, James. "Black Criminals, White Victims, and White Guilt." February 9, 2015. Accuracy in Media. https://www.aim.org/special-report/black-criminals-white-victims-and-white-guilt/.

Sowell, Thomas. "A Censored Race War." National Review. May 15, 2012.https://www.nationalreview.com/2012/05/censored-race-war-thomas-sowell/.

Steele, Shelby. "What Killed Michael Brown?" Video: Official trailer. https://youtu.be/ZIbAI1vEl-E.

Stieber, Zachary. "Undercover Videos Show Antifa Members' Combat Training: Watchdog." *Epoch Times.* June 13, 2020. https://www.theepochtimes.com/undercover-videos-show-antifa-members-combat-training-watchdog_3386535.html.

Svab, Petr. "Antifa Investigations Will Take Time to Be Effective, Former FBI Agent Says." June 10, 2020. *Epoch Times.* https://www.theepochtimes.com/antifa-investigations-will-take-time-to-be-effective-former-fbi-agent-says_3384143.html.

Taft, Victoria. "Worst Mayors in America Demand Congress Stop Trump From Ruining Their Riots." PJ Media. July 22, 2020. https://pjmedia.com/columns/victoria-taft/2020/07/22/worst-mayors-in-america-demand-congress-stop-trump-from-ruining-their-riots-n670250.

Tapscott, Mark. "Journalist Warns Congress Antifa Plans to Spread Violence Across America." *Epoch Times.* August 5, 2020. https://www.theepochtimes.com/journalist-warns-congress-antifa-plans-to-spread-violence-across-america_3451423.html.

The Negro Family: The Case For National Action, Office of Policy Planning and Research. United States Department of Labor, March 1965. https://www.blackpast.org/african-american-history/moynihan-report-1965/.

Unz, Ron. "Race and Crime in America: The unspoken statistical reality of urban crime over the last quarter century." July 20, 2013. https://www.unz.com/article/race-and-crime-in-america/.

von Spakovsky, Hans A. "Sanctuary Cities Put Law-Abiding Citizens at Risk." The Heritage Foundation. Dec. 9, 2015. https://www.heritage.org/homeland-security/commentary/sanctuary-cities-put-law-abiding-citizens-risk.

Watts, Marina. "Everything Candace Owens Has Said About George Floyd So Far." *Newsweek.* June 5, 2020. https://www.newsweek.com/everything-candace-owens-has-said-about-george-floyd-so-far-1508959.

Weber, Jared. "Support for Black Lives Matter movement has decreased significantly since June, local and national polls agree." *The Dallas Morning News.* Nov 4, 2020. https://www.dallasnews.com/news/2020/11/04/support-for-the-black-lives-matter-movement-has-decreased-significantly-since-june-local-and-national-polls-agree/.

Wilcox, Dale L. "How Our Suburbs Are Under Attack From Illegal Immigrant 'Sanctuary' Laws." The Daily Signal. September 25, 2020. https://www.dailysignal.com/2020/09/25/how-our-suburbs-are-under-attack-from-illegal-immigrant-sanctuary-laws/.

Wilcox, Dale L. "The Sessions DOJ is working to end the great asylum hustle." *The Hill.* July 20, 2018. https://thehill.com/opinion/immigration/397751-the-sessions-doj-is-working-to-end-the-great-asylum-hustle.

Wilcox, Laird. *The Watchdogs: A Close Look at Anti-Racist "Watchdog" Groups.* 1999.

Williams, Thomas Ph.D. "Newt Gingrich: George Soros Actively Working to 'Undermine the American System.'" Breitbart. Sep. 23, 2020. https://www.breitbart.com/2020-election/2020/09/23/gingrich-george-soros-actively-working-to-undermine-the-american-system/.

Williams, Walter E. "Is racism responsible for today's problems?" *The Sumter Item*. July 30, 2020. https://www.theitem.com/stories/opinion-is-racism-responsible-for-todays-problems,349100.

Williams, Walter E. "Who benefits from Democratic control of cities?" AP News. www.creators.com. January 23, 2019. https://apnews.com/article/race-and-ethnicity-archive-gerald-ford-cd60b6d9b1e34e20b9b0c19205c2cae6.

Xiao, Bowen, and Ivan Pentchoukov. "Other Far-Left Groups Exploit Protests for 'Revolution.'" *Epoch Times*. June 5, 2020. https://www.theepochtimes.com/antifa-other-far-left-groups-exploit-protests-for-revolution_3375358.html.

Index

E

F

G

X

Y

Z

Author Bio

Corey Lee Wilson was raised an atheist by his liberal *Playboy* Bunny mother, has three Anglo-Hispanic siblings, a brother who died of AIDS, baptized a Protestant by his conservative grandparents, attended temple with his Jewish foster parents, baptized again as a Catholic for his first Filipina wife, attends Buddhist ceremonies with his second Thai wife, became an agnostic on his own free will for most of his life, and is a lifetime independent voter.

Corey felt the sting of intellectual humility by repeating the 4th grade and attended eighteen different schools before putting himself through college at Mt. San Antonio College and Cal Poly Pomona University (while on triple secrete probation). Named Who's Who of American College Students in 1984, he received a BS in Economics and won his fraternity's most prestigious undergraduate honor, the Phi Kappa Tau Fraternity's Shideler Award, both in 1985. In 2020, he became a member of the Heterodox Academy.

As a satirist and fraternity man, Corey started Fratire Publishing in 2012 and transformed the fiction "fratire" genre to a respectable and viewpoint diverse non-fiction genre promoting practical knowledge and wisdom to help everyday people navigate safely through the many hazards of life. In 2018, he founded the S.A.P.I.E.N.T. Being to help promote freedom of speech, viewpoint diversity, intellectual humility and most importantly advance sapience in America's students and campuses.

The S.A.P.I.E.N.T. Being has two programs, the Make Free Speech Again On Campus (MFSAOC) and World of Writing Warriors (WOWW) to promote its mission and vision of sapience. The WOWW program plans to self-publish 50 *MADNESS* non-fiction textbooks in partnership with Fratire Publishing over the span of the 2020 decade in alliance with the MFSAOC program to start 50 chapters on America's high school and college campuses by 2030.

If you're interested in the MFSAOC Program and starting a S.A.P.I.E.N.T. Being club, chapter, or alliance please got to https://www.SapientBeing.org/start-a-chapter, e-mail SapientBeing@att.net, or call (951) 638-5562 for more information.

If you're interested in the WOWW Program and their 50 *MADNESS* series of textbooks from the S.A.P.I.E.N.T. Being, please check them out at https://www.FratirePublishing.com/madnessbooks, e-mail SapientBeing@att.net, or call (951) 638-5562 for more information.

Hopefully, this book was enlightening and your journey through it made you aware of the issues and challenges ahead of us. If it has, your journey towards becoming a sapient being has begun. If it hasn't, there's no better time to start than now. Come join us in creating a society advancing personal intelligence and enlightenment now together (S.A.P.I.E.N.T.) and become a sapient being.

www.ingramcontent.com/pod-product-compliance
Lightning Source LLC
Chambersburg PA
CBHW040833040426
42336CB00034B/3460